INSIGHTS

TO

Intimacy

Why Relationships Fail & How to Make Them Work

Christian Pankhurst

Published by:
Christian Pankhurst

Heart IQ is a trademark of Christian Pankhurst.

ISBN-13: 978-90-825466-0-6

Editor: Carol Killman Rosenberg
www.carolkillmanrosenberg.com

Interior and cover design: Gary A. Rosenberg
www.thebookcouple.com

Printed in the United States of America

To my mentor, Jerry,
who believed in me
before I knew how
to believe in myself.

Contents

———

BONUS: How to Become Sexually Magnetic

First Things First

To get the most value from the practices I'm going to reveal to you, it's best if you can actually *see* them in action. That's why I recommend that, before you get started with this book, you visit www.HeartIQRelationships.com and sign up for your complimentary home-study companion course using the access code myheartiq. In this course, I'll break down exactly how these practices work to give you an added dimension that can't be matched by reading this book alone.

You'll also receive additional resources, updates, and insights that didn't make it in the final book, as well as a surprise gift from me to you to support you on your Heart IQ Relationship journey. So, please take a moment to register and sign up to your free account using the access code myheartiq at www.HeartIQ Relationships.com.

First Things First

Who Is Christian Pankhurst & Why Should I Read This Book?

People are shocked at the beginning of my Insights to Intimacy LIVE seminars when one of the first things I tell them is, "You are me, cleverly camouflaged as you." Why would I suggest that? Because it's the most powerful relationship medicine you can take when you realize what it means. It's so easy to think of yourself as separate from others, and yet, my experience has been that, if I change what's going on inside, my outer world changes with it. Like Neale Donald Walsch says, "If you don't go within, you go without."

Our intimate relationships are profound mirrors to our inner conflict and unresolved issues, making them the perfect vehicle for our personal healing and awakening. It's not always an easy journey, but in my opinion, there's nothing more rewarding and important than mastering the art of intimate relationships.

Why? Because the greatest gift you can give to the world is to become a fully healthy you. . . . And a fully healthy you doesn't just impact *your* life, but it positively transforms and heals all those whose lives you touch, especially your children. Isn't that worth the effort and sometimes uncomfortable exploration of your inner world?

I believe this is more than just a book you pick up and read once. No one should climb Mount Everest alone; this book is your guide to reaching your relationship "summit" so that you can end the pain, disconnect, and suffering that has caused past relationships to fail and that threatens your current or future intimacy.

I know that if you use the practices you learn in this book, the insights you gain will totally transform your life and relationship. Don't just read this book. Study it as if your life depended on it. Then try out the practices and see for yourself. Now, you may be wondering if this book is for you if you're single. The answer is yes! Although I express many of the practices and concepts as if I were coaching a couple, everything you're about to learn can be applied to *all* your relationships and, more important, your future intimate partner.

I know I might be biased, but when it comes to relationships, this may be the most important book you will ever read. I understand that's a bold statement, but the fact is, this book provides the missing link between your *desire* for a harmonious and thriving intimacy and actually having one. As you've probably found out by now, those are two very different worlds.

No doubt you've read other books, listened to CDs, gone to courses, and learned about numerous techniques to improve communication and have more fulfilling sex or how to become a "better" partner or lover. But what happened? For most people, not much. Something changes in the short term, and then it's back to the status quo.

Good news! I'm going to share a practice that works at the core of the issue! You see, it all comes down to your relationship, to the part of you that feels unworthy and not enough. Once you can navigate your defense mechanisms and recognize how you project them on to your partner, you will discover the insight that leads to relationship bliss. If you want to learn how to open, you need to study how you close. You can learn all the best techniques, all the right things to say, but if you don't know how to manage the part of you that feels unworthy (which we all have, no matter how much "personal work" we've done), nothing you do will make a difference.

In the pages of this book, I will demystify for you why relationships fail and what you need to do to make them succeed. You will understand the root causes of intimacy sabotage and how to tap into ecstasy and joy through partnership. You will understand how childhood influences shape the very dynamics you experience in your relationships, and how these influences can lead to self-defeating thoughts that disconnect you from your true essence and goodness. You will also learn practical step-by-step strategies for increasing intimacy and joy with easy-to-follow daily, weekly, and monthly practices.

This book is split into two parts. In Part One, it's all about you, the individual. I'll reveal why, in so many moments, you believe you're unworthy and undeserving of love and what needs to be done to heal and access your intrinsic goodness. In Part Two, I'll lay out the actual heart-centered communication practices, that, when mastered, will help you navigate your resistance and heal whatever is standing in your way of having the relationship you so deeply crave. In the bonus chapter, I'll reveal how to use your sexual connection to deepen your intimacy while avoiding the common pitfalls of having sex with a closed heart. Throughout the book, I will also share just a few examples of the many letters and e-mails I've received from clients who have put these practices to work and achieved amazing results.

So what's my experience? Where am I coming from? The wisdom and practices I'm about to share with you emerged from the live study of group dynamics and interactions that I've had with thousands of clients who have attended my multiday seminars since 2003. In fact, at the time of writing this book, I've spent over 10,000 hours facilitating individuals and couples to open their hearts and to connect more deeply with themselves and others. I'm not saying this to boast, but to share that the wisdom I've gathered has primarily come from *direct* experience and not just from reading books or studying other experts.

From the experience and wisdom gathered during this time of intense facilitation and teaching, a unique method emerged, which I call "Heart IQ," or what some just refer to as Heart Intelligence. After years of requests from coaches, counselors, and therapists, in 2011, we opened our certification program, enrolling over one hundred practitioners in the first day! We now have certified practitioners working in more than twenty-five countries around the world, and you can find a directory of many of them at www .HeartIQ.com. If you're a professional wanting to learn more about certification, please visit www.HeartIQAcademy.com.

In 2008, I put my skills to the test by entering a national competition in the UK called "Britain's Next Top Coach." During the final round, I was asked to give a ten-minute session to a client and bring them to resolution while being filmed in a single take—no edits allowed. This recording was then posted online with other candidates and the viewing public had to vote on which coach they felt made the biggest impact. I won the competition with 52 percent of the votes from ninety-two different countries. Again, this may sound like bragging, but that's not why I'm sharing it. If the majority of all those who voted could see the value and impact of this method, surely there must be something to it. And, if that's true, isn't it worth your study so you can make it work for you, too?

My career in this field began as a chiropractor in 2002. I quickly had a sense that, for many of my patients, their physical pain was a symptom of an underlying *emotional* health issue. To test this theory out, I set up an experiment. I asked some of my patients to attend a series of evening workshops designed to help them connect to their emotional and energetic bodies instead of receiving my regular physical adjustments. I asked them to see if they noticed a change in their symptoms. The results were mind-blowing, and so much so, they put me into a disorienting tailspin . . . since I had just finished a five-year master's degree in chiropractic!

How could I continue to focus on low back pain when I knew I could make a bigger impact? Yet, how could I give up after such a huge investment in time and money?

I decided to do something, that looking back, was one of the scariest things I've ever done. I quit my well-paying job as a chiropractor, sold everything I had, and traveled to the United States accompanied only by my burning passion to help people. I knew I wanted to lead groups but was, at this stage, wholly inexperienced. The next step became clear. I needed a mentor, so I sought out some of the best seminar leaders, facilitators, and group dynamics experts in the world.

For the next four years, I studied and lived in Europe, Australia, and the United States while learning as much as I could from teachers I respected. I had the privilege of being the protégé of Neale Donald Walsch for a year in 2004 and to be personally mentored by Tej Steiner, a master at circle work. This was a time of accelerated learning for me as I got to absorb wisdom from my mentors and then instantly apply it and test it in my live seminars, which I was also running at the time.

However, in the summer of 2006, I discovered something that would change my life forever. A new teacher emerged, a teacher who is still with me to this day. I call it "Circle Wisdom." For those not familiar with this term, it's not as "woo-woo" as it sounds. Another way of describing it would be the group's collective intelligence. Basically, when you get people together and focus them on what they are *really* feeling (rather than on their stories, blaming, or what they are thinking), an amplified field is created that heightens the attendees' capacity to feel, become aware, and get clear. As I get to also sit in this field, the potent environment also heightens *my* clarity, insight, depth, understanding, and capacity to feel.

After spending more than 10,000 hours in this environment of real, authentic sharing and truth, the wisdom of the circle and the intelligence from the group have taught me more than I could ever have learned in a book or seminar. This is why, to this day, my primary work is all done in an amplified field where live group dynamics reveal the very things individuals or couples need to work on in their life and their relationship.

If this sounds scary to you, I assure you that there is nothing to fear. This is one of the most joyful experiences you'll ever have, and once you feel it, you'll want to create an amplified field in your own life. The good news is that this is exactly what I'm going to teach you in this book because with the right partner, you can create a sacred "container" from which you will experience heightened joy, love, clarity, insight, and direction. And isn't that what relationships are truly for? To feel more and be more than you can on your own?

The tragedy is that most relationships cause us to diminish our light, our power, and our gifts, and not enhance them. It's not your fault, nor is it your partners' fault, as you'll soon discover in the following pages, but it's going to require a commitment from you to do the work and look at yourself honestly. Are you in for that?

Good. Let's begin.

The Limitations
of This Book

This work is about taking risks. Not the crazy kind of risks that land you in a heap of trouble, like gambling your entire savings in Vegas or jumping out of a plane without a parachute. I'm referring to the risks that really make a difference in the quality of your life. Consider these questions: Will you risk living your deepest truth in spite of the conditioning set by your culture, family, church, or education? Are you willing to let go of everything you have become to stay true to yourself and true to the vibrant spirit of your heart? Can you risk opening yourself, showing your vulnerability to another in the face of rejection and failure? Will you risk exploring the shadowy corners of your being and risk feeling the depths of your emotional reservoir, touching the parts of you that you've long neglected until you can find peace with it all? Will you risk actually showing up in life and being present, rather than distracting yourself through habit, compulsion, or addiction?

Nearly everyone will say "yes" to the above questions while sitting comfortably in their chair, as no action is required. But the reality is that to apply what will be taught in this book, we need to get support and guidance from those who see beneath the defense, beyond the dynamic, and can hold a space of love, when we've lost the capacity to do that for ourselves. This is needed to navigate the inner shadowlands that are risky to confront if unsupervised.

I wish I could tell you there's a secret formula you just need to follow and you'll be done, simply by reading this book from the comfort of your home. However, this process is more than a set of skills and techniques. It's an awakening practice, something that is best studied live, in a safe, nurturing group environment, like at one of our Insights to Intimacy LIVE seminars. This isn't about my trying to sell you an event. I want to serve you and support you in transforming your life at the deepest level possible. When it comes to matters of the heart, you simply can't receive *everything* you need from a book, video, or online course, and anyone who tells you differently is misinformed.

If relationship health could be achieved by learning the right skills and getting the right information, then this book is all you would need to operate your relational life. The reality is that the very parts of you that are holding you back from having the relationship you want are in your blind spot and won't be accessible to you on your own. That's why I recommend you join our online community and use the home-study companion course to support you on this journey. If you've not already signed up, please do so before we begin Part One. Visit www.HeartIQRelationships.com for instant access using the access code myheartiq.

Inviting Your Partner
to Join You on This Journey

One of the questions I'm asked most often is how one partner who is interested in this work can convince a less enthusiastic partner to try it. I'm sure it won't surprise you to know that more often than not it's a woman asking this question in the hope of recruiting her man to these practices. There's a good news/bad news answer to the question.

The good news is that when approached properly, this can be the richest, most powerful question you'll ever ask your beloved. The bad news is that approaching it properly is not an easy task for many people. There's an underlying paradox, and it applies not just to this work, but to any change you want your partner to make, even healthy changes like getting sober, changing spending habits, or brushing their teeth before going to bed.

The paradox begins with a question you need to ask *yourself*. Can you, right now, right in this red-hot moment, accept and love your partner fully, completely, and unconditionally right where they are? This is a tremendously valuable question. If your honest answer is no, your partner is feeling that from you. Even if you never discuss it, the pressure to be something different is always energetically felt in the container of your relationship, and that pressure itself is the block that will keep your partner stuck in this area. Before you can effectively request that your partner join you in this work or make any other change, it's necessary to overcome your own resistance to the present situation. Sometimes the easiest way to achieve that shift is to put a time frame on it. Can you commit to accepting this person right where they are, loving them completely with your full, open heart, for a certain amount of time, knowing you will reevaluate your position then?

If you can, you have discovered the tool for creating miracles. When your partner absorbs this energetic shift in you—this position of "I love you and *accept you fully* if you do this, and I love you and *accept you fully* if you don't"—only then will change be possible for them. Your contingent-free love will fortify and inspire your partner in ways you can't even yet imagine. That is the essence of true invitation.

The truth of relationships is that we don't all grow at the same pace or in the same direction. It can be painful when you're growing rapidly and your partner is lagging behind. Even when it's not addressed openly, both of you will feel this gap widening between you, and it can strike fear in the heart of the partner who isn't growing. Often this fear manifests as defensiveness or stubbornness, an annoyance that things can't just stay the way they've always been between you. That's why open, raw vulnerability is so critical here.

When you're truly coming from a position of unconditional love and acceptance, you can point out this gap without throwing your partner into defense. You can say, in effect, "I love you and I want us to go to new heights, but I can't make that happen alone. Do you want to join me on this journey? Right now, I'm all in, and my full focus is on you and our partnership. But this ever-widening gap is too much for me to manage on my own, and I need you to work with me to close it. Even if we're working from different positions, at different paces, if we're both working to close it, we're going in the right direction. Otherwise, the gap will keep getting bigger. I need to know whether you care about that and want to help me close it, or you don't."

It doesn't mean you'll always get a yes. But from this position, something very interesting will happen. Either your partner will begin taking steps to join you, or you'll have new clarity around whether or not this relationship is serving you.

It may seem like a subtle distinction, but it's imperative that the invitation comes from an energetic position of complete love and acceptance of the current situation. If it comes from an energy of ultimatum, it will feel manipulative and only serve to increase the gap between you. You're not presenting this information as a threat—simply as an honest, raw assessment of what's going on from your position. It has to have the flavor of an exciting opportunity you can't wait to explore together. You need to convey a genuine expectation that your partner will happily comply. Otherwise, they'll pick up on your doubt and entrain with your negative expectation.

The thing you want to avoid at all costs is conveying the message: "You aren't good enough the way you are so I want us to do this in order to fix you/us." You want to instead seduce your partner into the vision you hold for something beautiful and grand and extraordinary. You want to entrain your partner to your genuine excitement at the prospect of creating this relational masterpiece together. From that position, the possibilities are truly unlimited. Go live them.

Introduction
to Heart IQ Relationships

Y ou know you want it. Deep down, you've *always* wanted it: a blissful, connected, magnetically charged love relationship with a wonderfully matched partner who sees you fully and adores you endlessly. Does it sound like a fairy tale? It's not. No matter what your current relationship status might be, you're about to gain access to that dream. The powerful, proven practices you are about to learn will unlock the romantic connection and deeper intimacy you've always longed to experience.

This relationship book is unlike any other. It will show you how to be in an authentic, delicious relationship with *yourself*, and you'll discover why that's such a critical precursor to being in a relationship with a partner. You'll recognize your long-buried truth as you blast through the all-too-common myths that have kept you from experiencing relationship bliss.

When you and your partner practice integrating the three synergistic components of a Heart IQ Relationship, you'll have the tools to transform your entire experience of life. You'll be:

1. Powerfully, naturally healing each other's past wounds and neglect.

2. Using communication skills that keep you deeply, meaningfully connected to your beloved and to yourself.

3. Enjoying a healthy sexual connection that provides an endless stream of aliveness and vitality for you both.

You may have heard the myth that personal growth is very much a solo, individual process. That's not true. Your optimal healing requires others. When you understand the principles of Heart IQ, which I will share with you throughout this book, your partnership becomes the catalyst to deep healing and the ability to feel unprecedented joy. Of course, it is not responsible for your joy or happiness, but your relationship provides the pathway to your next level of emotional healing and expansion.

A Heart IQ Relationship is built on extraordinary communication skills that will allow you to deliver your truth so powerfully and authentically that it instantly lands in your partner's heart. Likewise, you'll learn to receive your partner, skillfully offering reassurance while sharing whatever is moving for you (that is, whatever you are feeling, sensing, or thinking in the moment). The communication practices you'll learn with this book will combine into a single cohesive style of communication that will bring your connection to unprecedented heights.

The final aspect of a Heart IQ Relationship is potent, sexual magnetism and polarity with your partner. Sexual magnetism and passion is the piece that's so easy to lose in an ongoing partnership, and sharing a Heart IQ Relationship means knowing how to rebuild and rekindle it. When sexual energy gets repressed, it's rarely only about sex. When the passion is gone, much of the joy of life goes with it. You experience loss of drive and loss of clarity; your health may even start to deteriorate. You can't access certain emotions, and your apathy spirals into many different areas of your life. You'll be surprised to learn how important a healthy sexual connection is to your overall enjoyment of life and how easy it is to reclaim it.

Are You Ready to Embrace Change?

You're about to embark on a journey that will emphatically change your relationship—and your life—so let's talk for a moment about change. When I was a chiropractor, I was fascinated with the idea that a very small, subtle touch on a patient's spine can generate a profound change in their emotional expression. It's a nonlinear transformation; sometimes the smallest input can create a very large output in terms of seeing a difference in a person or situation.

I want you to keep that in mind as you progress through this book because talking less and doing less can quite often create the space for us to feel each other in new and meaningful ways that can transform our mind's idea about what is possible and open our hearts to a deeper love than we've ever known. Just as it is the spaces between the notes that create music, it's the spaces between the words and actions in our relationships that can create the most intimacy.

Even though the insights in this book promise profound change, you must understand that it is never your job to specifically change your partner. That's a trap so many of us fall into, but it just doesn't work. You're not here to "fix" your partner or your relationship because there is nothing to fix. Instead, your role is to practice loving "what is," without making "what is" wrong. Notice I said *practice*. This process of loving your partner unconditionally is not an easy task, especially when your partner activates your wounds and triggers.

Let me be frank and bust some myths for you early on. There is no such thing as a completely healed and whole human being (who's considered to be a "finished product"), nor is there such a thing as a perfect relationship, or for that matter, a perfect partner who's "the one" and perfect in every way. This is fairy-tale thinking, and although common during the honeymoon phase of the relationship, if it continues, it usually does more harm than good and indicates potential denial. The truth is that we're all works in progress, and because there is no one else on earth *exactly* like us, we need to have good communication skills to bridge the gap of misunderstanding and disconnection that inevitably comes up when two people come together.

The thing is, you and your partner are both perfectly imperfect, and your mission, if you choose to accept it, is to love each other *in* your imperfections. It's about loving each other for who you are *and* for who you are not. I think that's good news because if you can love the good, the bad, and the ugly, you free yourself from the prison of conditional love. Of course, just because it doesn't work to fix our partner, it doesn't preclude us from taking it to a dramatically more vitalized and enjoyable level.

Now please listen carefully: If you desperately desire to change yourself because you believe you're not okay as you are, you will *not* succeed. But if you want to change because your current circumstances don't match the person you know yourself to be, then you *can* change, successfully and sustainably. The same goes for your relationship. If you hate your relationship and believe it's irreparably damaged and broken, you're not in the right starting position to apply these concepts. You must first find the goodness at the core of your partnership (and yourself) and appreciate what it has brought you so far, before you can elevate it to the glorious heights it's worthy of. The simple fact that you are reading this book does illustrate your present devotion to your partner and your desire for a deeper connection and greater intimacy—so give these practices all you've got! (If you're not sure you're in the right relationship for you, you'll gain clarity on that as you read this book and try out the suggestions.)

We can't change by shedding or getting rid of any aspects or traits we don't like. It's all part of the totality of who we are, and we must embrace who we are right now without judgments to be able to move forward. Not being okay with any part of you is what keeps you stuck. The first step is to love yourself and embrace who you are right now to the best of your ability. You must first connect to your intrinsic value (that isn't dependent on anything or anyone) and expand your awareness of it, so that life can come about in a new way to reflect your new state of worth.

But I must warn you. Reaching for that connection with your core goodness might seem ironically challenging: The more you connect to what you want, the more your unworthiness will come up. Your unhealed subconscious is whispering, *Who are you to deserve this kind of divine relationship anyway?* It sucks, but it's all for the best really. The more your unworthiness surfaces, the more you can heal it. When you feel that unworthiness creeping up and you shine light on it, you can begin to digest it bit by bit, and it will come up less and less in your life.

Neale Donald Walsch says, "Whatever you try to get rid of; will get rid of you." It doesn't work to try to get rid of anything we don't like in ourselves or in our relationships, and it's impossible anyway. The effort to get rid of it will consume you because anytime you focus your attention on something, whether it's good or bad, you cause it to grow. That's why it's far more productive to focus on moving toward joy in your relationship than it is to focus on what's not working in a misguided attempt to "fix" it.

In the same way that it's impossible to get rid of anything, it's impossible to keep anything. If you get happy feelings and try to cling to them, your clinging will make them go away. It's like trying to grab water. Feelings are states that move through you in the present moment. It's impossible to keep any one state of being in your life full time, so intimacy requires learning to embrace, love, and support all of your authentic emotions (and your partner's) in the moment, as they surface.

I want to say this one more time to ensure it lands: Watch out for the subtle agenda you might be running to try to change your life and relationship because you're not accepting where you are right now. This can't be stressed enough. If your motivation for change is coming from not being okay where you are today, then the change will never stick, as you're starting out from a place of self-judgment where you're telling yourself that you should be further along or better in some way. This is what I call "push energy," and it creates tension and suffering. If you're hard on yourself and push yourself to grow, you will lose depth and will disconnect from your own joy and intrinsic value, eventually collapsing from the strain and burning out into a numbing malaise.

Therefore, improve your life and relationships from a place of self-love and love for each other. Connect to your longing for a deeper, more intimate connection while simultaneously appreciating all you have achieved so far, celebrating your decision to take your life to the next level.

If it feels like this is a lot to take in, don't despair. I'll be going into greater depth on all of these concepts throughout this book, as well as sharing many more, as we take these insightful steps to unlocking the greatest bliss you've ever known. Let's continue, shall we?

SUCCESS STORY FROM JUDITH & GRAHAM

Judith began her Heart IQ journey about a year before her husband, Graham, joined her. They are both now actively involved and have just celebrated their 25th wedding anniversary.

Judith says that Graham has changed since coming into the work: "He used to get stressed when things went wrong in our relationship because he couldn't fix them. I felt uncertain that I could share with him what I was feeling because I didn't want to cause him stress. Graham has learned the importance of just being there with me, which means that I could tell him what I was going through, knowing that he can hold me without needing to fix my pain."

Graham says that he has seen wonderful changes in Judith, too: "Judith is enjoying life more, both with and without me. We've both learned to say what we want, rather than what the other thinks we should want."

The couple was overjoyed to receive a message from their niece on their 25th wedding anniversary. Even in the midst of the pain of her own parents' divorce, she shared, "I would be happy as anything to have a relationship like yours."

Need help applying this in your relationship?
Visit www.HeartIQRelationships.com for FREE demos
and tutorials using the access code myheartiq.

PART ONE

How to Become a Healthy You

CHAPTER 1

Elevating Your Heart IQ

Our default state, as human beings, is *joy*. The only things keeping us from experiencing an endless stream of joy are the judgments we constantly run. It's as if joy were raining down upon us at all times, but we're only holding up a thimble to catch our share when we could be catching oceans of it!

Heart IQ is learning to watch and notice what closes us to receiving joy, so that we can choose to remain open instead. When we become aware of how we close, we need to start loving and accepting it with deep, sincere appreciation. The irony (and secret) to fully loving and accepting yourself is that this can only be fully realized through the power of being felt and witnessed by others. If you're someone who is attached to your independence, what I've just shared may not sit well with you. To think that you *need* others to love yourself goes against nearly all modern wisdom. It's true: Independence and self-sufficiency are incredibly important qualities on the journey of emotional freedom and health. But there comes a time when doing it on our own and being self-sufficient aren't enough. It's lonely and we soon crave deeper love that can come only from becoming interdependent, where we can be seen, felt, and appreciated by others while struggling in the swampland of our unworthiness.

Simply put, we need to hold two truths simultaneously: 1) I am whole and complete unto myself, and 2) I need others to fully thrive and heal.

The days of the independent spiritual practice are coming to an end. Working on ourselves by ourselves provides a slow vehicle of transformation, compared to the wonderful potential of growth through our intimate relationships.

Nearly all trauma from our past stems from feeling disconnected from important people in our life. The disconnect we feel shapes how we relate to and connect to others later on as we mature. As others were intricately part of the disconnection we felt, it makes sense that others will be needed to heal it. However, you'd be amazed at how many professional therapists, counselors, and healers still hold a notion that a one-to-one or solo practice or intervention can sustainably alter the patterns of deep relationship entanglement. We live in a relational world where our complex behaviors change and adapt to the different people who come into our lives.

You can't fully awaken on your own, and meditating on a mountaintop in isolation can only get you so far. The only way to master your inner world is to practice coming into peace with others, as they are mirrors and reflections of your own conflicting parts and the relationship you have with yourself.

There is a caveat though: Both partners need to be in a certain frame of mind, looking at the world through a particular lens, to facilitate this wondrous, mutual healing. Both need to be able to hold unconditional loving space for the other, free of judgments, resentments, unspoken needs, and unmet expectations. Rarely do we look at our partners through such lenses, and that is why many relationships are more harming than healing. Without the benefit of elevating our Heart IQ, we're likely to reinforce and solidify old wounds in one another. That's why the insights you will learn in this book are so imperative.

Where Do You Fall in This Spectrum of Relationship Scenarios?

No matter what your current relationship status may be, the insights in this book will transform your life. Becoming conscious of your starting point will help you create the road map to your desired destination, so take a moment now to read through the following relationship scenarios and see which one fits you best.

➢ Is Your Relationship in a "Bad" Place?

The purpose of a relationship is to help us access our joy. But it doesn't always seem that way when you're triggered, hurt, and in defense. If you've suffered trauma in the past or have been betrayed and believe you can't trust in your partner again, then it's time to inject some Heart IQ medicine into your relationship!

If you are considering separating or getting a divorce (and especially if kids are involved), don't proceed until you've read this book or attended one of my Insights to Intimacy LIVE seminars. You'll be amazed to discover that what had seemed like irreconcilable differences can turn into small blips that will be easy to navigate.

Since relationships are meant to bring up our old wounds, and we all attract the perfect people to facilitate our healing, there are instances where seemingly "bad" relationships are actually precisely what we need to further our personal awareness and emotional growth. Of course, there are other instances where separation *is* the highest and wisest choice, and when it's time to close a connection, you'll want to do it in the healthiest way—emotionally, energetically, practically, and spiritually. This is hugely important if you want to eventually open to a new relationship that is healthy and enriching. (You'll find complete instructions for consciously closing relationships in Chapter 11.)

➢ Is Your Relationship Doing "Okay," but the Spark Has Gone?

Many relationships survive, but most never get an opportunity to thrive. When two people in love commit to a long-term partnership, it's common for life, kids, stress, and entropy to get in the way of ever-deepening intimacy and connection. Over time, it's easy to let the duties and stresses of everyday life create a wall between you and your partner, causing you to grow apart. Codependent dynamics can kick in, where you lose yourself and forget who *you* really are! Life revolves around the family and children, but what about *your* dreams, *your* life, and *your* essence?

After a while, sex becomes just "okay," and you find it difficult to think of new things to talk about. You may notice that your roles have switched, and you now have to compensate for what your partner is no longer bringing to the relationship. The feeling is not an intense, "something is radically wrong here" feeling, but instead, it's felt as a subtle, numbing *dis-ease*. Things are okay, but something deeper, something you once hoped and longed for, is missing. Your heart knows it, but your mind keeps you busy enough to ignore it.

No longer. Don't settle for a mediocre connection when you have the chance to gain new insights that will allow you to launch your intimacy to new heights and relight the spark. How many more years are you willing to wait before the mundane becomes intolerable? Your children are learning everything about what healthy relationships look like from your example. With the practices you're about to learn, you can show them something new and different, something heart intelligent.

➤ Do You Want to See How Deep the Rabbit Hole Goes?

If you're in a vibrant, connected, and stable relationship with trust fully intact, you're going to love the insights you'll glean from this book. You'll learn what's possible for your relationship and rediscover the limitlessness of what you and your partner can accomplish together. The focus for you is not just about healing your past, navigating triggers, or finding your way back home after getting lost in your pain, but instead, it is to expand your intimate, sexual, and emotional range so that you can experience a depth of authentic love you never knew existed.

➤ *Are You Single?*

It's easy to think that relationship books are only for couples, but singles can get great value from the Heart IQ tools, too! Wouldn't it be useful for you to know what you need to be and do to attract a healthy, loving partner? And when you're in your next relationship, wouldn't it be amazing to already *have* the skills and insights to build the intimacy you crave without falling into the common traps that couples without this knowledge inevitably fall into?

Are You Ready for Real Love?

The answer is yes. Even if you're afraid you still have "baggage." Even if you feel you're on a self-development journey and you haven't yet quite "arrived." Even if you're not sure you've cleared the emotional debris from prior relationships. Right where you are, right now, is exactly where you're meant to be, and from this precise vantage point, you are a perfect candidate for the right relationship. In fact, one of the myths I'll be dispelling for you is the myth that you have to be "ready" for real love.

It's a bit of a chicken-and-egg scenario, really. Yes, it's true that you need to be willing to know yourself and work on yourself to have the kind of blissful partnership I'm promising here. But a common misperception is that you need to be totally "fixed," healed, and baggage-free before you enter into a new coupling or it will be doomed from the start. That is not the case at all, as you will see. In fact, the very best way to accelerate your personal growth is to be in a relationship, especially when you master the tools I'm about to offer you.

Yes, you will need to do personal work and you'll need to do relational work, but one does not need to precede the other. It's a delicate dance. We need to heal in order to have healthy relationships, *and* we need relationships in order to heal. We can gain insight on our own and come into ever more strength within ourselves, but we need relationships to fully digest our accumulated pain, transforming it into wisdom, peace, and bliss.

More Myths and Truths

Let's look at a few of the other relationship myths I'll be updating and shedding new light on as we take this journey together. The truths behind these myths were never taught to you when you were young, but knowing them as you develop these life skills will be an investment that will pay off in your relationship with your partner as well as in every other area of your life.

MYTH: "The quality of my relationship is determined by my childhood wounding."

TRUTH: It isn't your wounds themselves, but your relationship to your wounds that determines the quality of your romantic partnership. You don't need to know what happened in your past or who did what to you. No matter what trauma you may have experienced, the real power to heal comes from adjusting your relationship to that wounding. This is where you will reclaim your wholeness.

You don't even need to know what form the wounding took! You might be wounded from some invasive energy that was directed toward you as a young child. Or you might be wounded by neglect—the very common scenario of not having received the kind of clear, bright, unbridled love you were programmed to expect as a human infant. In either scenario, your wounding is something that will surface in your relationship and will require skillful handling. However, it's a myth to assume that your past could fate you to have problematic relationships. In this book, you will learn the skills to adjust your relationship to the wounding so that it can benefit—rather than detract from—your relationship health.

MYTH: "It takes a lot of hard work to create and maintain a successful relationship."

TRUTH: The more we learn to relax in each other's presence, the easier we can see, hear, and feel each other, and naturally meet in our longing to be connected. It's true that intimacy does require intense effort at times, but only in the sense that it can be difficult to circumvent our complex defense systems in order to do our own meaningful inner work.

Successfully upgrading what we've learned from the past comes from our loving and accepting *what is* first, without needing to change it, judge it, or make it wrong in any way. Creating what we want doesn't come from the fuel of fearfully avoiding what we don't want. Working hard in a state of worry and stress to fix your relationship's troubled areas will never bring you the kind of blissful connection you're longing for.

It's important to define a balance between the things you both need to do and learn and the things that you both need to feel and receive. Intimacy grows from the give and take of being and doing, receiving and giving, listening and expressing, learning and feeling, action and stillness. It's the art of "and-ness" rather than the "either-or" approach that most of us have been taught. Just like a garden grows from both sunlight and rain, intimacy needs both hard work and relaxation to flourish.

MYTH: "We need to discover and address the issues that block us from our joy before we can be more joyful."

TRUTH: We do not need to dig up our past to find our issues. When we move toward our joy, our long-standing core issues come up naturally. They're disguised as current-day judgments, arguments, misunderstandings, or hurt feelings. In reality, these disturbances are actually our old, undigested wounds that have been causing us to feel unworthy of being abundantly joyful and in love with life.

Of course there is value in self-analysis and continual growth. But an overemphasis on self-improvement can become addictive and swampy, trapping you in the heavy drama of defining your life by your blockages. This kind of hyperfocus doesn't serve you. A better approach is to simply move toward your joy, allowing your resistances to automatically show up. You don't have to go looking for your stuff; your stuff will find you!

It's possible to be joyful while acknowledging all your undigested, unfinished business. It's important to explore and acknowledge all of our parts—our best assets as well as our shadowy, predatory parts. When you get used to accepting these shadows, you can actually feel good about feeling bad. You can take these unacceptable parts of your past and transform them into the insights that lead to your awakening.

But here's a caveat on the other end of the spectrum: One can use the joyful presence of the moment to avoid dealing with the issues that need to be examined. I call it a "New Age bypass" when a person avoids pain and truth by claiming to have already "cleared" old emotional blocks. It's not really possible to "clear" negative emotions because negative emotions don't actually exist. What many call "negative" is really just a judgment of an energy that is either misunderstood or channeled in an unhealthy way. For example, some might say anger is a negative emotion. True, this energy can be harmful when we have a closed heart. However, when we do the work to embrace our anger (our power and the core inner fire that burns in each of us), our anger now becomes the foundation to our aliveness, sexuality, and healthy boundaries with others.

When you channel any quality, any emotion, through the awareness and goodness of your heart, the result is always beneficial. Therefore, if any emotion is creating undesirable feelings, behaviors, and results in your life, it's a clear message that there is a part of you in judgment and in conflict with itself, and thus your heart is partially closed. This is important for you to be aware of because awareness of your closure is necessary for you to open.

Again, you don't need to look for or focus on your "negative emotions" or parts of you that have closed down. Your disowned parts will surface in their own time, in their natural place within your healing journey. Moving toward joy is the first step, and then watching very closely how your energy, emotions, and thoughts try to derail your intimacy is the second step. This art of watching your inner world is called "tracking," and I'll be covering how to do this in a later chapter.

MYTH: "Letting my partner know what I'm really thinking and feeling will give my partner evidence to judge or blame me, and in the end, I will feel worse for having exposed too much of myself. Some things are better left unsaid."

TRUTH: The more we can track and express our internal thoughts and emotions as a real-time process in each other's presence, the more we can deeply feel each other in our living-breathing aliveness. That's the indescribable bliss of true intimacy! Who we are is continually evolving in each second, so to know each other at this level requires our willingness to expose our processes to each other as they are unfolding (not just when we're feeling clear after personal reflection). This means being willing to take a risk and share what you're feeling, thinking, and sensing in the moment, without giving any prior thought to how your partner will receive it.

However, here's a caveat: Although I recommend sharing your truest and deepest feelings and many of your thoughts with your partner, this does not translate into sharing absolutely *everything* you are thinking. For instance, if a sexual fantasy featuring your next-door neighbor suddenly pops into your mind, it probably won't benefit your relationship to share those details with your partner. Our minds move in mysterious ways and come up with all kinds of thoughts that don't bring meaningfulness to our lives. However, if this fantasy turns into an ongoing distraction or longing you wish to follow, then it is actually important to acknowledge your lack of presence and share the reasons for it with your partner.

Being willing to take this kind of risk translates into your choosing to trust yourself and your partner, rather than staying defended and censored in the way that you manage your communication with each other. The real risk is in allowing yourself to be seen and valued in the unfolding process of who you are becoming, rather than believing you need to "have it all together" and only share once you're clear, aware of your part, and in a good space.

MYTH: "In order to feel good, we need to avoid feeling bad."

TRUTH: It's very common to avoid feeling our pain. Perhaps we're trying to avoid getting lost in the drama, or we have a judgment that feeling our pain is bad or weak, or that in feeling it, we might feel something that makes us realize a truth we've been avoiding. However, it's of vital importance that we feel what is moving within us and that we get present to the wisdom and insight contained within it. This is not the same as dwelling in our complaints or being a victim to circumstances. It only means that if we are hurting, that hurt will not go away until it's felt and if we don't go within to feel it, we will act out and project our unconscious unfelt feelings on to others and the world.

The good news is that pain no longer feels painful when we embrace it! It is possible to feel good feeling bad. As you allow what you are feeling to move through you without judgment or story, you begin to learn how to use the energy of pain to inspire your creativity while deepening your ability to love and feel grateful for what you have. Pain is a source of power, and like the alcohol in the wine, it's what makes the wine rich—but too much will kill you.

7 Insights for Creating a Delicious Relationship

The following seven insights are vital for a successful Heart IQ Relationship. Each of them is essential on its own; however, the true power of this framework is realized only when each insight is integrated into a cohesive practice.

1. Connect to Your Joy

You must have a way to access your joy that is independent of your partner. Whenever your personal joy is intrinsically tied to another person, you've created a codependent, emotionally unhealthy relationship. Naturally, you don't want to go to the other extreme either and be completely indifferent to your partner's suffering. There is a balance to be found. You want to be able to empathize with your beloved, but also be able to access and open your own heart as an independent, sovereign human being.

2. Create a Safe Space

Safety is critical for depth. Therefore, if you want to experience a deep, loving, and authentic connection, you must explore what you need to safely open up to your partner. Everyone is different, and you will also need to discover how to access the unique key that will unlock your partner's heart, creating room for both of you to feel sheltered and secure in your relationship.

3. Communicate Effectively from the Heart

Heart-centered communication is one of the most essential life skills you can learn. It is sharing yourself in a way that allows you to navigate defense and get your needs met without manipulation and code. "Code" is my term for any form of communication that evades the direct truth you want to express, softening it with confusing language or burying it under manipulative hints and suggestions. It can manifest as sarcasm, hint-dropping, manipulative flattery, or even humor. It's terribly frustrating to be on the receiving end of coded communication, even though it's often delivered in an attempt to be polite or liked. When you master heart-centered communication, you receive others easily, creating a safe space for them to open and share more of themselves, and allowing intimacy to naturally expand.

4. Become More Responsive

Responsiveness is the natural spontaneous giving and receiving of love, attention, words, movement, sound, and touch when your heart is open. Becoming more responsive requires embodiment (an in-the-body awareness of what you are experiencing on various levels) and your uninhibited, spontaneous presence with yourself and another. When mastered, this skill is the most critical ingredient for thriving intimacy.

5. *Claim Each Other*

"Claiming your partner" means deciding that you are "all in" the relationship, at least for a given period of time, and being willing to open yourself fully to making it work. When you don't ask for what you want, it's easy to assume your partner is not "the one" and start looking for greener grass. Instead of owning, expressing, and allowing your needs to be met, you let an inner hunger grow in the shadows, which eventually expresses itself as "leaky" behavior. An important part of healthy relationships is sealing off the leaks to give intimacy a chance to grow.

6. *Be Vulnerable and Heal Your Trauma Together*

Relationships are a perfect vehicle for healing your past hurts, wounds, and trauma. However, if you can't track this dynamic when it surfaces, your partner will seem like the enemy, triggering everything you want to move away from. Understanding how our old traumas are activated within our relationships and how to navigate the vicious cycles of suffering and defense is critical to relationship success.

7. *Activate and Sustain a Healthy Sexual Connection and Passion*

A healthy sexual connection is not just about sex. It's about feeling alive and free in your capacity to feel your emotion and your sexual energy and share it in an uncontained, spontaneous way with your partner. Conscious, heart-centered sexuality can provide the springboard to new levels of joy you can't yet even imagine! Polarity—the dance between masculine and feminine energies—plays a crucial role in keeping the charge strong.

Aim for Mastery

With so many options for personal development and spiritual expansion, it's harder and harder for those genuinely on a path of transformation to find the real deal. How do you discern where to find real depth? From my own experience, *mastery* is the defining variable. Mastery happens by directing your focused passion and dedication into some part of your experience in a way that it becomes your own expression. It doesn't matter what you focus on, except that mastery must be your aim. Whether it's to be a masterful dancer, a parent, an entrepreneur, or a lover, your focus on mastery is the doorway to competence in anything you do.

Imagine a steep mountain. Two groups of people want to climb it and get to the top. The first group races ahead and begins the climb, reaching the foothills to enjoy the view. But when they look at the remaining climb ahead, they determine that the path is too difficult to continue. They come back down to search for an alternative route. They walk around the base and take what looks like an easier path on a different side of the mountain. On their second attempt, they reach the foothills again and enjoy the view from a different vantage point. However, their elevation has not changed, and they are no closer to reaching the summit.

The second group takes longer to get ready and prepares with in-depth training before venturing up the path to the mountain. When this group reaches the foothills, they have gained the necessary skill, courage, and trust to continue their journey. They have the inner resources to get them through the hardship. When everything around them tells them they can't go on, they access a force internally that says, *I can do this.* They persist and reach the top.

Now here's the interesting conclusion to this metaphor: Once you've reached the top of the mountain, you don't just see the path you took, but you also see that all paths lead to the top. Your perspective expands to behold all the possible ways you could have made it there. When it comes to life mastery, there are myriad paths to take, but all of them require a dedicated commitment to pushing through the uncomfortable, disappointing rocky spots. The question I want you to consider is this: What could be more meaningful, fulfilling, and joyful than dedicating yourself to mastering your relationships? In my opinion, nothing! I believe that this is the most rewarding journey you could ever undertake, and you can use this book as your road map.

"Safety" and "Comfort" Are Worlds Apart

Before going any further, there's an important distinction to be made so that you don't confuse safety with being comfortable. They are not the same thing. People who don't feel safe tend to cling to comfort, even when it dulls and numbs their experience of life. Imagine walking a tightrope. You're about to step from the edge of the platform onto the rope when you notice there's no safety net. If you fall, you'll die. Do you walk the rope? Probably not. But if you imagine looking down and seeing a safety net, are you more likely to take that step? Of course you are. A safety net actually gives you permission to explore your fear of heights. It's the same with the rest of life. It's only when you feel safe that you can finally open up to exploring your insecurities and venturing into the unknown territory of risk, adventure, and uninhibited self-expression.

Why is safety so important? It's because when you don't feel safe, you guard your heart, and love can't come in or out. Feeling safe gives your heart permission to open and allows you to feel your depth and truth. Consider one more metaphor: Imagine a castle protecting a beautiful princess. Surrounded by a thick wall and plenty of guards, the castle remains well protected from harm. However, while the defenses are up, the princess cannot know what it feels like to love, explore, and enjoy her life. She is trapped. When a threat approaches the castle, the guards keep the doors closed. A "lack of safety" has been detected, and the princess remains successfully unharmed. But what if the guards are overly responsive in their protection? What if a friend approaches the castle and the doors remain closed? Or worse, the prince himself? Of course, the opposite can also happen. What if the guards are sleeping and danger is allowed to penetrate?

We all have that vulnerable part inside us that is protected by walls of defense. Some of us have overprotective guards, and others let harm come straight through the door. Developing the art of true safety entails establishing an accurate and appropriate response to threat, so that you can open when love is present and close when it isn't. Therefore, the aim is not simply to open because opening is not better than closure. Both are necessary, depending upon the circumstance. Many people open too easily and quickly to those who don't yet deserve to hold the heart they've been given. In other cases, hearts remain closed after many years of genuine loving. To have the intimacy you crave, you must learn to take back control of your defense system so that you can feel safe in your own world while also providing a safe haven for your partner to relax into.

Safety, of course, goes much deeper and further than determining the appropriate and accurate response to threat. Safety goes straight into the heart and soul of your connection to divinity and all of life. My fellow spiritual teacher David Deida uses a lovely analogy: Imagine that you are represented by light streaming through a stained-glass window. You notice that some of the panels are broken and missing. Not happy with the imperfection, you go about trying to replace the missing pieces and repair the damage. This response represents how you sometimes try to fix yourself—thinking you are broken, imperfect, and needing to repair the damage from your past.

Then you notice that not much light comes through the window because the glass is so dirty and dusty. So you decide to change your life by exercising, eating better, and going to a yoga class. As a result, you feel lighter and more whole. Neither response is wrong; however, they're both based upon an erroneous assumption. Plain and simple, you are not the window that needs fixing or brightening. You are the light that shines through the window.

Whether or not you're broken or dusty, the condition of the stained-glass window makes no difference whatsoever to who you are. It does, however, make a massive difference in how you feel. It's one thing to know who you are as a concept and another thing altogether to actually experience the goodness of who you are. Therefore, to improve the experience of our lives, we must do the work in all three areas. We must dust ourselves off and discover what brightens us. We must repair and heal the wounds of our past. And, most important, we must awaken our sense of self so we can integrate the understanding that we are actually the light itself.

Out of this knowing, true safety is born. It is knowing irrefutably that life has your back—that you can trust that you are connected at a deep level to everything and everyone. This can't be solely an intellectual knowing; it needs to be a deep embodied awareness that you carry with you throughout your daily existence. When you can touch the place inside you that is bathed in safety, while tenderly caring for your wounds and shining brightly as you clean your body and emotions, then you will be one step closer to having unlocked your bliss. And the insight for this multifaceted unlocking is found within your primary intimate relationship.

SUCCESS STORY FROM MARC & NATASHA

Marc and Natasha met at a retreat after both being involved in the work for a while. Marc says, "I can be there in my weakness, in my collapse, in my smallness, and Natasha holds space for me. She allows me to be there without trying to fix or change me. I feel loved in that place, and that's creating change in every area of my life. Every day, I'm discovering new insights and new parts of me. I feel totally and utterly alive and wonderful!"

Natasha says, "Heart IQ has radically transformed my life from a very isolated experience to one where I feel very connected, loved, and supported in community. The work I've done in circle has allowed me to be in relationship in a way that I've never been able to do before, and this is what has remained and sustained, with no effort to keep it."

When asked what one ingredient has made the biggest difference, Marc and Natasha agreed: "The biggest thing that Heart IQ has contributed to our relationship is the level of safety. If we can't be a safe haven for each other, then we have no business being in this intimate relationship."

Need help applying this in your relationship?
Visit www.HeartIQRelationships.com for FREE demos
and tutorials using the access code myheartiq.

CHAPTER 2

Coming into Joy
Through Your Relationship

One truth I've discovered is that relationships are required for healing and growth. When you become romantically involved with someone, your combined energy creates a focused field that brings your incomplete "stuff" to the surface so that necessary healing can take place. Because it can be so uncomfortable to have the incomplete parts of us exposed, we will often make the relationship wrong for being the catalyst that it's actually meant to be.

I want to show you how you can assist your own healing by understanding the relationship dynamics that come up for you and how to expertly navigate them. When you utilize Heart IQ practices, your relationship will become the greatest medicine you've ever received, and more important, you'll realize that the whole process of healing together can not only be profound but can also be profoundly enjoyable!

This information is based upon one remarkable idea that you might want to adopt as your relationship motto. For me, it is a simple truth. *The purpose of relationships is to come into joy.* It's easy to think that people come together to learn from each other or grow or serve, but the reality is that we seek out relationships with others to feel joy, and we tend to leave them when there's an ongoing lack of it. It's true that many other agendas bring us together, but I'm speaking to the simple truth of why we crave to connect with one another—why we need the nourishment of intimate emotional, physical, mental, energetic, and spiritual connection with others.

It's vital to find healthy ways to be nourished in life because there's so much that each of us is here to do and share in this world. You are a priceless resource that deserves to be valued. And your romantic relationship is meant to be your home base where your value is cherished and nurtured every day. If it's not, then this could be the perfect time for you to explore why your relationship isn't the place where your roots feel safe to grow deep into who you are. You are a gift to be cared for, and it is important that you learn how to become a fully healthy you. This is the greatest gift you can give to yourself, your partner, your children, and the world. Making this commitment to yourself will change your life and give you the freedom to also become a fully healthy, vital couple. And with that, everyone wins!

If I'm Okay As I Am, Why Do I Need to Heal?

The first step in comprehending how relationships heal us is to understand why there is even a need for healing. Are we really all that damaged? The answer is complex.

At our core—which many call our "essence"—there is only goodness. It can never be taken, damaged, or turned into something "bad." When someone says, "They are rotten to the core" or "Deep down, they are evil," they are confusing the energy/behaviors arising from damaged parts with the deepest divine spark, which lives in everyone, no matter how destructive their unenlightened actions may be.

This is often a difficult concept to digest as many of us fiercely hold resentments and pain in relation to another's harming actions, and the only way we can justify our ongoing anger or hatred is to assume the perpetrator is intrinsically bad. It's a form of victimization and projection of our own lack of understanding of our own intrinsic goodness. We can only see in another what we can see in ourselves.

When you begin to see others as intrinsically good, although they themselves may be completely disconnected from this goodness, then you can begin to have compassion for their soul and the life circumstances that have led to their own inner separation. You become part of the solution rather than part of the problem. This idea is simple to write, but not so easy to apply in life.

So, if we're good at the core, why do certain people act the way they do? Why would an intrinsically good person rape, abuse, murder, or inflict violence upon others? Only people who are separated from their goodness can act in such a way. This separation was inevitably created early on by an environment of disconnection and remains in place as a background unconscious operating system. Basically, if we forget or lose touch with who we really are, we will begin to believe we are bad or unworthy, or worse, we will see the world and others as a target on which to project our inner pain.

Emotionally healthy individuals, on the other hand, can easily distinguish between their damaged parts, their unworthy belief systems, and their core intrinsic goodness. Most of us, however, lie somewhere between this place of deep forgetting and awareness. Some moments we feel okay, and in other moments, we can drop into a place of collapse, self-doubt, and unworthiness, ignoring our divine spark that lies beneath. Heart IQ, therefore, is a way to access and actualize our divine spark, and, like exercise, it is something that needs consistent practice.

As this topic of core unworthiness and intrinsic goodness is such an important concept, let's go deeper with it. When you were born into this world, you were bright-eyed and fully present. You were pure goodness and love (and you still are). You can see it when you look at any newborn baby. There is no badness, wrongness, or emotional deficiency of any kind. But as the baby goes through life, he or she inevitably experiences various forms of trauma and neglect. There is wounding to the child. Parents, caregivers, friends, teachers, extended family, and others cause suffering and pain, whether consciously or unconsciously. Often even with no awareness or intention to do so, people simply act in ways that negatively impact the growing child.

As young children, we don't have the ability to identify ourselves as separate from our parents. We hold the reality that "it's all about me." So when our parents are stressed out, unloving, violent, or emotionally stilted and disconnected, our nervous system feels that disharmony and personalizes it. As young children, we conclude that everything we witness has to do with ourselves. We confuse *feeling* bad with *being* bad. Even if the tension we're energetically picking up has nothing at all to do with us, any bad feeling expressed in the home makes us believe we are at some level at fault. Subconsciously, the child's experience is: *If I'm not feeling good, there must be something wrong with me.* Over time, we continue to accumulate self-doubt, heaviness, and negative conclusions about ourselves, and that accumulation is what I'm referring to when I talk about "core unworthiness."

Beliefs that generate our sense of "core unworthiness" begin to accumulate for different people at different times. For some, this process begins during the early years of childhood, and for others, it could be much earlier, as in the case of a traumatic birth or a stressful pregnancy, creating a disconnection between mother and child, even while in the womb.

During pregnancy, the child is completely open, with no emotional defenses whatsoever. Then that child is dramatically plunged into a world where so much of the environment is disconnected. Even in the most harmonious families, most parents don't know how to be completely present and *feel* into their child—in other words, how to be deeply, unconditionally empathetic. Even if we experienced a non-traumatic birth and a blissful connection in the womb, most of us experienced either direct or indirect wounding in our early formative years.

Direct Wounding vs. Indirect Wounding

There are two forms of wounding we receive in our early childhood and throughout our lives. The first is direct wounding, an intrusive form of wounding that occurs when something happens that should not happen. Something was said to us or done to us—maybe sexual abuse, physical abuse, or emotional abuse—at a time when we were wide open and trusting. This kind of direct, intrusive abuse smashes our sense of safety (our safety container) and forces us to construct energetic, protective walls around us in order to function and live our lives.

While direct wounding is horrifically common, there is another kind of wounding that is far more prevalent. This second type of wounding is so subtle that if you asked most victims of it if they had ever suffered abuse, they would say they had not. The basis of this indirect form of wounding is neglect. It's not being "gotten," understood, or appreciated; our feelings go unrecognized (we are not being *felt*), and we are not acknowledged for who we are at our core (we are not being *seen into*). It's being born into an emotional void, where our primary caregivers were not able to be in their hearts enough to create the kind of warm, safe container that human infants are programmed to require for their optimal growth and thriving.

We may have been fed, kept clean, and sheltered, but not sufficiently encouraged, uplifted, challenged in a healthy way, and/or permitted to be our full selves. This has been the case for most of us. In subtle, unseen ways, our hearts were neglected. We weren't given permission to feel and express the full range of who we were. When this happens, we create the belief that we don't deserve to have our needs met. We might go on to be outwardly successful, self-reliant, "normal" people, but our basic human needs remain unfulfilled. We often can't even identify that we have these needs. That's why it's so hard for many of us to navigate the confusing swamp of our own emotional truth.

Both of these types of trauma have an impact on our relationships, and both can be healed through our relationships when we have the skills to achieve that healing. Sadly, when those skills are missing, our relationships can actually further deepen these wounds, hence the importance of becoming skilled at the practices I'm going to share with you soon.

Of course, healing is always an ongoing process. It's the journey of coming into greater and greater acceptance of yourself and genuine love for yourself. It's never complete. It's not like you either love yourself or you don't; it's something you will always want to expand over time. Relationships give you the perfect arena for discovering what is causing the lack of safety and lack of self-love in your life. The issues triggered by your partner show you where you need to evolve and grow.

You've probably noticed that your core unworthiness is not triggered by everything equally. On many issues, it's likely that you hold your worth and value brilliantly, while on other issues, you collapse. Until healing has taken place, certain energies and emotional frequencies are always going to have the ability to collapse you whenever you come in contact with them. If you were bullied, hurt, emotionally attacked, or suffered any situation that erupted rage within you during your childhood, that event created a powerlessness deeply embedded in your system.

Your immature nervous system did not have the resources to deal with the pain, so it stored the pain away. At later points in your life, whenever a similar situation shows up, it will re-create the same symptoms of paralysis you felt during the original trauma. If the new situation carries the same energetic frequency of the old (even when it looks very different at surface level), it will reengage the part of your nervous system that remembers that unprocessed trauma.

Remember, others are always involved in your hurts. Each time in your life you've felt pained, it's been by another—either through direct or indirect wounding. As children, it's just not common for us to inflict self-harm. Usually we feel abandoned, rejected, emotionally or physically abused, violated, smothered, our boundaries crossed, or unhealthily merged because without meaning to, our parents have made us the substitute for the intimacy they lack in their relationship. In these situations, a child energetically feels the need to give and give, and often, a role dynamic is formed wherein they feel they have to represent the other parent. They can't relax, play, or voice their own authentic needs. In all of these scenarios, other people were involved in creating the wound, and that is why other people are required for its healing.

The only way to heal these long-buried traumas is to be fully felt and witnessed when we get triggered. We don't even have to remember the incidents that caused the initial wounding; we just need to recognize when we've been triggered and know that it's an opportunity, right there, and then to move *toward* our partner instead of following our gut response to move away. It's scary because we have to be vulnerable. We have to be seen in our pain, our weakness, our shadows. It's a risky business, and it's not for everyone, but those who take this journey will bring their lives and their partnerships to unimaginable heights.

Our Metaphorical Mask: S.T.U.A.R.T.

To cope with the disconnection from our own goodness and to relieve ourselves from the pain of feeling unworthy, we as children begin to develop relief strategies. A protective energetic membrane is created in response to our need to disconnect from the emotional pain or emptiness we feel. I call it a membrane rather than a wall, because like the cells in our bodies, this energetic membrane is an intelligent semipermeable layer that allows certain emotions and awarenesses in, while blocking out others it deems as unsafe.

It's out of this layer that we develop strategies and behaviors to protect ourselves from feeling the pain of not being enough (even though this, itself, is a false belief). It gets complicated, so for simplicity's sake, I've named this defensive layer S.T.U.A.R.T. (S.T.U.A.R.T. is an acronym for the qualities we must call on when our defense strategies kick in: Safety, Tenderness, Understanding, Awareness, Relaxation, and Trust. You'll learn how to cultivate these necessary healing qualities as you proceed through this book.)

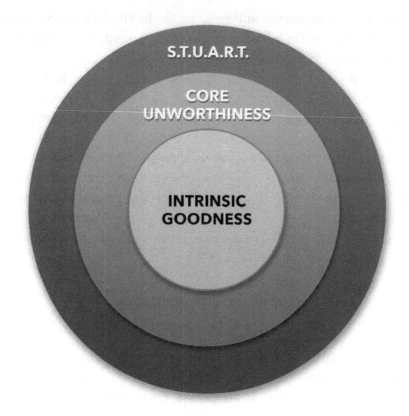

In the diagram, you can see what I call your "Awareness Hierarchy." The center of the diagram represents your core intrinsic goodness. Surrounding this core is a layer of unworthiness and pain that you have picked up via neglect and trauma throughout your life. Finally, surrounding your pain is your S.T.U.A.R.T., which keeps you distracted, heady, and numb.

It's a hierarchy because the first step to reclaiming your goodness is to become aware of how you disconnect from your pain. Then you must be willing to feel and be felt in your pain and thus surrender to it to allow your essence to emerge naturally and effortlessly, expressed to the world as your depth. If you try to skip this process and access joy without acknowledging and feeling your pain, you will experience what I call "Superficial Joy Syndrome," in which you will replace the missing range of relaxed depth with a high-frequency, tension-filled state, which is both exhausting to hold and to feel.

As we grow, we add to our repertoire of S.T.U.A.R.T. strategies. We find ways to leave our bodies, go numb, or emotionally check out through addictions and other avoidance behaviors. In adults, S.T.U.A.R.T. can be seen as the emotional wall between self and others, and also between conscious self and subconscious inner self. It's the metaphorical mask we wear, the persona we hide behind.

S.T.U.A.R.T. may seem like a hindrance to our joy, when in fact it is a good asset! It protects us from letting in crap and keeps us safe. But it also prevents the good things (intimacy, connection, and belonging) from being received. You don't ever want to get rid of S.T.U.A.R.T.; you want to make friends with it and become aware and conscious of your partnership with it.

Of course, for many of us, the original disconnect is amplified by direct trauma in the form of physical abuse, sexual abuse, or severe emotional abuse. This kind of pain is especially devastating because when children are abused, not only are they ripped open in their most sacred, vulnerable place, but the very containment that was supposed to protect them is now so damaged that it opens them up to further abuse later in life. It's important to remember in these instances that it is only the *container* that is damaged, not the essence or goodness of the individual.

Abused children lack the opportunity to develop appropriate boundaries; they don't have the resources to say no properly. Those who are sexually abused carry the shame of feeling dirty, and they energetically attract further unboundaried sexual encounters, all the while blaming themselves and feeling "slutty" and unworthy of goodness. Though it all began from an experience that clearly wasn't their fault, they don't have the resources to differentiate, so they take the guilt on as their own.

To recap, core worthiness originates with the loss of connection that results naturally at birth, grows stronger through the commonplace woundings of childhood, and is amplified when there is direct, intentional abuse to the child. This underlying lack of value, this energetic layer of unworthiness and disconnection, stays with us throughout our lives to varying extents. You become identified with this underlying belief that you're not okay. Even though at your core you are nothing but goodness and perfection (think newborn baby), a shell of unworthiness forms around that goodness. It feels bad to touch that shell, so you create a S.T.U.A.R.T. layer around it to protect you from feeling it.

WARNING: Be aware of anyone who tells you that they can "get rid of" trauma or remove your core unworthiness for good. The very therapists and healers who advocate such a promise often lack embodiment and the capacity to feel their own pain, blinding them from the deeper journey they themselves need to take. It's very alluring to think there is a quick fix for decades of abuse, neglect, and disconnection, but the very thought that your pain needs to be "treated" means you've fallen into the trap that you believe there is something wrong with you that needs fixing, when in fact, your very pain is the potential catalyst and source of your depth and power, once you understand how to transform it.

SUCCESS STORY FROM STEPH & AARON

It was during the Heart IQ shadow work processes at an Insights to Intimacy LIVE seminar that Aaron opened up to himself deeper than ever before. This connection with himself was the beginning of a turning point in his life. Two weeks later, he proposed!

Aaron says, "My defense mechanism was to just walk away, so I could find my own balance before coming back to try again. I realized what doesn't work about that habit is that it didn't give my partner a chance to feel what I was going through, so it left her in the dark and put a wall between us.

"Now, I can see the warning signs a lot earlier. I can better understand where things are going, I can feel more of where Steph is, and I'm also asking questions from a better frame of mind rather than going into a confrontational state.

"Before I couldn't hold space for my partner; it was just about what was going on for me. We would come at each other rather than giving each other space. Now, when we notice that this is not happening, we can remind each other to step back and tune in and reset to give us more space."

Aaron and Steph even recognized changes in their children and how they're relating in their own relationships. "It's empowered us as a family, as well as us as a couple. If it wasn't for this work, we wouldn't be together because we wouldn't know how to open to each other in the way that we do now."

Common S.T.U.A.R.T. Strategies

Let's look at what happens when people are running a S.T.U.A.R.T. strategy. Very commonly, they'll emotionally check out, leaving the vitality of their body to go into their heads. They're still there physically, but they aren't present in the moment anymore. They'll go numb and are no longer able to communicate their truth with ease. Many people live the bulk of their lives in this space, without ever knowing a deeper experience of connection to themselves and others.

An example of a S.T.U.A.R.T. strategy is continuous talking. It's a way of deflecting attention to avoid making an intimate connection, something that our S.T.U.A.R.T. finds threatening. Most of the time the person doing it is unaware of this strategy, but it feels very disconnecting to the person on the receiving end.

S.T.U.A.R.T. can also be activated, for example, when you're in a job that doesn't serve your highest, wisest self. You'll feel tired and lethargic even though you have no physical reason to be so exhausted. You may find that you judge yourself harshly for being lazy or procrastinating when, in most cases, it's merely a lack of alignment to what you're really here for. Discipline isn't necessary when you're following your heart. On the contrary, when connected to what you really want, inspiration will flow naturally and effortlessly to support you, and if you don't feel it, then perhaps your S.T.U.A.R.T. is telling you that you need to reassess some of your choices.

Ironically, S.T.U.A.R.T. can also *block* your healthy decisions as you approach a scary level of joy and happiness. You might have health problems suddenly come up just before you're about to take an important step in your life. Through no conscious effort on your part, you're sick and unable to go through with your plans. Yes, your S.T.U.A.R.T. can guide you and block you simultaneously! That's why you need to learn to track your strategies and take control of them.

Another way S.T.U.A.R.T. shows up is through intellectualizing. We speak with our head instead of our heart; we don't allow ourselves the time to really feel what's moving, acknowledge its presence, and share our present moment truth with others. This is one of the biggest ways in which we can see S.T.U.A.R.T. at work in our everyday lives.

"Bubble-bursting" is another strategy. You've probably noticed that some people will crack a joke or leave the room whenever an uncomfortable emotion comes up. They aren't able to be with what is happening. So, in this deeply intimate moment or this moment when something profound is about to be catalyzed, they'll either consciously or unconsciously burst the bubble because it's so uncomfortable for them. It's a self-preservative mechanism, as are all the S.T.U.A.R.T. strategies.

You may have heard the myth that we self-sabotage, but that is not what S.T.U.A.R.T. is about—even though it can feel that way at times. We don't use S.T.U.A.R.T. strategies because we subconsciously want to hurt ourselves. Putting limits on our abundance and joy, which some might think of as self-sabotage, is discussed in the next section. But do understand this for now: Our S.T.U.A.R.T.s were created as an emotional-energetic protection system, similar to a fuse in an electric circuit, that blows when too much current passes through. The fuse is not sabotaging the electronic equipment, it's *protecting* it. It's the same with our S.T.U.A.R.T. However, just as we can place the wrong fuse in a circuit (which will cause it to blow too soon or too late), our S.T.U.A.R.T. is also likely to be set incorrectly (it's usually downloaded from our family and culture). It's very likely to either be turned up too high, closing you off from the joy and intimacy that is trying to reach you, or it's turned down too low, where you are opening yourself up to people and energies too soon, which risk causing you unnecessary pain and suffering.

WHAT MAKES A SAFE ENVIRONMENT?

As you've learned, each of us in our first few years of life experiences a certain amount of safety or lack of safety. It's not an intellectual process; the young child isn't consciously thinking about whether or not they feel safe. The level of safety is registered in the nervous system, the emotional system, and the energetic system. The child is constantly tuning in to their environment and subconsciously determining whether it's safe to stay open. When they feel it's not safe, they begin to close and develop these S.T.U.A.R.T. strategies.

But what makes a safe environment? Many people think that it's the amount of love shown to the child that determines this safety, but this isn't the only factor. An often forgotten piece to the puzzle is that a child's sense of safety is not only developed by how much the parents love the child, but how much the parents love each other. It's the relationship between the parents that helps create the energetic container that provides the appropriate level of protection the child needs. Children are constantly "taking pictures" of how it is; that's how they learn. If their parents aren't able to truly feel their own emotions or to connect with each other authentically, they will accept this as the model of intimacy *and* protection they subscribe to throughout their lives.

For example, if your parents were unable to connect energetically, living primarily in a defensive mode, your S.T.U.A.R.T. will be cloned from this mold. They may not have fought, but if they were emotionally closed and unable to really feel themselves and be fully present with you, then you would have felt alone and thus unsafe and hence your S.T.U.A.R.T. emerged to help manage the emptiness and pain. That is why some people have "stronger" S.T.U.A.R.T.s than others. Depending on early experiences and the severity of trauma and neglect, your S.T.U.A.R.T. will be programmed accordingly.

The good news is that your S.T.U.A.R.T., with good tracking and awareness (along with taking inspired action), can be overridden with a new enhanced intimacy program! Cultivating a safe environment now that you are an adult is well within your reach, and you can safely begin lowering your defenses with the insights you gain from the tools and practices offered in the upcoming chapters.

Are You Limiting Your Abundance and Joy?

Have you ever noticed that you become uncomfortable when things are going too well for you? Does it feel like there's only a certain amount of goodness, love, and attention you're able to accept in your life before you start to close down and subconsciously defend against any more goodness? It's the case for most of us, though we generally don't recognize it on a conscious level. We all have a threshold for the amount of success and joy we can let in before we start to trigger defense mechanisms that actually lower our vibration to prevent any more of that which we really want from coming to us.

You may be reading this and thinking, *No, that's not me. I don't do that.* But have you ever found it difficult to receive a compliment and really absorb the positive message? You might say, "thank you," and listen and be polite, but do you truly let the words into your heart and receive them? For example, if someone told you, "You're so great," you might instantly say, "Thank you; thank you for saying that." It's a very subtle deflection, but that rushed, quick rebound of energy is actually a S.T.U.A.R.T. strategy. You didn't pause to fully absorb the positive attention that was being offered to you because, on a subtle level, you found it uncomfortable. Instead, as soon as it came at you, there was a defense saying, *Let me deflect this energy with a quick "thank you" so that I can feel comfortable again.*

A more extreme example of this dynamic is the all-too-common scenario of a partnership wherein one partner feels unworthy of the love and devotion shown by the other partner. It can feel baffling to the loving partner when the object of their affection breaks it off for no apparent reason. The reason, often unconscious to both of them, is that an abundance of unconditional love becomes tragically uncomfortable for a person who feels subconsciously unworthy of it.

Why Do We Defend Against Feeling Too Much Joy?

For what reason do we limit our abundance and happiness? The answer is simple, but it requires a deeper awareness of our emotional landscape. One of the first things to understand is that our mind has labeled and compartmentalized our different feelings into a long list of emotions, each with a unique name (such as happiness, anger, or sadness) and a story of how they should be used. However, the reality is that this long list of separate emotions is merely a mental framework and that the true nature *behind* all these feelings is a single source of emotional fuel.

This fuel is like electricity. It is neither good nor bad. Yet it can be used to light up the world or destroy and burn. This is critical to understand. We may feel stuff that doesn't feel good and we might act out in unhealthy ways when certain emotions rise to the surface, but we must remember that the energy itself behind what we're feeling is wholesome and pure. We must learn to separate the energy behind a particular emotion from how we use that energy in our lives; otherwise, we risk condemning and judging parts of our emotional range, thus repressing them and creating shadows that will wreak havoc in our relationships.

Here's an example: Jane is a passionate woman with a huge abundance of life force energy that she doesn't know how to manage. She lets her unconscious lustful desire run her life, and she injures many hearts on her journey because she is unable to remain faithful. One day, the shame, guilt, and regret are so big that she decides she's had enough and disciplines herself to a spiritual practice in which she abstains from sexual encounters, ensuring that she never feeds her hunger. Months pass, and she notices that her sparkle is gone and her exuberant spirit has diminished. What's more, her craving is getting worse. Her shame keeps the hunger hidden, and she begins to act out in secret.

Eventually, Jane turns to Heart IQ for help. Through Heart IQ, she learns that she has been confusing her passionate sacred life force energy with how she has been using it. She has concluded that because this energy injured others on her path, that the energy itself is wrong, that her sexuality is dirty and should be hidden from the world, which only makes the situation worse. Jane's work is to learn how to separate her unconscious *actions* from the pure passion gifted to her, so that she doesn't continue to repress her sexuality and turn it into a shadow addiction.

With this understanding that emotions are invented labels in the mind and that there's just one source of pure energy behind them all, let's look at this final piece of the puzzle:

If you want to increase your joy, you need to be open to feeling more of *everything*.

If you want to open the floodgates of joy into your life, be prepared to open the floodgates to whatever is in your system that needs to be felt. Do you get why it might be scary to be intimate and joyful now? Intimacy and happiness require you to open your heart, and when you open your heart, you will inevitably contact your unworthiness as well. In fact, the more you open to joy, the stronger your core unworthiness will come up as you are getting closer to your goodness that lies beneath it.

This is a good thing, I promise! When it comes up, you have an opportunity to digest it by being witnessed and held by your partner. Remember, it's a myth that you can digest core unworthiness on your own. Your core unworthiness was created from the disconnected hearts of others, so others will be needed to reconnect you back to your goodness.

The art of Heart IQ, therefore, is to get good with all your emotions, all shadows and all aspects inside you, so that you don't have to fear contacting anything, so you are free to go for joy, happiness, and abundance without your S.T.U.A.R.T. kicking in and without your fearing what lies beneath it.

Managing your S.T.U.A.R.T. is actually surprisingly simple. You don't have to fix anything. You don't have to go back to your childhood to try to repair any damage. All you have to do is practice receiving loving attention with an open heart. How do we learn to stay open? By watching how we close. If you can take notice of how you go numb and emotionally check out when confronted with abundant affection or admiration, you will have the power to begin choosing to intentionally stay open instead. The Heart IQ tracking method you'll be learning soon will help you achieve this awareness and insight.

THE UNDERLYING CAUSE OF ADDICTION

Addictions are created in a response to either feel more alive or feel less pain when we can't or don't dare to open our heart and access our true power. Addictions are fed by shame, guilt, and unworthiness and are a direct indication that we are disconnected from our intrinsic goodness. Addictions represent a block to receiving energy and love from two primary sources: 1) our connection to divinity or source, and 2) the love and attention from others. As our core unworthiness takes hold and we forget our own goodness, we block out energy from these sources because we feel we don't deserve to be loved. All of us need to feel love enter our hearts in order to thrive; when we shut love out, we begin to starve. Therefore, the strategies we use to seek alternative ways to receive *without having to open our hearts* are called addictions.

Addictions are created to replace the vacuum where love should have been. They become the vice we use to self-soothe our pain. In this sense, our addictions are appropriate and were put in place to protect us. Once we have learned to receive love and to connect with our own inherent goodness, the addiction will move on. This is why it's impossible to simply remove an addiction; it will always get replaced by a new addiction because there will always be a need to fill that emptiness.

An addiction is defined as anything you do that you do not have any conscious control over that has a negative consequence on you and others in your life. So it's not just about substance abuse. Something as benign as filling all your hours with busy activity can be an addiction, a way to avoid facing pain.

Make a list of all of the ways you limit your joy. Be as specific as possible. How do you go about avoiding intimacy? What are your compulsions that you don't have control over that keep you out of your heart? How do you avoid confronting the part of you that feels unworthy of love? How do you avoid opportunities that would lead you to your stated desires?

Making this list will powerfully move these dynamics from your subconscious up into the light of your conscious awareness. Once you know they're there, you can watch for these tendencies to surface, and when they do, you can deliberately choose to override them. It will be uncomfortable at first, but the more you do it, the easier it will get.

Own Your Goodness

Most of us do not habitually walk around bathed in the awareness of our inherent goodness and value. We've all done things in the past that have caused us to register shame, but there is no need to turn that shame into our self-definition. Shame does not stick to a self-loving person. If you recognize that you're carrying shame, it's important to ask yourself, "What part of me was in charge when this shameful event occurred?" Was it a part that actually wanted to do damage or hurt someone, or was it a part that just deeply needed to do that thing? Can you see that in hindsight, if you knew what you knew today, you wouldn't have done it and it was simply a lack of awareness and maturity that led to this action?

Often it's the fearful part of us that causes us to act in ways that generate shameful feelings. It's helpful to try to see those actions as mistakes made by a good person, rather than becoming identified with the actions themselves. When you're in touch with your inherent goodness, you understand that even good people can suffer from poor judgment, becoming hijacked by parts of themselves that are not representative of the whole.

It's impossible to feel long-term guilt when you own your goodness. Guilt can only stick to an identity that thinks it's bad. When you can acknowledge your mistake, learn from it, and make sure your new actions come from a new awareness, everyone benefits.

The alternative is to wallow in your guilt until it defines you, which will result in your creating more actions to support that identity. You need to recognize the separation between what you did and who you are. In Heart IQ, we call this "uncrossing your wires."

Do It with Joy

Core unworthiness is running in the background all the time and your S.T.U.A.R.T. is keeping you nice and numb so you don't have to feel it. But take a moment to tune in and feel what's moving beneath that background static. Can you feel it running within you right now? Can you honestly look inward and identify the areas of your life where you feel that you are not enough? It becomes so imperceptibly woven into the fabric of our daily routines that it can go undetected unless we make a point to recognize it.

Do you sometimes feel incapable of performing your work as well as you'd like? Do you berate yourself when you do things to "screw up" friendships, relationships, or projects you're working on? Do you have a vague, tugging sense that no matter how much effort you put into your parenting or your career or your love life that somehow you aren't ever getting it just right?

If you base your sense of self-worth on service or performance, you'll never feel you've done enough. When we identify too much with what we do, we start to believe we *are* our service, and then if we ever stop or slow down, we feel shame, guilt, and lack of worth. What if we made joy, instead of doing, our purpose? What if we understood that serving and being served need to be in balance for us to bring our greatest gifts into the world? In truth, both are equally invigorating, spiritual, and required for coming into the heart and living an awakened life of sustained happiness.

Now that you understand how your relationship is designed to heal you and bring you into the joy that is your birthright, it's time to delve more deeply into the basic tenants of the Heart IQ healing philosophy, the topic of the next chapter.

SUCCESS STORY FROM SUE & SIMON

Sue, Simon, and their four children appeared to have an idyllic life from the outside. Sue was the first to discover the work of Heart IQ on her own: "When I came to the retreat, I didn't even know if I wanted to continue my relationship with Simon. By that time, I had lost my ability to know what I was feeling."

Sue then persuaded Simon to join her at an Insights to Intimacy LIVE seminar, and it was a move that saved their relationship. She says, "At the seminar, we looked at what was going on together, and I began to feel my love for him again. I realized that it never went away; I had just lost my ability to feel it."

Simon had his own realizations: "I had the opportunity to wake up, to change, and to step beyond the baggage of my past. I realized that I wanted to ask this wonderful woman to marry me again, and so at the 2012 Heart Summit, in front of 300 people, I asked her to marry me and renew our vows. That resulted in one of the most incredible days of my life, when we renewed our vows in circle, in front of our favorite people in the world!"

Sue added, "Amazingly, our kids have received an enormous impact from our new relationship. They are more settled and solid, knowing they have that rock underneath them, which is Simon and me. They are inspired by us and what we've rediscovered, and they now have a new benchmark from which they can create their own amazing partnerships."

Need help applying this in your relationship?
Visit www.HeartIQRelationships.com for FREE demos
and tutorials using the access code myheartiq.

CHAPTER 3

The Heart IQ
Healing Philosophy

Wherever you might be on your own journey toward self-love, you're going to need to suspend your self-judgments to the best of your ability while practicing the Heart IQ healing philosophy. The core philosophical tenant of this work is that sustainable change can only occur when we accept who we are, *as we are*, without making who we are wrong. It's only through loving "what is" that the space is created for breakthrough and transformation.

You are intrinsically good. So is your partner. No one is so deeply wounded and damaged that there is badness inside them. But we all do carry some degree of core unworthiness. We think we're not okay, and then we project onto others that they're not okay.

As you will see in this chapter, there is no such thing as a negative emotion and nothing needs fixing. Anything you or your partner feels is simply what's authentically moving in that moment. When you allow whatever wants to move within you to move, it feels cathartically releasing. It feels good. When you let yourself feel angry or sad, simply surrendering and allowing the fullness of the emotion can feel fantastic. Once we can accept and embrace those emotions in ourselves, we're better able to allow them in another.

There Is No Such Thing as a Negative Emotion

You have a physical body as well as an emotional body. Exercising and consuming nourishing, life-giving foods can help to amplify your aliveness from a physical perspective. But to create a healthy, juicy emotional body, you need to practice your ability to connect fully with the broad spectrum of your feelings, and you have to be willing to be utterly honest about where you stand, emotionally, at any given moment.

Thinking positive thoughts and using positive words aren't enough. If the words and the forced thoughts don't jibe with your truest inner feeling, the energy won't match. Sadly, we're often more authentic in our doubts than we are in our positive thinking, but we've been conditioned out of the ability to give our true spontaneous response. We mask resentment with smiles, thinking we can fake our way to our joy. It just doesn't work.

We've been taught that connecting intensely with our negative emotions is unhealthy, overly dramatic, counterproductive, and downright dangerous in terms of what we might unwillingly attract. It's a myth. The truth is there's no such thing as a negative emotion. An emotion is simply an energy that flows through you, and every emotion is a gift. Your suffering is not caused by the emotion itself, but by your resistance to feeling it! Pain is not sadness, anger, or grief. It's your resistance to those things.

The more you are able to experience your emotions and let them freely flow through you, the more enjoyable each emotion becomes. It's not inherently better to feel happiness than it is to feel anger. Happiness just feels better. We have judgments that certain emotions are poisonous, but they're really not. Anger, for example, is one of our most powerful tools for creating change in our lives. We can use the raw, honest juice of anger to manifest magnificent things.

I want you to stop judging any emotion as bad. Little by little, begin practicing letting yourself express each of your authentic emotions more fully. The degree to which you make any emotion wrong is the degree to which that emotion is holding you back in life. You've suppressed your emotions in the past because you haven't had a safe container for them, so it's nothing to beat yourself up about. It's the normal, healthy reaction to not having ever felt safe enough to lower your defenses and express yourself in all of your fullness. The tools in the upcoming chapters will allow you to create that safe container within your relationship.

Often there's a fear that giving in to our sadness will lead to depression. But nearly all cases of mild depression are actually caused by the absence of emotional fuel. It happens when you've become so numb that you no longer have the ability to connect to your juice, your fire, your inner source of vitality and aliveness.

It's indescribably liberating when you finally release your obsession with attempting to control your emotions! Trying to get rid of undesirable emotions is an allopathic model that's no different from the Western medical practice of removing cancers or cutting out unwell parts of the body. I'm asking you to instead trust in the healing process and perfection of the body itself. No emotional surgery is required here.

See if you can shift into a habit of welcoming your feelings, whatever they are. It's a fascinating practice when you train yourself to be witness to it. Observe yourself first wanting to get rid of some troublesome thought or feeling, and then remembering to fully accept it. Know that the voice of doubt and criticism will always be there. Learn to observe it without becoming affected by it.

Now, I want to make clear that while all *natural* emotions are healthy and worthy of your embrace, the suppression of them can transmute them into unhealthy, dangerous by-products. Love, envy, anger, fear, and grief, in their naturally arising states, are all beneficial to feel. When we repress them, however, they become unhealthy transmutations of themselves.

Repressed anger becomes rage, an unnatural, dangerous, destructive force. Repressed sadness becomes depression, or a void that cannot be filled. Repressed fear turns into panic, an often debilitating state from which it's difficult to function. Repressed envy becomes jealousy. Even love, when it's not allowed to flow freely and naturally, can turn into unhealthy programs of possessiveness and need. All of these are the unnatural consequences of suppressing perfectly natural emotions.

You Heal It by Feeling It

As strange as this sounds, in order to heal, we need to *feel*. That includes lowering our S.T.U.A.R.T. defenses and feeling our core unworthiness. Why? Because when you feel your unworthiness (and are able to authentically share that experience with another), it transforms into your *depth*. If left unfelt, it remains a heavy obstacle in your life, preventing you from having the relationships and experiences you want. If you dare to feel it and be felt in it by others, this very energy will be transformed into your rich potential for deepening and widening your emotional-energetic range.

The more deeply you can feel, the more *joy* you can access because joy can only be felt in depth, just as light can only be seen in the presence of darkness and hot can only be experienced in the presence of cold. Contrast is needed to feel alive! Thus, our core unworthiness is like stored potential fuel to run our joy-engine!

We avoid the stickier areas of our relationships because we fear that looking into them honestly and openly will cause us pain. We avoid pain because it sucks to feel it. But whether or not we accept any situation as painful is actually more within our control than we think. Once we get the hang of embracing our emotions, whatever they may be, we lessen the pain they can bring us. Once we understand that every instance of sadness, anger, shame, or regret is a golden, gift-wrapped opportunity for growth and ultimately for expansion into greater realms of joy, we can choose to simply leave pain out of the equation.

CORE UNWORTHINESS AND THE PAIN BODY

How is it that the trauma or neglect experienced during our earliest years sticks with us and interferes with our present-day relationships? Eckhart Tolle calls the energetic body where we store all these traumas the "pain body." Our pain body stores emotional-energetic memories of undigested events that were too intense for our nervous system to process at the time, and thus we unconsciously stored them away, frozen in time, waiting for the day when we have developed enough safety and resources to deal with them. I say frozen in time because these memories store not just the emotional temperature at the time but also the age we were when the trauma occurred.

This is why you can get triggered by your partner and suddenly feel like a seven-year-old, running the same emotions you experienced as a child. You've activated your pain body, and in that moment, your higher awareness and open heart are not accessible, making intimacy and loving communication very difficult. When these distorted memories of injured value get reactivated through interactions with your partner, the natural instinct is to want to defend this disempowered version of you. This type of trauma, or undigested experience, is in all of us. And while awareness of it can lessen its impact, the unavoidable fact is that, at times, everyone falls victim to the pain and misery of feeling the effect of these past memories surfacing and getting in the way of intimacy.

It's important to remember that a pain-body response is only activated when there's uncertainty around your own value based on a past memory. Even though it's not enjoyable to feel triggered by your pain body, it's a signal that this part of you is ready to come to the surface to be healed. Left unchecked, your childhood triggers will derail your relationship, but with the right practice and skills, you'll be able to give these parts of you nourishment and safety. They will need to be integrated back into your system, under the command of your adult, mature self.

It's important to remember that pain-body trauma itself is not what gets in the way of a couple's connection. It's the unconscious relationship that each partner has to their pain-body trauma that undermines the couple's potential for intimacy. Every aspect of their intimacy can be a healing influence that can help to digest the pain and clarify the confusion around the injured value that each of them still holds. The memory of injury will always be there, but the influence of that injury can become a gift of clarity, conviction, and purpose when held by the certainty of love.

WARNING: I want to remind you that we often unconsciously attract a partner who is a perfect pain-body match, creating the potential for both parties to get triggered simultaneously, leaving no one to hold loving space. It's important not to jump to the conclusion that there is something necessarily wrong with your relationship just because you get triggered deeply and frequently.

Anger Is Healthy When Channeled Through the Heart

Every raw emotion is healthy when it's expressed through your heart. When it's not, however, these energies can be hurtful, poisonous, and damaging to all concerned. For example, anger that is not expressed through your heart (and therefore is not connected to your value or goodness) can cause you to lash out and become passive aggressive or manipulative.

For anger to be healthy, you first need to be in deep connection with your own intrinsic essence; you need to have a genuine love of self. When anger is expressed from that kind of wholeness, it's simply a tool to help you maintain healthy boundaries. Weak boundaries are one of the direct consequences of identifying strongly with your core unworthiness, and people who do not know how to uphold healthy boundaries usually have an unbalanced relationship with anger.

For many of us, the word "no" is egregiously underutilized. We need to have a generous amount of "no" in our lives to make room for the "yeses"—the things we do want. Being able to say no is an example of having appropriate self-love. When we go year after year without that level of self-love, and we don't know how to say no, we inevitably have our boundaries crossed again and again, until our "no" is finally expressed as rage, aggression, and sometimes violence. In some cases, it goes buried beneath our consciousness and is expressed as passive aggressiveness.

When we learn to make that critical connection with our deepest essence and begin loving ourselves, our anger becomes a completely different thing. We may not even recognize it as anger. Suddenly, what we once expressed as anger is just fire, passion. It's self-assuredness and confidence. It becomes the energy of our clear "no." It can still be powerful and intense, but it comes with a heart connection that feels self-empowering and empowering to others. That doesn't mean our anger won't still potentially trigger those around us and may even collapse those who are not in touch with their own anger. But if that does happen, we'll have the clarity and compassion to deal with it appropriately.

We're Triggered by Our Most Potent Stored Energies

Potent energies like anger and sexuality have high potential for triggering old wounds within us. As I mentioned previously, a lot of people end up confusing the energy they feel in their in-the-moment body with the way that energy has been used in the past. For example, if anger has been instrumental to your core wounding, as is often the case, it's likely that it's been difficult for you to strike a healthy balance with anger, either by suppressing it excessively or expressing it excessively. Anger then is more likely to become an emotion you judge harshly in yourself.

To connect with that inner vitality and aliveness that I like to call our "juice," we have to examine our relationship with those energies within us that we've made wrong, so that we can accept them as the pure, raw, beautiful fuel they're meant to be. I know it's difficult to fully grasp this concept, but everything that has ever happened to you has been for your benefit. That's true of everyone, even in what we consider to be horrible circumstances. If seemingly "bad" things happen, it's so that we can evolve by experiencing that contrast and desiring something different. However, just because this is true does not mean we should avoid the pain of what has happened. This is a perfect example of where we can go into a New Age bypass. If something terrible has happened, it's easier to check out, leave our bodies, and tell ourselves (or more commonly become a teacher and share with others) the spiritual wisdom of perfection, the benefit and the gift of everything that has happened, rather than deal with the pain the injury has caused.

Can you see the risk of falling into this trap? Nearly all spiritual teachers and healers go through a phase of New Age bypass as they try to find their authentic voice. So, yes, it *is* true that everything that happens in your life has a potential benefit for growth and expansion, but before that truth can land and impact you, you must first fully commit to the healing process of feeling all your parts, including the parts that feel hurt, victimized, vulnerable, and enraged. Until those parts have been given voice, any spiritual sugarcoating will only act as a Band-Aid.

Looking back on your own life, I'm sure you can see how your most painful circumstances are also the ones that have created the most depth within you. More than the fun, easy times, they have shaped the person you are. As you create greater contrast, you expand your potential for greater joy. In fact, I don't consider joy to be a separate item on the emotional spectrum list, as it's the *result* of full allowance and acceptance of *all* your emotions. As I've mentioned already, joy comes when you accept and embrace *all* of what you are feeling, rather than it being a feeling unto itself.

Joy emerges naturally and effortlessly when you relax into the unconditional love of self; it's the net energy you feel from the potential difference between your deepest hurt and your deepest bliss. The more pain you've felt and can own, the more exquisite bliss you are poised to create for yourself. If this doesn't register, reread this section until it does; it will change your life. Finally you can end the rat race. Joy is no longer something you strive for or chase; it emerges when you stop looking for a way to feel "better" and instead begin enjoying and loving where you are.

Healing Through Relationship Issues

Here is where it gets really interesting: When we are becoming more intimate with a partner and more ready to lower our defenses and "let our partner in," we have a deep inner knowing that our joy and our wholeness lie somewhere in that general direction. But on our way to uncover it, we get a surprise. We think that lowering our S.T.U.A.R.T. defenses will give us direct access to joy, but our joyful innermost core is not the layer we hit first. When we access the vulnerability to lower our defenses and let our partner in, the first thing we feel is pain, as we come up against our pain body, that energetic layer of unworthiness, shame, guilt, and un-deservingness.

When you're in a relationship, your partner of course has a S.T.U.A.R.T. defense system, a layer of core unworthiness, and core goodness as well. You relate to each other from those three layers of your being. When you fall in love, you create an energetic container that surrounds both of you. It feels safe within the container, so you start to lower your defenses. Relationship containers create an amplified field, so every emotion is heightened. As you open more and more fully, lowering your S.T.U.A.R.T. defenses, something will inevitably take place to trigger an old, unhealed wound that's been tucked away in that insidious layer of unworthiness.

It feels bad, and you don't like it. It feels like there's something wrong with the relationship, when in fact, this feeling has surfaced because there's something *right* with it. It's a precious opportunity to be held, witnessed, and loved right where you are. This is how you will digest your core unworthiness so that you and your partner can come together in divine union. You'll need the tools and insight to navigate that digestion. Fortunately, I've dedicated my life to developing systems and practices to help couples do just that, which is what I'm sharing with you in this book.

Why do you think receiving is so hard? You learned the reason in the previous chapter, but let me remind you: It's because when we allow ourselves to deeply receive, we touch that belief system that tells us we're unworthy. Lowering the first wall of resistance—our S.T.U.A.R.T. strategies—is not enough (see page 43). We need to recognize that our goodness lies beneath that subsequent uncomfortable layer (our core unworthiness), and we need to consciously lean into it until we can feel through to our worth and our deservingness. That means we must be fully present to the emotions it brings up for us, unconditionally accept those emotions, and integrate them into our experience so that we can then go deeper.

This is why we can't truly heal alone. We need others to trigger us into revealing what is there to be healed. We can learn to love ourselves (and certainly that is a worthy goal for everyone), but to become free of our long-buried undigested wounds, we need to be on the receiving end of love from another as well. We may initially deflect that love when it starts to bump up against our core unworthiness, but if we dare to let that energy from another in, it will begin to dissolve that unworthy layer at last. The more we can be felt there, through the beautiful witnessing energy of the other's acceptance, the more we heal. As the loving, attentive energy hits this layer, our core unworthiness contracts and self-implodes, eventually becoming absorbed back into our connected self and allowing us to snap back into wholeness by remembering who we really are.

When we feel that calling to be vulnerable with our beloved, we're instinctively aiming to experience the wholeness and goodness that lies at our innermost core, but to get there, we have to first make our way through the sticky, painful layer we've accumulated over it. The more we can understand that it's just part of the process, the more quickly and easily we can move through it. Without understanding these dynamics, we run away as soon as we touch that uncomfortable layer. We need to invite the discomfort and celebrate it instead. It's just a signpost that we're moving in the right direction, and the more we can relax into the process, the better.

Here's the good news: There are no complicated hurdles to leap or hoops to jump through. Whatever needs to be healed within you is precisely what will surface in the form of relationship "issues" when you are in romantic partnership with another. It's beautiful, really. Every perceived offense, every time you feel slighted, and every miscommunication is an attempt by your greatest inner wisdom to bring you into contact with the exact issues you need to digest in order to connect with your own core goodness.

WHY DOES MY STUFF COME UP EVEN MORE WHEN I'M IN LOVE?

This is such a valid concern, so let's take another, but deeper, look. As intimacy begins to grow in your romantic partnership, you naturally feel ready to lower your defenses and let your partner into those places where your joy has been safely guarded. You begin to unlock the inner doors to those parts of you where you've been longing to share yourself. But, as you open, it doesn't go as you hoped: The first thing you feel is pain. Remember, it's not pain from your present-moment relationship; it's pain connected to your layer of core unworthiness. *This* is the layer your S.T.U.A.R.T. strategies have been protecting you from feeling.

I get how unfair it feels to reencounter this pain at a time when you're finally feeling safe enough to bare yourself to another. But there's a good reason why this stage of healing needs to happen first. It's only when you can be present and not overwhelmed by this pain that you can finally free yourself to know that who you are is separate and distinct from how bad this pain feels.

The tough part is that the reactivation of pain can happen so fast that it goes right under our conscious radar. This makes it easy to associate any bad-feeling memories with the relationship. But remember, this feeling has surfaced, not because there's something bad or wrong with your relationship, but because there's something *right* with it. You are finally in a place, inside yourself and in connection with another, where you have enough safety and vibrancy to face what has been too threatening to digest in the past.

You finally have the chance to feel what it's like to be genuinely loved as you are. This is the real potential for healing that your romantic relationship holds—a kind of divine union that is created when two people take the risk together to follow their hearts into the unknown territory that lies behind the locked doors of their S.T.U.A.R.T. defenses.

Recognizing Common Pain-Body Triggers

Your pain will be triggered whenever your partner does or says something that reawakens an old wound within you. It may cause you to feel sad, hurt, defensive, or even just simply annoyed. Until you've begun this work, you won't have any conscious awareness that the current situation has anything to do with any prior occurrence. It will feel as though your pain or annoyance is purely and justifiably about the situation at hand. The truth is that the situation at hand would not be triggering you if you did not have a past trauma stored in your energetic body that matches the frequency of the current issue.

I've worked with couples in my Insights to Intimacy LIVE seminars long enough to have identified the following list of very common pain-body triggers. See if you or your partner can relate to any of these triggers:

- Your partner uses a "tone" with you—for example, a demeaning, dismissive, or patronizing tone. It could be any tone of voice that triggers a bad association from your past. Even an overly sweet tone could trigger the pain body of a person who experienced inauthentic sweetness as manipulation or insincerity.

- Your partner accuses you of something without giving you the benefit of the doubt.

- Your partner interrupts you or doesn't listen to you; you don't feel *felt* by your partner.

- Your partner rejects you sexually, or you feel ignored or dismissed.

- Your partner talks to you as if they know what you're feeling without asking you.

- Your partner gives you "leaky" attention, resulting in your not feeling safe because your partner is being ambiguous. You might think, *Does it even matter that I'm here?*

- Your partner compares you to someone in their past or to all men or women in general.

- Your partner criticizes or diminishes you.

- You are not being acknowledged, seen, or recognized, feeling that your partner is not present with you and is distracted. (An example of this is the partner who, after listening to your heartfelt personal sharing, immediately gets up to take care of chores.)

- You are the recipient of your partner's emotional projection or your partner uses you as an emotional punching bag.

- You know your partner is upset with you, but they won't tell you why. Your partner might be thinking something along the lines of: *If you don't know what you did to hurt me, then I'm not going to tell you.* You are being made to feel like you've messed up without being given any guidance on how to make it better.

- Your partner hangs on to the past, bringing up past painful scenarios over and over again without resolution.

- Your partner doesn't remember important dates like birthdays and anniversaries.

- Your partner is unable to take charge when you need them to. An example is a partner not stepping up when the other needs to be protected, reassured, or assisted.

- Your partner communicates tit-for-tat—in other words, your partner justifies their own neglectful, hurtful, dismissive, disrespectful, or negligent behavior by pointing out *your* bad behavior with various versions of, "You've hurt me, too!" This also applies when one partner gives feedback, but instead of receiving it, the other partner says, "You do that to me all the time!"

- Your partner speaks to you in absolutes, telling you that you "always" do something or "never" do something.

Ongoing Management of Your Pain Body

By now you have an intimate understanding of what your pain body is and how the pain body shows up for healing in our interactions with others. That understanding alone will transform your life and your relationships with all the people in it from here on out. The pain body is a tricky entity, so I'm going to give you a few more suggestions on managing yours and recognizing it when it rears its ugly head.

When you're in your pain body, you always think that what you want is for the other person to act differently. It feels completely like it's all about that person. Your happiness has crossed over into the other's responsibility. When you're in your pain body, you've put responsibility for your own contentment outside yourself, in this case onto your partner. Once you recognize this has happened, you can choose to reclaim responsibility for your own joy, and that takes away much of the pain body's power over you.

When you find yourself blaming and feeling like a victim, see if you can pause long enough to recognize that you've been emotionally hijacked by your pain body. Just acknowledging and breaking the pattern can be tremendously healing. Let your partner know you've just interrupted your own pain-body cycle and ask for support. Maybe you'll want to just sit silently together, hold each other, or look at each other in stillness, until the energy dissipates.

The pain body literally is a field of energy that, if you stop feeding it, will eventually dissipate of its own accord. You could make agreements in advance to breathe together, move together, just be still, or whatever you've determined in your "pain-body agreements." You can commit that no matter how much you want to argue and prove your point and keep the energy alive, you won't, choosing instead to focus on what you want the outcome to be. You can write out these agreements with your partner, or you can establish them verbally. The point is just to have an agreed-upon plan of action that you establish at some neutral point in time when neither of you is currently triggered by your pain body.

When your pain body is activated, the desire to be heard, validated, and come out on top can feel almost like a spell that's been cast over you. It's like you're possessed, hijacked by it. You might have the feeling, *This isn't even me. I don't know where this is coming from.* That's how you know it's your pain body that's taken over. You can get out of the spell more quickly if you accept it for what it is, so don't fight against it and don't try to avoid it. Just call it out. Know that it won't last forever. The more you can accept it, understand it, and be the observer of it instead of the victim of it, the more quickly it will dissipate so that you can feel and be yourself again. If both of you are aware of how and why this happens, you'll be able to give each other the space and understanding to move through your pain-body experiences with minimum distress and damage to the relationship.

What you resist persists—especially when it comes to your pain body. The worst thing you can do when it's taken you over is to continue talking. That's how you feed it; so once you recognize you're having a pain-body episode, just know that nothing that comes out of your mouth is likely to be constructive or healing. Nonverbal communication is one of the best ways to leave your pain body and come back into yourself again. Find the little tricks that work best for you to bridge your way back to your partner. If you've both been triggered and you're walking together, maybe the one who can come back the fastest squeezes the other's hand or holds out a finger. There might not be a finger that comes back right away, but eventually there will be. Experiment with your own sweet, simple gestures to let each other know you're ready and willing to reconnect whenever the other is.

You need to both constantly be asking yourselves, "What is it that I really want here?" Because what often happens is that we get so caught up in our pain and defending our hurts to each other, that we lose sight of the only thing that actually matters—what it is that we want. Once you bring your attention and focus to what you want your relationship to be like, chances are you'll discover that you both actually want the same thing. When it comes right down to it, we all want a harmonious, joyful relationship that lets us feel valued and loved. Practicing putting your focus on what you want will help both of you pull yourselves out of the pain-body experience and into healing.

MANAGING PAIN THAT ISN'T ALL YOURS: COLLECTIVE VERSUS INDIVIDUAL PAIN

While each of us has an individual pain body created from our respective past, there are also vast fields of collective pain that serve to connect certain groups of people. Races that have been discriminated against and unfairly treated might share a collective pain. Women share collective pain when they band together to express the suffering they've felt from sexism or simply from cold or brutal treatment by men. Men share collective pain when they bond in their fear of women's judgment or abandonment.

While great comfort can be found in commiserating with those who understand your particular brand of misery, there is also a danger to this sort of camaraderie. Unlike other opportunities to digest old trauma so that it can be felt, seen, and cleared, focusing on collective pain with other similarly wounded compatriots can actually do more harm than good.

When a collective trauma is this deep and vast, it can become like a bottomless pit of negativity. Bathing in it only serves to reactivate it, not heal it. While there is certainly a time and place for bonding with those who understand and share your trauma, I urge you to use careful discernment regarding how much energy you invest in this practice. If your time with your tribe leaves you feeling heavier and more identified with your grief, you need to acknowledge the unhealthy activation it's triggering. Any bonding situation that leaves you feeling lighter, clearer, and more connected to humankind on the whole is one worth pursuing.

Recap What We've Covered So Far Before You Learn the Skills

Always remember that we are here to experience joy. Joy is the reason we enter into relationships, and reaching for joy is what allows us to heal on a deep level. Any time we take insightful steps toward our joy, we unwittingly cause our core unworthiness to surface because we don't feel worthy enough to *be* joyful.

Also remember that many people believe humans who do evil things are evil at their core, but this isn't true. All evil comes from disconnection from one's intrinsic core goodness. This disconnection happens at a very young age, after trauma and/or neglect has occurred. We disconnect from our goodness, and we begin to build an identity around feeling bad and empty all the time. We confuse how we're feeling with who we are, since a child in their formative years takes *everything* personally. If the parents are in pain, the child will take on that pain. If the child is hurting, the child will think they are the cause of it.

Thus, when a child feels bad because of trauma or neglect, over a period of time, a heavy weight of unworthiness is born, like a ball and chain hanging around their ankles. After a while, the child develops S.T.U.A.R.T. strategies to disconnect from those feelings of unworthiness (who wants to feel unworthy all the time?). They are the ways in which we disconnect from our disconnection and defend ourselves from feeling unworthy.

Healing is all about acceptance and learning to love what is. When we're able to do that, we tap into joy, and the joy itself is what heals us. To heal ourselves, we don't need to fix anything or figure out who did what to us; we only need to learn how to connect to our joy! Excited to learn how to do this? In the next chapter I walk you through the first part of the process using an exercise called Heart IQ Tracking.

SUCCESS STORY FROM THOMAS & ALET

Thomas and Alet came into Heart IQ as a couple. When asked how this work has contributed to their already solid union, Thomas says, "It brought us home. What touches me so much is that it's so natural—meaning that it's not a method where we have to follow procedures. It simply resonates with our basic human needs and feelings—and it fits effortlessly into our everyday life and gives it more splendor."

Alet offered, "I've gained a tool to get smoother and easier access to what I feel in myself, as well as discernment about what I feel in my partner. I have learned a language in which I can express it more clearly. Tracking helps us both to see what's going on more quickly—and when it has to do with our past rather than what's happening between us right now. I feel that we've grown, not only as individuals, but also as a couple. Our connection has deepened and expanded."

They both admitted to feeling immense joy as they've been able to witness the changes in each other: "Thomas is more aware and therefore, speaks to me more directly, staying more present in our exchanges. Now I get to have more of him—his emotions, words, and embodied expression and that brings me so much joy!" Thomas adds, "Alet has exploded with radiance, clarity, and joy for life. I see her in an incomparably free place, beyond the limits she has been wrestling with before—which fills me with incredible joy!"

Need help applying this in your relationship?
Visit www.HeartIQRelationships.com for FREE demos
and tutorials using the access code myheartiq.

PART TWO

How to Become a Healthy Couple

CHAPTER 4

Heart IQ Tracking: Your Personal Practice First

Accessing consistent joy in your daily life can be complex. It's not easy to zoom your focus out far enough to see the big picture, the grand design, and to understand that there's a divine perfection running through it all. I've devised a system of processing your moment-to-moment reality that helps to make it a bit easier. It's called Heart IQ Tracking.

Heart IQ Tracking is primarily about gaining insight into what's causing your *resistance* to your joy, what's getting in the way, and which thoughts and judgments are keeping you from loving what is. When you track well, you have the key to joy in any moment! You're in touch with your goodness and you're observing what's moving within you in real time while you're feeling it. I'll soon be going into much further depth on how to build your tracking skills with a partner. For now, I want you to focus on your *personal* practice of Heart IQ Tracking, which means learning to pay attention to what is presently moving for you and learning to separate the *content* from your *relationship to the content.*

The Content and Our Relationship to It

"Content" refers to whatever we're noticing within our current experience, as well as whatever feelings we're having about a particular topic, theme, or concern that happens to be "up" for us right now, such as health, career, or love life. It's a present-moment awareness of what's occupying our energetic focus.

The next piece to track is our relationship to that content. What are the judgments, thoughts, or beliefs we're holding about the content itself? What judgments are causing us to feel resistance to *what is*, that is, resistance to what is currently moving for us? An example would be a belief that your current weight is unacceptable or that it's better to be in charge of a situation than it is to be at the effect of it or even that it is better to be happy than it is to be sad. The truth is, all of us are running judgments all the time about everyone and everything around us—most especially ourselves! It's extremely valuable to practice making this distinction between the content itself and our relationship to it.

For tracking to feel joyful, you need to stay aware of both the content and your relationship to the content. These are both critical components of the tracking. You must track the truth of the content, *and* you must track the judgments, fears, doubts, and any other inner dialogue you're running as it relates to that content. When only one of these is tracked, your tracking will feel heavy and incomplete, but when both are tracked together, it will feel joyful and satisfying.

Then, sometimes we need to engage a second-level track, where we notice how we are judging the judgment. Here's an example: *I'm feeling sad (the content) and I'm running a judgment that it's weak to feel sad (relationship to the content), and as I track that, I can see how I'm making myself wrong for having this judgment and not loving myself as I am (second-level tracking).* When you're tracking properly, you'll feel a sense of relief, as though you've laid down a heavy burden. If your tracking doesn't feel good, you're not going deep enough with it.

All those different "parts" of you we've been talking about contain the vital pieces of information that make up your own divinely personal jigsaw puzzle. Each one represents a different level of your reality. Only by listening to all these pieces can you effectively see the bigger picture and know your next move. As you practice Heart IQ Tracking, you'll build your skills for integrating the wisdom from all aspects of your being.

Do you want to see a demonstration of the Heart IQ Tracking process in action? Visit www.HeartIQRelationships.com and put in the access code myheartiq to learn more.

The Art of Embodied Awareness

"Embodied awareness" is the result of being embodied while tracking, and it's the Holy Grail of Heart IQ as it creates a relaxed, charismatic, and engaging presence that is open, responsive, and highly impactful in the world. To have an enriched life is to be able to see the big picture while simultaneously remaining fully present to each of its nuances. It's one thing to intellectually report, "I'm feeling sad because of what you just said." That statement could come across as flat and defensive. But to say it while simultaneously feeling the real-time juice, or emotion, behind it is to be tracking like an expert.

Heart IQ Tracking with embodied awareness means not only can you see the bigger picture but you can also zoom in at will on its various details. Pretend you are a building with multiple floors, each floor representing a different facet of your reality (such as your body, emotions, energy, intuition, or thoughts). Now pretend you are in a helicopter hovering alongside the building, allowing you to see the entire building from the outside. Since you can't see into the levels from this outer perspective, you can remain detached emotionally while viewing this building in its entirety.

While this view can be an asset in allowing you to see the bigger picture, it can also cause you to disconnect from the emotional reality of being a human being. So you'll want to be able to go into each level, move around there, and see how it feels. Heart IQ Tracking is being in the helicopter, but also being capable of walking into the various levels with enough emotional maturity to objectively witness what's there.

Mastering Tracking

Effective tracking involves going inward to honestly answer three questions:

- *What am I feeling right now?*

- *What am I longing for, or what do I need to come into a greater feeling of safety and joy?*

- *What is holding me back from feeling the way I want to feel?*

These are clear questions you can ask yourself in any moment. The more you ask them, the more comfortable and automatic they will become. You'll be astounded at the clarity, insight, and freedom this habitual practice will bring you. You can use these questions by yourself or with your beloved, but you'll find that within the amplified field of your relationship, the answers become more accessible. All emotion shows up more abundantly and presently in an amplified field, providing you are in rapport with your partner. If you are both triggered, tracking becomes virtually impossible.

Another way to approach tracking is by checking in with yourself on five different levels: physical, mental, emotional, energetic, and intuitive:

- To check in with your physical body, simply pay attention to where you might have aches or stiffness, and how tired you are, and whether or not you're thirsty or hungry, etc.

- On a mental level, notice what you're thinking about and paying attention to.

- On an emotional level, check to see if you're primarily feeling sad, mad, glad, happy, bored, angry, etc.

- On an energetic level, ask yourself, "How alive do I feel right now? Can I feel my life force coursing through my body? Or do I feel more numb, checked out, vacant?"

- Finally, check in with the intuitive part of you by noticing whether or not you're presently open to guidance from the wiser part of you.

At every level, you want to witness whatever judgments are spinning in your mind about what you're noticing (tracking the relationship to the content). We're almost always in judgment about something, and just bringing that to our own awareness can be tremendously powerful. We tell people we don't judge because we think spirituality is a judgment-free zone. But it's a spiritual veneer. We all judge, all the time; we judge everybody and everything. The question becomes: Do you change how you relate to people because of it, or are you beyond the judgment? Does it close you? Limit you? Do you treat people differently because you judge them? There is power in owning and claiming your judgments about others. But there is no power in needing to share those judgments with them.

When you recognize, internally, that you're running a judgment, try saying to yourself, "How interesting that I'm judging like this. Since this is what I'm holding about this person, I'm going to talk to them and see if it's true." Then try to remember that every person you attract into your life is a reflection of some aspect of you. Every judgment you make about another, good or bad, is simply a reflection of a judgment you hold about yourself. When you can make that connection throughout your day, you become masterful at your own emotional healing. And your romantic partner will always be your biggest, most accurate mirror for clearing and balancing whatever needs to be healed within you.

The enormous advantage to learning the skill of tracking is that it allows you to see what is actually present for you so that you can change it into something better if you'd like. You can't change anything in your life that you don't first clearly see and accept. I've worked with change throughout my career because my clients have always wanted to change, to release old patterns and programming, fix their relationship problems, improve their finances, etc. My first company was called "Embracing Change." I did a lot of good work, but once I'd supported my clients in changing, the change wouldn't stick. That's the problem with all personal development, actually. Eventually I realized something about my clients' longing to go from point A to point B. Most often, it was not born of a joyful longing, but born of a judgment that A is no good, so B must be much better. Change born from that position simply does not hold.

I soon discovered that to truly serve, I needed not only to inspire change but also to first inspire deep acceptance with the starting point. Only from that position have I been able to coach my clients into the kind of sustainable joy they long to experience.

Become a Student of Your Own Emotional Reality

To track well with embodied awareness requires deliberate attention to the fact that you have emotions that run through you every day. Unless you bring this fact up into your conscious awareness, your emotions could easily slip completely past your consciousness radar. Once you've become aware of them, the next step is to understand that your emotions are a completely natural part of who you are.

One telltale sign of a person who is afraid of their emotions is how fast they move. I don't mean physically; I mean through life. Watch how some people move from country to country, job to job, relationship to relationship, never settling in. They're like stones skimming across a glassy lake. A stone will bounce across the water's surface as long as it has enough speed, but if it slows down, it sinks to the depths of the pond.

I know this phenomenon firsthand. Before I learned the skills I now teach, speed was my asset and my liability. I'm a sprinter, so I love to go fast, but as all sprinters know, you can't sprint long distances. Short bursts, with rest in between, are what keep a sprinter going. My Achilles heal was sprinting, and sprinting, and then sprinting some more without taking the necessary breaks to let my system adjust. The consequence? My body would shut down and get sick. I'd be forced to rest. One way or another, life was sure to give me what I needed, and I finally gained the capacity to acknowledge and honor my emotions.

It's a skill that is vastly underutilized by the majority of us, but we do have the ability to witness feeling our emotions *while* we're feeling them. When we practice the art of witnessing our emotions while simultaneously feeling them, we begin to see how our emotions are connected to sub-personalities. Different aspects of us are trying to get our attention, competing with other aspects. We begin to realize that there are some things we can easily feel, and others we can't.

This observation marks an important step toward authenticity! If you can discern which parts of you are active, you'll be able to communicate that to others, thus improving intimacy and rapport. It's completely normal and human to want to avoid sharing parts of us that we feel are weak and unacceptable, but it's only through shining light on them that they can be digested and dissolved, especially with a loving partner to witness us.

Heart IQ Tracking Leads to Authentic Living

To begin accessing that most genuine you, you need to consider and embrace the possibility that you currently are *not* the most freely authentic version of yourself that you could be. If you're reading this saying to yourself, "Well, I'm completely real, so I don't need to bother with this part," I'd invite you to look a bit closer. Most of us do not realize how inauthentic we are in many moments throughout our day. It's nothing to be ashamed of; we've had countless reasons throughout our lives to identify ourselves with things that don't reflect our deepest truth.

Furthermore, when we get tied into our feelings, making our feelings into who we are, we have no access to our full authenticity. To make any progress toward connecting to our essence, our core goodness, we must first see the truth about how inauthentic we can be about some things in life. The idea is not to judge ourselves, but to just hold that awareness in a space of acceptance, understanding, and self-nurturing.

There's a beautiful irony in the fact that to become authentic, we must first accept our inauthenticity. Likewise, the only way to become less judgmental is to acknowledge how judgmental we are. As I mentioned earlier, there's this idea out there that judgment is not spiritual, but I would argue that it's far more spiritual to be real than to claim to be free of judgment. Remember, any trait you try to get rid of will get rid of you. To become less judgmental, we must first admit that we have judgments, and then we can decide not to attach any weight or focus to them.

Becoming more real means learning how to witness and manage your instinct to go into defense. When your partner makes an observation about you, it's always best to go into an honest inquiry around the suggestion. Our instinct is to jump to a defense position whenever the suggestion is about something we'd rather not see in ourselves. However, it's always better to look for a thread of possibility that there's truth in the suggestion because only in recognizing our hidden wounds can we heal them.

To become more connected, you must first acknowledge your disconnect! To be internally secure, you must first acknowledge your tendency to go into defense. It's never a black-and-white scenario, but to move in a positive direction on the spectrum of authenticity, you must first recognize where you currently reside on that spectrum.

Being genuine enough to amplify your joy requires some dedicated introspection. For most of us, it's not easy to touch the truths that lie deep within us alone, and that's where committed partnership comes in. Your energy speaks louder than your words. Often, your partner can feel something unresolved in you that you yourself are not even aware of. Intimacy creates skilled bullshit-detectors, and often a caring partner will be able to tell you when you're not coming from your most authentic self.

*　　*　　*

Your personal practice of Heart IQ Tracking will not only increase your awareness of what's moving for you and what's blocking you from feeling joy but will also naturally make space for your relationship to expand. What's more, when each partner in the relationship practices their personal tracking, the possibility for a deeply intimate relationship increases a hundredfold. Then, by sharing these experiences in real time with each other through relationship tracking (the subject of Chapter 6), your relationship can reach unfathomable heights. But first, you'll need a solid foundation for communicating from your heart. So, let's take a look at those skills in the next chapter to prepare you to start tracking together.

SUCCESS STORY FROM SARAH & GEOFF

Sarah and Geoff met at a Heart IQ event in 2012. Geoff lived in Canada and Sarah in the United States. Through their Heart IQ journey, they learned how to tune in to what they want and follow their hearts to take the risks they needed to take in order to share their lives together. They got married in 2015.

Sarah says, "Because we both have a better understanding of what healthy masculine and feminine energy looks like, we've learned how to relate to each other in new ways. We could both make parts of those expressions wrong in the past. Now, I notice that I can relax a lot more in my feminine energy because Geoff has more confidence to stand strong in his masculine energy."

Geoff relates, "Sarah is definitely owning her power in a new way, which is super exciting to me! Also, she's so much more willing to go into places that were 'off limits' before, like sharing her vulnerable heart with me, and taking risks where she wouldn't have in the past. It's in those moments of deep sharing with her that I completely light up!"

Need help applying this in your relationship?
Visit www.HeartIQRelationships.com for FREE demos
and tutorials using the access code myheartiq.

CHAPTER 5

Laying the Foundation for Heart IQ Communication

Before you can jump into the communication practices that are about to change your life forever, there are some foundational pieces that must be established. One piece I'll share with you in this chapter is a method for creating safety within the container of the relationship. As we've discussed, safety is an irrefutable requirement for opening into the bliss of deeply connected partnership.

The other piece is a set of laws you'll need to keep in mind while practicing Heart IQ communication. When two people become a couple, they establish an energetic field between them, and there are six immutable laws of this field that I have watched play out thousands of times in my retreats and in my work with couples. Just absorbing the information in these six laws alone will begin to transform the way you view your partnership. (We'll be delving further into each of them throughout the remainder of this book.)

The 6 Laws of Emotional-Energetic Couple Dynamics

1. **You are me cleverly disguised as you.** This first law states that both partners will grow and evolve through the healing of either one of them. If we are in relationship together, you are my medicine. We have attracted each other because we are mirrors, symbiotically poised to evolve together. As you allow me to support you in your healing, I get value as well because as you expand

your emotional range and grow, I grow, too. We are tied to each other on this journey. You benefit from my efforts, and I benefit from yours. As I realize that you are, in fact, me cleverly disguised as you, I can practice treating you as I would like to be treated. As I remember that you are me, I can be more compassionate with you as a practice of being more gentle with me.

2. **Whatever I repress, you will express for me.** A relationship is an energetic container. Though each of us represents an independent field of energy, there is additionally a field of energy that contains us both, and that field is healthiest when both partners are able to feel and express the full range of their emotions. If I am not able to do that, my partner will end up expressing the parts of the range that I don't own in myself to balance the emotional-energetic deficit that I create in our relationship. This shift occurs unconsciously, even when it's not my intention.

For example, if I cannot own my anger, my partner will begin expressing more anger because I have created a deficit of anger within the energetic container of our relationship. Balance can be restored in my partnership when I take the time to reconnect to myself and my own experience so that I can access and directly express the full range of my emotions. Once I am in touch with all of my emotions and able to express them clearly and directly, my partner will be able to stop taking up the slack.

3. **What I like in you, I like in me. What I don't like in you, I don't like in me.** It is a fact that our partners will trigger us, in both large and small ways. We experience a trigger as an annoyance with something our partner says or does, or as a perceived offense or slight toward us, or anything that hurts our feelings, bugs us, or makes us feel anger. What is really going on beneath the surface is usually not seen until we are taught the skills to identify it.

Triggers are gifts from our subconscious. At the subconscious level, I get triggered when my partner exhibits a trait that I have suppressed within myself, having made it "wrong" for me to own this particular trait. The truth is that we are all human, and we all have all of it within us, but due to the conditioning of our core unworthiness, each of us has certain characteristics that we bury and suppress out of fear that we will become this "wrong" thing.

A trigger happens when you reflect back to me states of being that I have worked hard to avoid. Since I have a subconscious belief that these particular qualities, traits, or states of being are wrong, it pains me to see them expressed in my partner, and my instinct is to make my partner wrong for expressing them. These states that I've suppressed are my "shadows," and they are parts of me that I need to come into balance with and accept in myself in order to heal and become joyful and whole.

All states of being are beneficial when they are channeled through the heart and felt and expressed directly. When our shadows are brought into the light, they are transformed into our greatest gifts. Therefore, our partner holds the key to our deepest shadow work and our most profound healing.

4. I can only be present with your emotion to the degree that I can be present with my own emotion. If my emotional range is limited, there will be certain emotions that aren't accessible to me in my own life. If you have access to a broader emotional spectrum, you will at times express emotions that I am uncomfortable with because I have not owned them within myself.

For example, if you are expressing sadness, and I'm not okay with allowing myself to express my own sadness, then your expression will trigger my need to protect myself. As a result, I will either become annoyed by it, or go numb because I've determined that this emotion is out of the range of what feels safe for me to experience. As we continue to practice supporting each other in our healing (by witnessing each other with unconditional love while we process our triggers), we will both naturally expand our comfortable emotional range.

5. When we're in resonance, what moves in you moves in me. Resonance naturally occurs when our connection deepens to the extent that our hearts become synchronized and we entrain with each other. It's a state of being so tuned in to each other that we sometimes think the same thoughts, feel the same feelings, and see the world through the same lens. Resonance can be deliciously enjoyable, healthy, and beneficial for growing intimacy; however, there is also a danger of becoming unhealthily merged.

When each partner does not maintain clear emotional-energetic boundaries, we can lose ourselves in the presence of each other. When I begin to make your needs more important than my own, I lose sight of the fact that no matter how deeply connected we are, I still need to feel me and what I want in this moment so that my heart has its own voice.

6. Clarity is needed for both pain to digest and for love to land.
Energy and emotion love specific direction. Vague statements such as "I love you" can be made more energetically potent when they are delivered with more detail and specificity. Statements like, "I love the way your hair feels," or "I love the way you prepare our meals with such care and thoughtfulness," are likely to land more deeply than less targeted expressions of love. Likewise, it's best to express your pain with as much detail as possible. If your pain is expressed ambiguously (for example, "You've hurt me"), it will create more defense in me than if it were expressed more specifically (for example, "I'm feeling hurt by your rejection of my lovemaking advances last night.")

Understanding these six laws will transform the way you relate to your partner. They provide the framework for a blissful Heart IQ connection and a foundation for the communication techniques that will ensure an authentic, ever-evolving relationship. Another necessary component to this foundation is *safety*.

Opening Requires Safety

The very first practice for creating the communication habits that will transform your relationship entails establishing a bubble of safety around your union. The ways in which couples have traditionally attempted to create safety are not what you'll find in this book. Following a traditional model, we might make agreements to never hurt each other or challenge each other, to always strive to agree with each other, and to manage ourselves so that we take care not to do anything that might potentially cause our partner to feel unsafe. These are agreements based upon restriction. They have a suppressive effect on the energy of the relationship. Restrictions focus on what we can and cannot do, which reflects the unspoken idea that we must prove our love to each other in tactical, regimented ways.

It's like saying, "Your love is valid to me only if you prove it by doing what makes me feel good, and not ever doing anything that might make me feel bad about myself." It's a codependent practice of placing your own value and worth into the hands of another for safekeeping. It gives each partner the illusion that they should have the right to control and manage the other's behavior, energy, and attention to ensure they never have to feel bad.

The agreements I'm suggesting have the opposite effect. They will help unearth a sense of freedom and joyful abandon for both of you, which is far more juicy and conducive to a blissful union. It's about feeling safe enough with each other to expose our unsafety. It's allowing ourselves to be seen in those places where we are not fully connected and developed in ourselves. It's like saying, "I feel safe enough with you to expose and explore where I feel unsafe in me."

With the 6 Laws of Emotional-Energetic Couple Dynamics as a backdrop, we create sacred agreements to help us define the boundaries and freedoms we both require to feel accepted and loved exactly where we are, while also agreeing to stretch ourselves to discover how much more we can become. Safety allows for depth of intimacy. It lets us feel okay about relaxing and dropping deeper within to discover a more intimate place of connection with the world and ourselves. It's only through this flavor of safety that we can relax into our deep longing to trust another, and soften enough so our partner feels invited to join us in the rich, vast space of our undiscovered self.

Conscious Relationship Agreements Breed Safety

Why is it that relationships feel so inherently *un*safe to so many of us? Perhaps it's because we've been hurt in relationships before. Perhaps it goes back to the events that contributed to our core unworthiness, as discussed earlier, when others said and did things that caused our world to feel less and less safe and comforting. Many people feel so much un-safety around the idea of being in a relationship that they remain intentionally alone and emotionally restricted their whole lives.

I believe one of the main reasons that relationships feel so unsafe to us is their unpredictability. By nature, a relationship depends fifty percent on another person's intentions and affections toward you, and to a great extent, you have no control over those factors. But what if there were a way to ameliorate some of that un-safety so that you could more easily lower your walls and embark on the soul-nurturing journey of becoming vulnerable and emotionally ripe with a partner who is ready to facilitate your growth and evolving?

There is a way. It's by setting intentional agreements together. Starting a relationship with conscious agreements is the best way to create a safe container for your souls to play together in. To access joy and healing, you must feel safe enough to be fully you in the presence of another, and making relationship agreements is the best way to establish that safety. We often establish relationships without ever clearly speaking about the parameters on which they're based. We make assumptions, and we assume our partner is making the same ones. It might even feel scary to articulate these assumptions with each other. But the truth is that the more you speak to the unspoken, the safer you will feel.

The kind of agreements I want you to make are not about setting up rules to limit your expression and opportunities, but are instead designed for your liberation, to open you both up to the deepest wells of intimacy and love. We'll go through the biggies now one by one, and at the end of this section, you'll find a summary to share with your partner when the time feels right.

1. Do You Agree to Strive to Become a Fully Healthy You?

As I've mentioned, the greatest gift you can give to your partner is to become a fully healthy you. If you're always focused on what your partner is doing and worrying about how to help your partner open, you're not taking the most direct route toward serving the relationship. If, on the other hand, you commit to focusing on your own vulnerability and your own opening, the relationship will flourish.

This is true not only in couple dynamics, but in all relationships. The greatest gift parents can give their kids is to become a fully healthy couple by being fully healthy individuals. One of the biggest mistakes I see when I coach parents is that they have become totally focused on the children, with no attention or energy left for nourishing the relationship between each other. They think they're doing right by their kids, when in fact they may be sending them an unhealthy message. A child's nervous system registers safety based on how well the parents' relationship is functioning. A child learns love best not by being loved, but by observing love.

2. Do You Agree to Openly and Honestly "Take Space"?

When you feel an emotion moving within you, and you're willing to share that with your partner in real time as it unfolds, we call it "taking space." Taking space nourishes our human need to express and reveal ourselves, and to feel valued in that expression. It's a sense of, "I get to be just as I am. My value is intrinsic and nothing can take it away. I am valuable just being me."

You can also take space for things you've planned in advance to discuss, but even then it's most effective and heart-centered if you can do it by describing what is moving for you in that moment, through the process of Heart IQ Tracking (which I shared in Chapter 4 and will discuss with regard to couples in Chapter 6). It's important to commit to being as real as you can possibly be with your partner in every moment. Agree to be willing to share what's moving for you—what you're feeling, wanting, and needing.

3. Do You Agree to Lovingly "Hold Space" for Your Partner?

When your partner has opened up to you, resist the urge to fix, offer advice, teach, or rescue. The best service you can provide your beloved is the practice we call "holding space." Holding space nourishes our human need to feel accepted without the condition of being understood. It's like saying to your partner, "Even if I don't completely understand where you are in your process or experience, I want to understand, and even without understanding, I can still hold you lovingly and unconditionally in the place where you are, and even feel delighted in holding you there."

Holding space is more than being a good listener. It's giving your full attention and support to another person as that person tracks and shares their internal reality. It's not about jumping in and getting involved. If you want to rescue, that simply means you want to rescue something in yourself. When you hold space, you're in full acceptance of whatever is being shared, even if it triggers you. You can share your feelings around being triggered when it's your turn to be open and vulnerable.

Having said that, you do not want to be quiet and passive while holding space. There is a difference between interfering in what is being shared and offering your spontaneous, supportive response. As your partner is talking, you want to respond with frequent small words of confirmation, nods, perhaps gentle touches, and maintained eye contact. If you understand on any level what your partner is saying, or even if you can only relate to a fraction of it, you want to express that understanding with your nonverbal and briefly verbal cues. Only do what is authentic for you, but in any way that feels genuine, do your best to make your loved one feel heard, seen, and "gotten."

Being on the receiving end of uplifting spontaneous response feels sublimely validating and fulfills our human need for acceptance. It's like saying to your partner, "Whether I like what's happening right now or not, I can relate to where you are. I get you in this place." Be open and generous with your spontaneous response. When the time is right, state what is moving within you in reaction to the sharing.

4. Do You Agree to Resolve Conflicts Quickly and Directly?

The more skilled you become at quickly and directly sharing whatever discontent or other emotion is moving within you, the better your chances of having a vital, successful ongoing relationship. You might be afraid of triggering your partner's anger or even of losing the relationship if you speak your mind, so this practice can be a real challenge for some people. It is absolutely critical, however. Without developing this skill, you run the risk of losing polarity together. The juice evaporates, the sexual magnetism fades, and gradually what was once a fiery, passionate connection becomes a cordial, lazy, weak bond based on familiarity and routine.

When a conflict first comes up, it's fluid. It's easy to move and easy to clean up. The longer you ignore it, however, the more dense and solid it becomes. It gets heavier, gradually transforming into an unwieldy obstacle that prevents you from being present or feeling any light, genuine joy. Only when we deal with conflicts immediately, while they're still in a fluid state, can we spare ourselves this extra burden on our partnerships.

When circumstances prevent you from being open and direct at the moment of your triggering, you'll still want to clear that energy with your partner as soon as you possibly can. Don't sit on it hoping it will go away. You'll only be re-traumatizing that bit of your pain body that was ready to come up for healing. If the conversation feels especially difficult, you may need to bring in a third party to facilitate, such as a counselor or close friend. Just make sure it's someone you both trust to have your best interests at heart.

When sharing your trigger, be careful not to make your partner feel wrong or judged. Instead of bringing up past evidence to reinforce your position and make yourself seem right, speak only about what is moving within you in the present moment. For instance, you might take note of what your body feels like. Is this trigger bringing up anger for you, or does it feel more like disappointment and sadness? Are you nervous to discuss this topic? Are you doubting yourself? Are you concerned about your partner's reaction? When you begin to understand that any judgment of your partner is really a judgment you hold against yourself, you'll become more compassionate and you'll be able to use those judgmental moments as powerful opportunities for self-growth.

5. Do You Agree to Practice Heart-Centered Communication?

In the upcoming chapters, we'll be going into great depth about how to communicate from your heart to keep your relationship blissfully invigorated. But right now for our purposes of making agreements, the main thing to focus on is to maintain compassion for your partner, even when you are angry or deeply entrenched in your pain body.

When we're triggered, it's easy to fall into lazy patterns of speaking in absolutes. Resolve to remove from your vocabulary the words "never" and "always." It's highly unlikely that your partner "never" or "always" does anything, and those kinds of blanket statements only rile up the receiver and ignite positions of defense. You want to carefully choose ways to articulate your authentic feelings that allow you to simultaneously hold the intention of energetically moving toward your partner, not further away.

One very valuable phrase to incorporate into your communication toolbox is, "There is a part of me that feels . . ." As I discussed earlier, there are always different parts of you at play and your reality is seldom one-faceted. Acknowledging this during your communication with your partner will soften your message and make it easier for your partner to absorb without going into defense. Using the terminology, "A part of me feels . . ." is far more effective than saying, "I feel." The latter language sends your partner the message that the totality of you feels that way, when in truth, whatever you are feeling is always representative of just a part of who you are. When you share something as a part of you, you make room for the other parts to also have voice.

In your communication agreement, you'll want to agree to close your conversations consciously. Even if unexpected life events interrupt your discussion, it's important to come back to the incomplete conversation and complete it as soon as possible. It's also a good idea to acknowledge the incompleteness in the meantime so that you can feel connected even in your incompleteness.

6. Do You Agree to Steer Clear of Relationship Detractors?

One thing that makes relationships feel unsafe is the concern that your partner won't keep your secrets. Being open and vulnerable with another requires an agreement that your relationship specifics will stay contained within the relationship. When issues arise, the most important person to talk them through with is your partner, and if you've agreed in advance that you won't talk to any outsiders, it's more likely you'll turn to each other.

There may be times, however, when you or your partner feels the need to process something with a trusted person outside the relationship. Having an agreement in place about who that person might be for each of you will allow you to maintain the feeling of a safe container. So your agreement might be to have no third-party talk, or it might be that you each have a particular person or people with whom you can process, preapproved by the other partner.

The idea is to limit this kind of interaction to people who genuinely want the relationship to succeed. That way, your partner doesn't have to worry that you're off bitching about them with someone who is likely to fan the flames of your discontent. The agreement should specify that any discussion with others be in the spirit of helping the relationship to work better, not tearing it down.

In general, the most successful relationships are maintained when neither partner talks about the other negatively with those outside the relationship. That includes analyzing and assuming things without asking your partner directly. Complaining to others about your partner makes the relationship's energetic container "leaky." After a while, these venting sessions feel like a heavy weight you drag around. They create a wall between the two of you, built from even the tiniest repetitive breaches of uncontained venting. Practice sharing *light* about your partner in all circumstances, and you will see the *light* growing in your relationship.

7. Do You Agree to Honor Each Other's Pace?

A safe relationship container is one in which boundaries are respected and made clear. Agree to never push your partner into emotional areas they don't want to go into. All healing has its time, and you can trust your relationship to bring up what's ready to be undertaken for each of you at precisely the right moment. It's okay to lovingly invite your partner to stretch a bit, especially if you see where a blind spot might be potentially holding your loved one back from reaching full authenticity, joy, and wholeness. But if your gentle nudge is resisted, you have to let it go.

I often coach couples in a situation where one partner is ready to be fully open and vulnerable, but holds back because the other partner isn't in the same place. The partner who's ready to share will push and dig, creating a confrontation where none is necessary. There are some instances when more pushing is warranted, which I'll go into later, but for the most part, you want to honor and respect your partner's wishes regarding when to do healing.

If you are feeling triggered and are ready to be vulnerable about that, allow your partner to hold space for you and love and support you, right where you are. Don't be concerned if you're the only one ready at the moment. You're setting a valuable example and paving the way for the day your partner arrives at this point. Remember that your healing always creates healing for both of you. And if you're the partner who isn't there yet, practice holding space for the one who is. Gently imagine yourself in your partner's position and offer the same compassion and safety you'll want to eventually have offered to you.

8. Do You Agree to Not Police Your Partner?

In personal development circles, there's lots of talk about accountability. There is value in deciding on something you want for yourself and asking another person to make you accountable for making progress toward your goal. That other person, however, should *not* be your romantic partner—and vice versa. Let's say for example that you want to lose ten pounds. If you put your partner in charge of reminding you about your diet, the simple act of enjoying a meal together can become a potential point of contention. When we put ourselves in the role of school monitor, watching our partner's every move and looking for opportunities to catch and redirect, it's just not a sexy situation. That kind of policing is very depolarizing to a relationship. It's better to get that kind of accountability support from a trusted friend or group, not from each other.

9. Do You Agree to Reach Consensus?

Reaching consensus means making sure that your partner feels safe and considered before you proceed with anything. When you have consensus, one partner will not railroad the other or become a dictator over the activities of the relationship. For instance, one partner won't make major purchases or plan out all the details of a holiday or vacation without first consulting the other.

Of course, there may be some areas of your relationship where you'll both agree that one of you will take the lead, and that would be a caveat to this agreement. Maybe one of you loves to cook and plan meals and the other one loves culinary surprises. It wouldn't make sense in that scenario to make sure every meal is agreed upon in advance. Maybe you've decided together that one of you will be in charge of car maintenance or laundry, and you give carte blanche to that partner in those particular areas. But it's likely that certain aspects of the relationship will still function best with consensus, such as child-rearing and where and how to spend your quality time together.

10. Do You Agree to Create Space for Sharing?

When either partner has something meaningful to discuss, it's very important that you both give that discussion the proper time and space. You want to avoid any distractions or interferences, so it's best not to attempt this conversation over a meal, in a car, or in any kind of situation where others are likely to interrupt you. Don't ever have a serious discussion when you are drunk or have been using drugs; you won't be conscious and present and able to give it the respect it deserves. Likewise, just before bed is not a good choice if you're tired. The important thing is to be sure to allow enough time and to sit and be fully present to each other.

When you take these extra steps, you ensure that the conversation will move you into greater connection, whatever the content of the sharing. If you're the one who has something to say, be sure to take responsibility for your experience by tracking your feelings and thoughts in the moment. Speak in the first person (for example, "I'm noticing that I hold a lot of anger around this topic.") and avoid accusation and blame. Remember that your partner is a mirror, and see if you can express your authentic truth in a way that will promote your healing.

11. Do You Agree to Do Daily Check-Ins?

"Check-in" is a practice I learned from one of my mentors, Tej Steiner. It's a practice of setting aside a few minutes each day to be in authentic communication with your partner. Just knowing that you both value your intimacy enough to intentionally schedule it into your day creates a wonderful sense of being honored and cherished by each other. It could be just five minutes each morning before you get out of bed or fifteen minutes when you get home from work, or it could be both. It's just an opportunity for each of you to look within and track what's moving for you with the intention of sharing it with the other. The time it takes to do this will vary from day to day, and from couple to couple, so experiment to find out what works best for you.

Knowing you have regularly scheduled opportunities for genuine, heartfelt communication alleviates some of the potential stress of having to officially ask your partner to take space for you when you have something to share. Of course, if you have the opportunity to address concerns as they arise, it's always best to do that.

12. Do You Agree to Notify?

It seems like a simple thing, but so often when we're very close to someone, we forget to extend the simple courtesies we routinely offer to others. An agreement to notify each other on a regular basis will eliminate so many common relationship arguments. For example, if you have agreed to meet your partner somewhere at a specific time and you're running late or your plans change, notify your partner. Don't just show up late; it demonstrates a lack of respect for your beloved, which, even if you scoot by without reprimand, will begin to deteriorate your partner's sense of being valued and honored by you.

13. Do You Agree to Commit?

Safety is threatened in our relationships when we feel insecure in our commitment to each other. If you're always worried that the other partner has one foot out the door, it will be impossible to access the kind of vulnerability that allows healing to occur. Since the concept of commitment itself feels unsafe for many people, a good idea is to decide upon a set time period for your initial commitment.

This feels like an odd concept for many of the couples I've coached, but it's actually a quite effective way to create safety without all the ambiguity of the more commonplace ways couples approach the issue of commitment. Once you've both decided you want to be "all in," the next decision becomes: "For how long?" You could decide that for the next two months you will be completely devoted to each other and the relationship. Or maybe six months feels right to you or maybe it's just two weeks.

This works because when you assign a specific boundary of time to commitment, the commitment increases. When you say "forever," it's not as powerful. Men, especially, respond particularly well to any situation that provides an end to the mission—a reward, a goal, a medal. The idea is not that you part ways after the time period has elapsed, but that you then evaluate the relationship together and honestly communicate where each of you stands with it.

Most likely, you will then agree to another commitment period from there or establish some sort of recurring all-in-check-up schedule. Eventually you may stop doing it once you feel established as a long-term, committed couple, but it's a wonderful way to increase intimacy at the start of a relationship or later if the relationship falls into a fragile state.

14. Do You Agree to Close with Integrity?

The truth of most relationships is that they eventually end. Most of us have several, if not many, romantic partnerships throughout our lifetimes, and the only one that doesn't end is the one we happen to be in when we die. So it's important to have a plan for healthy closure, even if you never need to use it.

What often happens is that the relationship goes on for some time with a certain degree of unconsciousness and lack of connection, which means one or both partners are not having their needs met. Since they haven't been putting care and focus into maintaining a mutually nourishing container, the container becomes "leaky." From this vulnerable position, one partner could easily become attracted to someone else and might explore that relational possibility in secret, only coming back to break it off with the original partner once the new situation is established.

This is an all-too-common unhealthy scenario and will almost always result in problems with the new relationship. The way to do it consciously is to first put care and effort into maintaining the connection and polarity with the original partner. If that becomes difficult, and you do find yourself attracted to a third party, you need to recognize that the attraction is a signal that there is something lacking in the original relationship.

Look inward and do the work to figure out what that lack is, and bring it up with your partner. Let your partner know that this lack in the relationship is a real problem for you, and if it can't be remedied together, you will want to end things. After an authentic exploration with your original partner, if the lack can't be addressed, then you close consciously with that person before beginning the new relationship. (You'll find complete instructions for consciously closing relationships in Chapter 11.) It may seem unsavory to discuss breaking up when that's the last thing on your mind, but if you both agree that if the time does come, you will create a healthy, conscious closing, it will create more safety in which you can be vulnerable and flourish.

Our Sacred Relationship Agreements

The following agreements serve each of us in our intention to open more to love and deeper intimacy in our relationship. These agreements do not restrict us; they liberate us.

1. The greatest gift I can give to you is to be a fully healthy me. Given this, I agree that I am here in this relationship for me, and you are here in this relationship for you.

2. We agree to take space and to authentically communicate what we're feeling, wanting, and needing. We agree to share what's moving in the present moment, rather than collecting evidence that verifies past reality.

3. We agree to hold space for each other and not attempt to rescue or fix. We agree to give a generous spontaneous response. (I agree to let you know that I am feeling you to the best of my ability in any moment.)

4. We agree to confront and resolve our conflicts as close as possible to the time the conflict occurs. If we get stuck, we agree to bring in one or more others to witness and support us with regaining our clarity.

5. We agree to communicate only in heart-centered ways and avoid using the words "always" and "never." We agree to close our conversations consciously. Even if unexpected life events interrupt our discussion, we agree to come back to our incomplete conversation and complete it as soon as possible, and to acknowledge the incompleteness in the meantime so that we can feel connected in our incompleteness.

6. We agree to speak of each other only in uplifting ways to others. If either of us needs to privately share our upset that relates to our relationship with a third party, we will choose to confide in those friends who are fans of our relationship. We agree to only confide in friends who will not take sides, but will listen with an

open heart toward both of us if we are experiencing challenge in our connection. We agree that those friends are: _____ _____.

7. We agree to not push each other. I honor you in being who you are, and who you are not, in any given moment. I also agree to invite you to stretch if I see that a blind spot is potentially holding you back from being your full self.

8. We agree to not hold each other accountable. Instead, we agree to hold ourselves accountable and to ask for support when we need it.

9. We agree that we will make decisions and take action together, unless we agree that one of us is designated as "the lead" related to a specific decision or action.

10. We agree to create uninterrupted sacred space for meaningful discussions when we have something important to share.

11. We agree to daily scheduled check-ins to be in authentic communication.

12. We agree to notify each other if we need to break or change the time agreements we make.

13. We agree to be fully devoted to this relationship for _____ months as of _____ (date). When that time period ends, we agree to give dedicated focus and attention to our choice to be in this relationship and make any adjustments and improvements that feel right at that time. We may establish a new commitment period from that point, or additionally agree to check in regularly—every _____ months, to review these agreements and adjust them accordingly so that they continue to serve both of us.

14. We agree to follow our couple wisdom—even if it means breaking these agreements following a conscious close to our relationship.

Signed: _____

_____

Incorporating the 6 Laws of Emotional-Energetic Couple Dynamics into your understanding of what a romantic partnership is and combining that with your sacred relationship agreements create a solid launching pad for incorporating Heart IQ tools into your daily interactions. The most important tool—aside from your personal Heart IQ Tracking—is Relationship Tracking, which is the subject of the next chapter. Read on to discover how you and your partner can take your relationship to the next level.

SUCCESS STORY FROM STEPHANIE & DAN

Stephanie and Dan met at a Heart IQ event. Each had been involved in Heart IQ for two years prior to meeting each other, and both had previously been in twenty-plus year partnerships. Through this work, Stephanie and Dan were able to start their new relationship journey together from a heart-intelligent framework.

Dan says, "Heart IQ has helped me to let go of old habits and patterns around communication, vulnerability, intimacy, and the safety I feel in sharing myself with another. For example, now I can relax and share what I'm feeling and thinking with my partner, without the fear of it somehow being used against me. We still have our moments of not being connected, but now, I have the understanding to partner with Steph in a way that can transform those moments into some of the most wonderful and healing experiences of my life."

Stephanie agrees and says: "Heart IQ has made all the difference, not only in me but in the clarity and expectations that I bring into my intimate relationship. Being in this work together has given us a single track on which to be together. Heart IQ gives me and us a clear track to come back to amidst the confusion of daily life and healing, so that we don't lose sight of that deep and certain place of love that has brought us together. I wouldn't want to take this journey without it, and having Dan in my life is a much bigger reward than any risk I have to take to face what challenges me."

Need help applying this in your relationship?
Visit www.HeartIQRelationships.com for FREE demos
and tutorials using the access code myheartiq.

CHAPTER 6

Relationship Tracking: Your Primary Communication Tool

Do you want to see a demonstration of the relationship tracking
process in action? Visit www.HeartIQRelationships.com
using the access code myheartiq to learn more.

The communication practices you're about to learn in this chapter will give you the insight to do two critical things: First, you will use them to establish, maintain, and expand the intimacy between you and your partner as well as other significant people in your life. Second, you will use these tools when you need to repair intimacy that has been damaged or broken. (Remember, neither you nor your partner is broken or damaged in any way; it's the level of intimacy that requires fixing.)

The foundational tool you'll begin practicing is relationship tracking. Heart IQ Tracking is an internal experience, and relationship tracking means deliberately making that experience external so that you can share it with your beloved. It's the most direct route to a partnership rich with intimacy, magnetism, and juice. When you apply the skill of Heart IQ tracking to your relationship, it's absolutely magical. Imagine being able to communicate to another the internal commentary of whatever is going on for you, in the moment, while you're in connection with that person. You have a pure awareness of what's moving within you, and the ability to fully feel it as you witness it, without getting uncomfortably caught up in the drama of it. You have the skill to authentically share this internal process with your partner and be fully received and met in that place. That is the bliss of real intimacy.

Present Your Position with Clarity and Simplicity

When you're tracking properly with your beloved, everything is simply what it is. You don't get bogged down in defensive habits like speaking in make-wrong absolutes to try to wound your partner. Even when you're hurt, you don't come at your partner with the energy of "You always hurt me!" Instead you have the clarity to say, "A part of me is feeling hurt and I'm noticing the part of me that would normally want to make you wrong for that . . ." As we've discussed, using the phrase "A part of me feels . . ." is tremendously beneficial because it helps your partner to be much more receptive to whatever it is you're expressing.

Even though it seems benign enough to simply say, "I feel . . ." when you want to express what you're feeling, the truth is always that it is only a part of you that's feeling that way. You are a fantastically multifaceted being! There are countless parts of you that you could choose to access in any given moment. While you're in dialogue with your partner about a grievance you need to share, you will want to give authentic voice to the *part* of you that is feeling the grievance, but that part is not all of who you are, and it helps the communication immensely to recognize that.

Relationship tracking works best when you can stay light about it. This means you'll want to speak from a place where you can own your worth and feel your heart open and responsive. You may be feeling diminished and victimized about what's not working in the relationship. You may feel guilt about the part you've played in its trouble spots. While expressing what's not working to your partner, you'll want to deliberately stay connected to your own goodness and worth. If your pain body is activated, you'll find this practice to be very difficult.

Relationship tracking is a heart-centered communication practice, so you want to try to stay focused on what you want and what you feel. Most of us have a tendency to share our thoughts, ideas, and analysis through the vehicle of story telling. This kind of sharing from the head is always based in the past or future, and that's fine, but the primary content of your sharing needs to be more immediate than that, and centered on your present-moment longings and what you're experiencing.

Relationship Tracking Begins with Acceptance

The first step in relationship tracking is to become aware of all the ways we're in resistance and how we're not in a state of loving acceptance of what's going on for us. The second step is to share that and be felt and witnessed in it. When another feels your guilt, shame, or authentic needs, it's so incredibly healing. We require that attention from another in order to come into self-love, contrary to what you may have heard. You may have been told that if we need others to validate our reality, we're in a position of weakness and dependency, and that it's not real self-love if others are involved.

It's true that we can survive by taking care of ourselves, but it's simply not our optimal state. We're not designed to be islands. We are communal creatures. On a human level, we are tribal in nature. We need each other to reflect back our okay-ness in the places where we don't feel okay. As you've learned, others caused our wounding, and others are needed to undo it.

It's not about being overly dependent, needy of attention, and perpetually asking, "Do you love me?" It's about being able to track and realize, "This is my wounding; this is my pain; this is my longing." It's about having the courage to vulnerably share that realization within the amplified field that allowed it to surface, so that the witnessing of it can soothe the wound like a nurturing balm, and the rewiring can take place at a cellular level. This is how the nervous system begins to understand that the self-judgments and unworthiness beliefs aren't true. This is where self-love can grow and flourish.

Tracking allows different parts of you to become activated simultaneously. As we've discussed, we all have that energetic pain body that remembers all the traumas we've had since birth in the form of undigested, unclaimed "vibrations" that keep us feeling unworthy. These vibrations are "banked" when we're too young and immature to process them, and they become frozen at that young age so that later when they're accessed by our triggers, we sometimes revert in our energy to that very young age. Sometimes these parts need to be given full voice.

In my case, I was never given permission to just *be* in my anger. Whenever I expressed anger I was hit or told to be quiet. So as an adult, when I'd feel anger rising inside me, another part of me would pop up saying, "Careful now, Christian. You know what happens when you get angry. You won't be loved." Only in the beautiful safety of an amplified field created by two heart-conscious partners has the first voice of authentic, healthy anger ever been able to overcome that second cautionary voice. Knowing it's okay, and even encouraged by my beloved, to have my real feelings, I'm able to heal. The same will be true for you.

With relationship tracking, we get to feel all of those different parts. It's possible to have lived within just one of those parts for the last decade or even for most of your entire life. You can be in a part of you, not the whole of you, for all that time. You could live in a checked-out energetic part that numbs you and keeps you from ever touching your emotional depths, or you could live in your pain body and allow your S.T.U.A.R.T. to create drama after drama as a distraction from your truth.

The purpose of relationship tracking is to learn to love what is. That's the reason we do it. Being held in the unconditional love of your partner while you track your reality is what ultimately releases you from the judgments and *resistance to what is* that have been blocking your joy.

Communication Is a Dance

Whenever two people are communicating, there's one who's taking space and one who's holding space. Ideally, the conversation smoothly alternates between space-holding and space-taking for each of you. When you're simultaneously competing for space, there will always be some disconnect, and it will be difficult for either of you to have your needs met. Relationship tracking will revolutionize your communication with your partner by providing a structured system for *taking space* and *holding space* for each other. If you and your partner have made the sacred relationships agreements in the previous chapter, you've already set the stage for this essential process.

When you hold space really well, there's an internal stillness, a presence that feels like an invitation to your partner. It requires you to have achieved a certain level of okay-ness with who you are, since the more you can be comfortable with yourself, the more you'll be able to make your partner feel felt. Holding space effectively means being able to monitor your own triggers and defensiveness (your S.T.U.A.R.T. strategies) for the sake of the other. It means being generous with your supportive spontaneous response. You want to clearly demonstrate that you are receiving what's being said, even if that means being a bit animated to make sure your partner feels you feeling them. That's what gives the space-taker the freedom and confidence to continue. Anyone who feels they're communicating into a void won't want to communicate for very long.

As important as it is to practice your space-holding skills, the very best thing you can do to improve your communication is to dedicate yourself to being a good space-*taker*. That means having the confidence to claim all of who you are in the moment. You start by being clear and direct about wanting to take space so that your partner knows you have something to share. Then, once you have your partner's undivided attention, you can't buckle. Having the full loving attention of your partner can easily trigger core

ACTIVE LISTENING IS NOT THE WAY

I dislike the traditional practice called "active listening." You may have come across it if you've ever done any couple's counseling or retreats. Practicing active listening involves sitting silently while your partner says everything they need to say, and then when they're done, repeating it all back to them and asking, "Did I get that right?" It can feel very rigid and robotic and can leave the partner who has shared feeling unfelt. If you're generous with your spontaneous response, your partner will feel heard without this awkward structure.

unworthiness. Unless you can connect to your inherent goodness and worth, it can be hard to receive that kind of focused, loving attention. Don't waffle. Don't let your mind wander to how your partner will receive what you have to say. Just track and share with directness and vulnerability.

If your partner isn't giving you enough spontaneous response to put you at ease, or if you just find yourself needing more, it's fine to invite more participation from the space-holder by pausing and allowing room for longer responses. You can even state directly: "I'm going to pause here, even though I have more to share with you, because I'd love some sort of response from you right now."

Intimacy requires a certain degree of balance. You both want to bring all you can of yourselves into your communication practice. If either of you consistently takes up too much or too little energetic space within the container of the relationship, balance will suffer and intimacy will be lost. Imagine a box that holds two inflated balloons. If one of the balloons is barely inflated, the other balloon may overinflate to fill the space within the box. If one partner is not bringing enough juice, enough of their own authenticity to the exchange, the other may reactively begin taking up all the space. That can leave the first partner feeling even further diminished, and like there's no room for them to take space and be heard. Both need to be aware of the need to bring their full selves to the partnership.

The beautiful dance of intimate communication requires the ebb and flow of giving and receiving; if either party is incapable of either one of those things, there's no circuitry; no completion, no intimacy. Communication that's delivered must have somewhere solid to land, so you have to practice fullness in your receiving. When you share, you've got to share with all you've got, bringing your juice, your mojo, your rawness. Sometimes that won't be easy, when you're in collapse* or you're triggered, but you still need to bring as much of you as possible to the communication.

How to Be a Better Space-Taker

Taking space is all about tracking and vulnerably sharing your tracked reality with another. It's the ability to notice what's moving in you, giving yourself permission to fully feel whatever is there without getting so *involved* with what's there that you become collapsed by it. You're in witness mode, yet you're not detached, disconnected, and robotic. You're giving yourself permission to feel what's real without becoming hijacked by it or connected to the drama of it. You ultimately know the whole experience is healing and powerfully strengthening for the relationship, so you can relax into it somewhat, even while enduring the discomfort of it. You're an embodied observer.

Skilled trackers have good discernment. They can track what's going on with self and another, and tell the difference. They take responsibility for what's moving. They stay present. If they notice some old story is running, they track and share that. They speak in "I" language, unapologetically reporting what's real and true, with directness and courage. You need enough space inside you to do it; you can't be so close to what's moving in you that you buckle

---

* Collapse is what we call a state where you have lost connection to your heart and power and have lost the ability in that moment to track effectively. For example, when I was fourteen, I was attacked outside a nightclub and started to experience terrible panic attacks after the event. Although I was "fine," when I went back to spot where it happened a few years later, my knees gave in and I burst into tears uncontrollably as my nervous system activated the dormant undigested pain. In this moment, I went into collapse.

under the pressure of it. When something is difficult to track, a good tracker disclaims that openly. It's called "tracking the track," and it sounds like this: "I'm noticing that this is really hard for me to share. A part of me doesn't feel open right now. I'm tracking a fear that what I'm going to say may put you in defense."

Remember, Heart IQ Tracking is an internal experience, and relationship tracking means deliberately making that experience external so that you can share it with your beloved. When you feel blocked, you can even say, "I'm tracking a block right now." Just identifying that will begin to dissolve the block. Keep it in the here and now. Say to yourself, "Right now what I feel I want is . . ." What's your fear? What's your need? Get in touch with both of those, and communicate the answers. The best question you can repeatedly ask yourself is: "What's moving for me right now?"

Relationship tracking can take some practice because most of us have been conditioned to believe that communication in relationships is about rehashing events. The energy gets quite dense when you only share content, beginning conversations with: "Last night when you did this, I didn't like it because . . ." It's easy to be too much about the content, and not enough about the observation of your experience of the content. But your connection to your partner hinges on connecting through your observer space; it's not really all that dependent on content!

In fact, another valuable way to approach tracking is to divide it into three sections:

➤ First, you share any fears, resistance, or judgments about what you want to share.

➤ Second comes the actual sharing itself.

➤ The third piece is to then share how you're feeling about having shared that content.

It may sound like a cumbersome process, but actually following this three-step formula creates enormous lightness and connection.

It's a guaranteed way to make sure you're communicating your fullest truth in this deeply intimate, charged moment with your partner.

Sometimes, of course, sharing your experience will necessitate some external explanation, but even then, the tracking should come first. A good tracking habit to develop is to solicit invitation from your partner when you want to share anything other than what you're wanting or what you're feeling. You pave the way for this "head-centered" communication by saying something like, "I'm feeling defensive and closed right now. I feel disconnected from you because I'm running some energy over something that happened last night. May I share it with you?"

It may sound unnecessarily formal, but getting a buy-in from your partner will automatically make them more likely to offer reassurance and responsiveness, and make you more likely to feel felt and heard. Giving your partner the opportunity to invite that kind of sharing will prevent them from feeling attacked by it. If they agree to hear it, you can actually be in your anger, be in your sadness, and be able to feel it and express it fully without your partner feeling ambushed. Venting isn't bad; it can stimulate polarity. But you need to get an invitation to vent by first tracking and sharing your present-moment feelings so that your partner can better hold space for you.

If you don't have a healthy relationship to anger, this kind of directness will be challenging for you, but it's actually the kindest thing you can do for your partner. Holding grudges is devastating to the health of your relationship. Being passive-aggressive with your energy is cruel, depolarizing, and damages the integrity of the sacred container of your intimacy. Even sugarcoating your complaints is demeaning and shows a lack of respect for the partnership. Everyone knows that "feedback sandwich" technique, where you say something nice, then comes your truth, all wrapped up with a compliment on the other side to soften the blow.

It's so much better to create the kind of partnership that allows you to safely and authentically share both your negative and positive reactions to your beloved in the moment, as you are feeling them. Since it takes some dedication, keep reminding yourself to be honest about your experience of tracking itself. When you're "tracking the track," be sure to share what's *not* moving as well as what is moving. The best way to avoid conflict is to track your own defense and be honest about it. You say, "I'm in defense right now" or "I'm numb" or "I feel too emotionally exhausted to do this well" or "I feel scared we're not connected." When you're feeling disconnected and you're able to own the disconnect, it's like you've emptied the vessel so that it can be filled with joy. When you're keeping the disconnect to yourself, there's no room for joy to enter.

Always be as clear and articulate as possible. Don't say, "I feel sad about it," assuming your partner knows exactly what you mean by "it." Say, "Part of me feels sad about XYZ." Even if it seems like you're being repetitive, it will keep your communication clean and clear. Being repetitive is better than being misunderstood. When you feel your frustration, anger, or impatience building, state that before you speak. Say, "Part of me feels a lot of frustration right now, so I want you to know that what I'm about to say may come out strongly, and I don't want you to feel attacked. . . ." Doing this allows your partner to feel valued and loved in advance, and gives you more freedom to speak plainly.

Sometimes your partner will try to take your communication off in a tangent, especially if they've been triggered by something you're saying and their S.T.U.A.R.T. is trying to protect them from experiencing some old pain. It's up to you to pause and say, "I want to hear that, and I'm happy to go there with you, but can we first address what I was saying here? It's important to me to share this with you and I don't feel complete with it yet."

The better you get at relationship tracking, the more you'll sense that your partner sees exactly what's going on in your mind. Even in the midst of extreme discord between you, this creates incredible intimacy. You'll be amazed at how juicy and blissfully connected this method of expressing yourself, and even expressing your anger, will make you feel.

How to Be a Better Space-Holder

When you're holding space and you notice your beloved tracking especially well, be sure to point that out! Chances are this is pretty new stuff for both of you, so don't hold back your praise and encouragement. Say, "Wow, I really felt what you said just there. That felt really real. Thank you for that." The more you reinforce your partner's heart-centered communication, the harder they'll work to keep it up, so compliment good tracking whenever you see it!

Keep in mind that you are in the supportive role when you're holding space. Pauses are good and necessary for the space-taker, but a common mistake is to listen for the pause so you can jump in. Many of us have triggers around being misrepresented or mis-quoted, so you might feel the need to correct an inaccuracy in the space-taker's reporting, or to point out they've misunderstood something, or otherwise attempt to take them out of the experience of what they're feeling. It's important to refrain from doing this while you're holding space. Let the moment pass, and continue to receive your partner. You can always bring it up later if you want to clear up a misunderstanding, but trying to do it while your part-ner is vulnerably sharing can have a shut-down effect and make the sharer feel invalidated.

Also, watch out for intellectualizing.* I don't want to make it wrong because we all have that tendency now and then, but if you notice yourself going into your head, track it and reveal it. Just say, "I'm coming from a heady place right now; I don't think my heart is very open," and then your partner will at least know not to take it personally.

At times, certain emotions and frequencies expressed by your partner could cause you to shut down. It means that it's an area

---

* Intellectualizing is speaking from a disembodied place where the speaker may sound rushed, they are not "dropped in," they are not feeling themselves well (little pause or stillness). It's more of felt sense where a lack of peace and stillness emanates from their communication. It's not impulsive, rash, or destructive though—it just feels "heady."

you have trouble accessing and accepting within yourself, so it will be uncomfortable for you to witness it in your partner. If you notice yourself going numb, share the potential of that kind of trigger with your partner when it's your turn to take space, and see if you can come to any awarenesses together that would help you to heal in that area.

There will be times when you simply vehemently disagree with something your partner is sharing. Holding loving space for your partner doesn't mean you must be in agreement with what's being said. Let your partner finish, and then practice saying something like, "I hear you and I appreciate you sharing that. That doesn't match my reality. That doesn't feel at all accurate to me, but I understand that it feels accurate to you, so I'm glad you're sharing that with me. Given that we don't share a reality on this topic, what steps can we take to have both of our needs met from here?"

Acknowledgment is the critical cornerstone of space-holding. It means accepting and appreciating your partner's willingness, courage, essence, and good intentions no matter what the content of the communication may be. You can find appreciation simply by witnessing the amazing internal movement that both you and your partner are always constantly experiencing. At any given moment, you might be having five critical thoughts about what your beloved is saying, but you can still appreciate that they're speaking their truth. Even when you're talking about something extremely challenging, that should only reinforce your appreciation for your partner and whatever they're being courageous enough to share with you.

Never forget, as you are holding space, that all healing within the relationship provides medicine for both of you as individuals as well. Your partner is your mirror. As you provide the space for your partner's healing, you, too, are healing, even when you don't recognize it in that moment.

SPEAKING FROM THE PRESENT WITH PRESENCE

The essence of tracking is realizing that *you* are neither the content of what you're tracking, nor your experience about what you're tracking. You are the ever-present, joyful witness to it all! *You* are simply the pure, embodied awareness of your unfolding moment-by-moment reality! Being able to un-identify yourself with the content of your track is essential to maintaining the presence and lightness that characterize good tracking.

When tracking, it's critical to speak about the present moment *and* to speak with presence. These two qualities of presence and present-moment communication are what make tracking come alive. Speaking "with presence" happens when the individual who is tracking takes responsibility for their energy levels while tracking. That person needs to *bring* energy to the track, rather than being at the center of what they are tracking. No matter what their emotional state may be, the tracker speaks with directness, aliveness, vitality, and juice. They are *bright*.

For example, let's say I'm feeling sad and I begin to track my sadness. If I'm not present, I could easily get lost in my sadness and speak about it with a tone and energy that is a match to it. I would literally be tracking from the *part of me* that is sad. This is not proper tracking. Tracking is witnessing what we're feeling while we're feeling it. It's having the emotionally maturity to step out of the sadness to speak about it in a matter-of-fact way. This skill actually allows us to enjoy the experience of having the sadness without becoming identified with it. The process is not always easy, but with dedicated practice, it's possible to bring this kind of *presence* to all our interactions.

Speaking in the present moment entails watching out for storytelling and justification. Whenever the discussion deteriorates into stories from the past or worries about the future, present-moment awareness has been lost. It's natural for this to happen from time to time, and the answer is simply to keep tracking when it does. If you notice yourself going into collapse, speak your observation to your partner. You might say, "I'm noticing I'm losing presence. I'm noticing I'm being triggered by this right now, and I'm finding it really hard to stay in my juice, in my aliveness. I'm being pulled into wanting to go into the story so that I can victimize and blame."

The incredible thing about tracking is that simply by naming and speaking about this collapse, you'll automatically feel your juice and your presence returning so that you'll be able to move forward with clear, effective tracking.

The role of the receiving partner is to hold space for whatever naturally needs to unfold, offering a constant stream of reassuring responsiveness. It's incredibly healing to communicate with presence, while keeping our focus in the present-moment awareness of what's currently moving for us.

Confirm Your Partner's Reality by Tracking Together

Some couples avoid the vulnerability of tracking together because they fear that what they divulge will cause rifts in the relationship, when in fact the opposite is true. When there's something you're experiencing that you're not giving voice to, your partner will sense it energetically. Because of the nature of entrainment, your partner will have to energetically "hold" the tension of your unexpressed emotion. Holding these unexpressed tensions for each other can become a terrible drain on a relationship.

Often, all we need to feel solidly connected to our partner is to have our reality confirmed. Nobody likes feeling patronized or "handled," even when it comes from a desire to protect us. The truth will always feel cleaner and more conducive to real intimacy. Confirming your partner's reality is difficult when your partner is in self-judgment, but it can be tremendously healing. For instance, Partner A might say, "I'm such a failure." If you, as Partner B, genuinely feel the opposite is true, you could certainly say, "You're not a failure; you've had many successes." But if that isn't your truth in that moment, your inauthenticity will be felt and your partner will feel even worse. It's far better to confirm their reality with something like, "I can tell that's what you're believing about yourself. I want to reassure you that's not the case, but I think

I'm actually entrained in your judgment right now. I'm running it with you. I don't want to be, but that's where I'm at." While harsh, it will be confirming their reality because if you're feeling that judgment with them, they'll be sensing it. It will actually make them feel better to have their reality confirmed. The golden rule of tracking together is: truth trumps everything.

PRACTICE YOUR TRACKING SKILL ON OTHER TOPICS

Many couples fall into a pattern of making all of their conversations about the relationship itself. It's much healthier to ensure you make time for each of you to talk about your own life—your experience and feelings that have nothing to do with the relationship. It's an opportunity for your partner to simply hold space for you and get to know you better! Particularly when you are new to tracking, you may find it challenging to track yourself while immersed in your painful, entangled relationship issues. Practicing your tracking skills on other topics is a great way to solidify them before embarking on your relationship issues.

Relationship Tracking and S.T.U.A.R.T. Strategies

As you are learning how to be a good space-taker and space-holder, and you and your partner are practicing your new skills, it's important to understand that you will encounter pitfalls from time to time—courtesy of S.T.U.A.R.T. There are several S.T.U.A.R.T. strategies that commonly come up during relationship tracking sessions. These S.T.U.A.R.T. defense mechanisms, as you know, arise when we're afraid to feel the pain that might result from expressing our truest, most vulnerable selves. You'll want to watch for these pitfalls to intimacy and avoid them as much as you can. If you notice one popping up, you'll need to call it out for what it is and consciously redirect your attention to focus on what you want to feel with your partner.

1. Thinking You Know Best.

In any couple, it's rare that both people are equally heart-intelligent. One almost always needs to lead. Every group needs facilitation and leadership, and every couple does, too. But that doesn't mean that whoever's list of personal development credits is longest gets to be life coach to the other one. In every instance, the one who leads needs to be the one who is the clearest, least triggered, and most in their heart *in that moment*. That's likely to change from situation to situation, but if you've both been learning and practicing the techniques in this book, you'll want to have mutual faith in each other to take the lead in implementing them.

Agreeing in advance that either one of you is welcome to take charge when the other is in emotional collapse will most often lead to swifter, better application of the heart-centered principles that will restore you to relationship bliss. You just have to be careful to maintain a peer relationship, even as one of you is taking the lead. When we know something or have an idea or opinion that's quite strong, we want to tell the other what they should do. Suddenly we're in a therapy dynamic. The partner becomes the coach, the therapist, the person with superior knowledge. The second you fall into that trap, you are no longer peers, and you will decrease the sexual magnetism within your relationship, effectively de-polarizing your connection.

You're on a gradient, and that does not work for intimacy. Intimacy can only work within a peer-based dynamic. You want to live in the question, not in the answer. You never want to be in the position of saying to your partner, "I know who you are." Instead, you want to be curious and open, always asking, "What more is there to learn about you? What mystery are we on the brink of unraveling?"

If your partner falls into teacher mode with you, be delicate about pointing it out. If you can do it authentically, try saying something like, "I appreciate what you're saying; I can tell it's important and I want to receive it. I know your intention is loving, but it's causing me to feel tension. What works for me, what opens me to receive you, is when you give me your truth through what you're feeling, instead of explaining it from a teaching perspective."

Appreciation builds rapport, but it should never be used as a strategy. If you have a genuine appreciation for any part of what your beloved is doing, by all means express that, but only to the extent you mean it. This is true for any time you are at odds with your partner. If you can find something to authentically appreciate, stating your appreciation will form the bridge that will allow the stickier part of your truth to be better received.

2. Sidestepping Truth with a New Age Bypass

Our search for enlightenment and spiritual mastery can unfortunately become dangerous when we use it as a clever protection mechanism to keep us from being real. The New Age bypass can be a huge derailment to our relationship tracking success when the need to appear spiritual overrides the objective of being raw and open in our vulnerability. The New Age bypass is also one of the most common reasons people get stuck in their spiritual journeys and stagnate in their growth. They read a book and then begin preaching from a shallow perspective of incomplete truth. They would read, for example, that "we are all one," and that "all of life is an illusion." They'd begin to disown their humanity, transcending their pain to live in a checked-out, disembodied malaise. Their lives become flat and juiceless reflections of their pseudo-spirituality.

Another common example is the trite statement, "You create your own reality." This is probably the most confused and misunderstood concept in personal development. When used as a New Age bypass, it allows you to justify just about anything without taking personal responsibility. If I hurt you and you come to me with your hurt, I could simply say, "That's your stuff, not mine.

Why have you created that for yourself?" This response reveals a lack of maturity and awareness and is a sign of a closed heart. People say things like that to keep themselves away from having to own their shadow and be vulnerable and real.

A final example I'll share (there are thousands) is when someone thinks that becoming enlightened and spiritual means no longer having needs. They turn into an independent zombie, aloof and superior. They carry an air of: "I am peace. I don't need anything or anyone to be happy. I am love. Blah, blah, blah." Sadly, these people are usually the ones who have the most needs, yet have experienced growing up in an emotional desert, so their needs are completely unknown to them. Without an early environment that made it okay to feel, to express, and to have their needs met, they have disowned their capacity to feel their own needs and wounds as adults, and their ability to express what they really want in an interdependent way. The result is that the very people who need this work the most are the ones most likely to ignore it.

The most complete truth, of course, is that there are no absolutes. It is true that we create our reality (we have control), *and* it's true that we create none of it (we need to surrender). It's true that we are all one with the universe, *and* it's true that we are human beings, clearly individualized and each living our own human experience. It's true that we need nothing to be happy, *and* it's true that we have needs that must be met in order for us to thrive. These appear contradictory, but they are not. Each truth makes sense depending on whether you look at it from the human realm or the spiritual realm, and we are all full-time inhabitants of both.

3. Storytelling

Storytelling takes place when we cover up our real emotions by focusing all our energy on the story about what has taken place. While it's true that there will be times when telling a story is important for clarity when sharing our truth, we often end up using that story to stop ourselves from feeling what's real for us. Whenever you notice you or your partner habitually clinging to a story, know that a S.T.U.A.R.T. strategy is at work. Our stories often feel comfortable to us because we've habitually defined ourselves through them, but they keep us in an un-empowered victim role that doesn't serve our joy or our relationship. Recognizing our stories and their accompanying drama gives us the opportunity to consciously detach ourselves from them so that we can identify with a deeper truth about who and what we really are.

4. Drama

Much like storytelling, drama is an emotional overindulgence of a memory. It's almost as if we get high on the terrible thing that's happened, whether it's an emotional event, something someone said, or even something innocuous that we've imbued with meaning. We put our attention on this thing and we grow it until it becomes an addiction. Even if we can objectively observe this imbalance, we're pulled again and again back to that drama point, like an anchor of comfortable pain. Those who feed on drama are the ones most likely to create it in their lives. It's often unconscious, of course, but if we're not getting our needs met, we'll find ways to receive the emotional-energetic deficit of our closed heart by some other means. Whether it's addiction, codependency, or creating drama, they all share a common outcome: They feed us enough to momentarily comfort our pain, while perpetuating an inner emptiness that can never be filled. Eventually, this need runs so deep that we can't even identify it anymore. It becomes a need with no name, making it harder to meet it and heal.

5. Fast-Talking

Fast-talking can be a S.T.U.A.R.T. strategy for people who find comfort in using words to get to the bottom of things. These people feel that "talking it out" is the best route to finding resolution when a crisis arises, and in their effort to speed their way out of discomfort and into harmony, they share everything that crosses their minds at lightning speed. We can get a lot of information across with fast-talking, but it forces us to skip over much of the depth of what we're expressing.

Fast-talking becomes a S.T.U.A.R.T. strategy when we use it to gloss over our deeper emotions and keep the conversation at a more intellectual level. This strategy is often seen in those who were stifled as young children. Since they carry a subconscious fear that they don't deserve to take up much space, they rush to express as much as they can as quickly as possible. It can be alleviated by the space-holder reassuring the fast-talker that what they're sharing is important and deserves all the time in the world.

6. Excessive Baby Talk

Some couples adopt a sweetness of expression that resembles sugarcoated baby talk. It's not necessarily a bad thing when used in moderation, but when it's excessive, it's often a S.T.U.A.R.T. strategy that keeps them from being in a magnetically charged, sexually connected state (often known as polarity). When your childhood trauma was in the area of neglect, there will always be a part of you that craves a return to the age of neglect so that you can get what was so heartbreakingly missing at that time. Typically, those in that situation will attract a partner with a similar background so that they can both go back and nurture each other in this neglected area. But when baby talk is habitual, it can become a S.T.U.A.R.T. strategy for avoiding the more grownup aspects of our relationships. Since babies don't have sex drives, relating through baby talk can disastrously decrease the polarity we feel with a partner. It might feel soothing, relaxing, or nourishing in small doses, but there are consequences to using baby talk too frequently.

THE RELATIONSHIP TRACKING PROCESS

As you can see, there is a lot to keep in mind when learning the invaluable skill of relationship tracking. Here is a step-by-step guide you can refer to until it becomes second nature to you.

STEP 1

Partner A

Tracking your reality and sharing your truth: Partner A tracks out loud by sharing their truth around what's going on for them in their life. They can speak to anything that feels important and "up" for them right now in this present moment. This can include dreams, visions, fears, doubts, longings, and hunger.

- What's something you want your partner to understand about you or an area of your life that you want to be felt in? Imagine that your partner has asked you, "What do you want me to know about you? It can be big or small or seem meaningful or insignificant. Just share with me what's moving around inside you—the stuff I wouldn't know without getting to crawl inside and feel you."

Acknowledging judgments: If you're noticing tension or self-judgment, speak to it as part of what you're tracking. Describe it. Where is it in your body? What is the feeling? What is the judgmental voice saying?

- For example: "I'm noticing that as I share about my goal, I'm starting to feel scared and I have this belief that I'll fail so why talk about it?" Or, "I'm noticing how exciting it feels to finally be sharing this with you, but I've also got a voice telling me, 'Don't say too much! You'll take up too much time and he'll get bored and then you'll just have to shut down again.' That is not what I want. I want to share it all with you."

Embodiment: If you're tracking that you feel numb, discon-nected, or in pain, you can still decide to add some juice to *how* you're expressing what you're feeling, rather than being resigned to expressing *from* that disconnect or pain. In Heart IQ, we call this "embodied awareness." Just do your best to notice what's going on for you and bring your focused energy into speaking about that.

- For example, you might say, "Wow, I am feeling so numb right now!" Instead of giving in to the numbness and express-ing yourself in alignment with it, you're calling it out and even registering surprise that you would feel numb when discussing something you do care very much about.

Shadows and S.T.U.A.R.T. Strategies: If you can, track your defense mechanisms at play. What shadows or S.T.U.A.R.T. strategies are you noticing? What's happening that's making you feel closed or disconnected?

- For example: "I want to tell you about this fear I've been running for the past few weeks. I feel like it has a grip on me, and I'm starting to not feel safe within myself. I've noticed how much I want to convince you that I'm doing okay when you've asked me about it lately *(your S.T.U.A.R.T.)*. It feels hard for me to let you see how shaken I've become by this fear. I'm afraid you'll think I'm really unstable, and maybe even crazy *(your shadow),* and I'm afraid that will make you question whether or not you want to be in a relationship with someone this crazy."

Partner B

Being responsive: Partner B is holding space and being respon-sive to Partner A. This is a practice of acknowledgment that entails being present, engaged, interested, and focused on Part-ner A. You must be available with your energy, and you must demonstrate that with your body language, facial expressions, and emotional and verbal response. Being acknowledged and received with generous, authentic, and uplifting responses gives Partner A the opportunity to feel "felt."

- Here are a few examples of spontaneous responsiveness:

  Small comments like: "I get it," "I see what you mean," or "That feels good to hear!" or "Wow, really? That's so cool!"

  More comprehensive yet still brief: "It feels really good knowing where you're at. I love being able to feel you."

- Here a few examples of nonverbal acknowledgments:

  Nodding your head

  Smiling

  Facial expressions that reflect your partner's emotional state

Validating another's reality: It's important for Partner B to validate Partner A's reality. That means agreeing to the realness of what your partner is experiencing, whether you agree with that reality or not. This is not about responding only when you feel your partner is "right." It's a more unbiased offering of confirmation. It shows that you're willing to make space for what's being expressed as your partner's truth, and showing that you value it as such.

Offering reassurance: If Partner A shares something that is difficult to reveal or takes courage to expose given that they have had to step beyond fears and insecurities to share it, it's very important that Partner B reassures Partner A that this sharing has been deeply received.

- For example: "Thank you for telling me that. It means a lot to me to learn that about you *(reassurance)*. I can imagine how hard it was for you to tell me that, knowing that I might reject you once you did *(validating partner's reality)*. I'm really glad you shared that, and I love you even more for making sure we don't have secrets between us *(reassurance)*."

- Or "Given how isolated you've been since our move, I can totally see how you could feel rejected with me having to work so much lately *(validating partner's reality)*. Even though my work is demanding a lot of me, I do think about you throughout my day. I miss us having more time together, too, and I'm really craving to feel more connected with you right now *(reassurance)*."

Remembering "less is more": Partner B is offering Partner A encouragement, taking care not to hijack the space by engaging with lengthy responses that would refocus the attention and the flow of energy onto Partner B instead of keeping it on Partner A. Reassurance should be no more than six or seven words. If you start going beyond a sentence, you're now taking the space, and if this happens without your partner's consent, it will feel like a "hijack," decreasing the intimacy between you.

Tracking the experience: Only after Partner B has acknowledged, reassured, and validated the reality of Partner A, Partner B will then track their own experience in relationship to what's been shared.

- For example: "I'm noticing that I didn't keep up with all the details of your vision, but I feel really energized right now by the emotion of what you shared and how you shared it. It feels really good to feel you so open and excited!" Or, "Wow, I feel a tingling warmth moving throughout my body as I hear you speak your truth!"

- Again, less is more, so keep the description brief unless permission is asked and granted to go into a lengthier response. For example: "I got a really strong image while you were sharing. Do you feel open right now to me telling you about it?"

STEP 2

After Partner B shares, Partner A can share again about what they're noticing in the present moment as they receive Partner B's response. Do they feel more open and relaxed by receiving this response? Do they feel more defensive or scared? Do they feel tension over being held accountable for taking action on what's been shared? Partner A tracks and shares these findings until they feel complete.

STEP 3

Partner A and Partner B switch roles.

You may need to go back and forth several times until you both feel complete. You'll know you're done when you feel intimately connected to your partner, with no energetic blocks between you. Thank one another for giving the relationship this precious time and attention. The next chapter will provide more practices for deepening your tracking experience.

The more you and your partner engage in heart-centered relationship tracking, the more adept you will become at speaking your truth and feeling heard and felt—and allowing the space for your partner to do the same. Your understanding of each other will deepen, and, as a result, you'll be creating a more intimate bond. The safety container in your relationship will grow ever more expansive, and you will be ready to share even more of your juice. Are you ready to do that? Are you ready to go even deeper? Read on.

SUCCESS STORY FROM ANNA & DAVID

David says, "Heart IQ made an impact in our relationship right from the beginning. We started this relationship setting up some agreements so that we could share how we really felt with each other and not unintentionally play games as we were getting to know each other. One agreement was that each of us was responsible for sharing if we wanted the relationship to go in a specific direction. This helped us both to not assume what the other was thinking and feeling, and both actively move our relationship in the direction we wanted. This clarity brought about a lot of safety for us both, which meant that our connection moved really deep, really fast–because our relationship space felt clear and simple.

"I've experienced the drain in my past relationships of having to 'translate' what I understand about myself and what's moving between me and a partner who's not engaged in her own journey. That's brought me a huge degree of dissatisfaction and disappointment, and a disturbing amount of strain trying to convince and persuade, rather than having a partnership where we speak the same language. With both of us being in Heart IQ, it feels so natural to understand each other. We 'get' each other, so it's much easier to be on the same page!"

Anna adds, "Heart IQ has helped me and my partner to understand our triggers, so that we don't take things so personally in our interactions. Even better is that we can now hold space for each other in the times when we do lose track of ourselves and get more lost in our stuff. We can find our way back much more easily!"

Need help applying this in your relationship?
Visit www.HeartIQRelationships.com for FREE demos
and tutorials using the access code myheartiq.

CHAPTER 7

Deepening the Connection with More Heart IQ Practices

As you can see, a deeply connected partnership requires openness. Striking the right balance between receiving and giving (or holding and taking) will allow each partner to be moved *and* to spontaneously show the other how they are moved, in real time. A deep, meaningful connection depends on being open *to being opened*. It requires building the capacity to fully feel and poignantly receive the love and attention that is offered to you. Heart-centered communication is more than just one person offering information and the other receiving it. There's a third component that allows the communicator to deeply feel that the message has been received. It's not an A-to-B equation, but an A-to-B-to-A equation.

Love relationships depend upon this three-part communication dynamic. Love is what it feels like to feel you feeling me. It's not simply me sending love to you. It starts with me feeling the love within myself while I focus on you. Next, *you* get to feel me feeling that love within me, and as you do, there's an exchange of energy that occurs. You have to let that energy from me in, and then I have to feel your receptivity of it.

I'll restate it another way: When I embody love and I'm looking at you, you can feel love because you feel *me in love*. It's not a direct transmission of energy from me to you; it's you witnessing me in a particular energetic state and opening to me in that state. If you witnessed me without openly receiving my energy, the circuit would not be complete. You let it in; you feel how good it feels to *feel me* in my love for you, and I then get to *feel you* there. There's giving, receiving, and then understanding that the receiving has happened. Again, it's not A to B, but A to B to A.

The Challenge of Receiving Love

Here's where the circuitry gets tricky. Receiving love is not the easiest thing for most of us. Remember, it goes back to our core unworthiness ("Who am I to be on the receiving end of such pure, abundant love?") and also our tendency to live within a truncated emotional range. Do you recall the fourth Law of Emotional-Energetic Couple Dynamics? It states, "I can only be present with your emotion to the degree that I can be present with my own emotion." In other words, I can only feel in you what I can access in me. In accordance with that law, you can only receive another's communication, or love, to the extent that it corresponds with what you're already allowing within yourself.

This is where so many of the couples I've coached have come into rocky terrain in their relationships. When they first attracted each other, they were vibrating similarly, meaning they had similar capacities for loving and receiving love. When one partner goes through an emotional growth spurt and the other does not, the result is one partner with the capacity to love on a much higher level than the other partner is capable of. The partner who has grown may be trying in earnest to shower the other partner with more love than ever before, but the still-limited-in-range partner simply can't receive that much love; nor can they begin to return it.

I hope you're starting to understand why it is so vitally important that you learn to expand your emotional range. Your current emotional range determines, not only your ability to see into and feel others, but also your level of responsiveness—your ability to receive another's love. When you expand your range, you get to connect more fully with your partner, along with everyone else you interact with in life. The beautiful thing about this paradigm is that you're never done! You can continue to stretch into more and more glorious ranges throughout your entire life.

Emotional Range Expansion Creates Relaxation

The primary benefit to expanding your emotional range is that when you have that capacity to feel all of you, and you're not afraid to feel your entire being, and there are no parts of you unexplored, untouched, or unexpressed—you will feel relaxed. That allows others, and especially your partner, to relax in your presence. Without achieving this state, whatever I repress, you will have to express. Whatever I hold on to that is not digested (not felt by me) will be felt by you. You won't know why you can't quite relax with me.

I cannot hold space for you and let you feel what you're feeling unless I'm okay with that in me. If I'm not okay with that in me, I will make you feel wrong. But when I'm okay with all of me, just being in my space will make you feel safe, light, and felt. Wouldn't you love to feel more felt? Wouldn't you love to have someone to hold space for you so you can feel and express all of who you are? Everyone wants more of that. But it's impossible for you to give that to another if you don't do this work.

Energy wants to flow. After a period of time in an intimate romantic relationship, an energetic container is created that holds you both. Energy moves in this container in a specific way, so if you are repressing something in one area, it has to balance itself in another. If one of you is unskilled at intimacy, the other one will have to pick up the slack and do all the work on intimacy in order for the relationship to stay alive. If one of you is irresponsible, the other may be forced to become extra-responsible, and start to resent that over time.

Here's an example: My client's ex-husband had a habit she couldn't stand: He did not always express himself in a kind and courteous way to strangers, often using a superior tone with store clerks and waitstaff in restaurants. My client realized that, without it being really conscious for her, she was constantly being driven to balance out his actions. She'd be over-the-top sweet with service people everywhere, hugging and getting into deep conversations with these strangers, wildly overtipping, and doing basically anything she could do to try to compensate. She didn't recognize what was going on with her until she learned about the "Whatever I repress, you must express for me" Law of Emotional-Energetic Couple Dynamics.

This kind of imbalance creates insecurity in relationships. It's like you're a puppet with your partner's deficits pulling your strings. Becoming aware of this dynamic gives you the opportunity to take conscious control of it and address it in your tracking sessions so you can bring more balance to the partnership.

Communication Styles Are Learned but Are Open for Rewiring

Communication is the cornerstone of any successful relationship, yet heart-centered communication can be quite challenging because most of us are not in our hearts most of the time. Nearly all of our cultural programming has conditioned us to live in our heads. Our natural style of communication will be whatever style we learned in our earliest years from our parents. What did you see as a child? How do you remember your parents communicating?

I grew up in an emotional desert. My parents never fought; they were quite passive with each other, but there was a vast energetic void in the home and I never knew where I fit in. I felt like a ghost, like my energy wasn't ever fully recognized, and yet I was very lively. When I had my temper tantrums, they seemed alarmingly loud in that quiet environment.

Maybe you grew up in a loud, demonstrative home, or maybe one of heavy silence and coded diplomacy. Maybe you endured an emotionally abusive environment, or one with frequent physical violence. Both extremes can be damaging: the dramatic, intense household with doors slamming and anger flying, as well as the emotional desert where feelings are swept under the carpet and boat-rocking is not permitted.

Your inherited communication patterns directly influence how you shape your own adult communication and how you relate to your partner, even if you consciously object to your parents' communication style. The good news is you can unlearn those patterns and rewire them. But to do that, you have to first become fully aware of those dynamics. You have to know yourself well enough to be able to discern which parts of you are in defense. You have to be aware of what moves in you, and what doesn't move. You have to develop the skill of authentically transmitting what you feel to another with directness and without code.

Remember, "code" is any kind of indirect communication style that gets in the way of pure, honest expression. A benign example of coded communication would be the wife who says to her husband, "It's cold in here; don't you think, dear?" What she wants is for her husband to adjust the heat in the home to make her more comfortable, but instead of asking directly, she makes a statement that she hopes he will internally translate, getting the "hint," and taking the steps to meet her need. Most of us learned some degree of either drama or coding (or perhaps even both) from our parents, but in either case, it was simply our parents' unconscious mechanism (their S.T.U.A.R.T.s) for creating safety. They didn't know any other way.

Safety is such a dominant, primary human need that people will do anything to try to get it. For some, it means avoiding all those dangerous-feeling emotions at all costs and sweeping everything under the rug. For others, it means attempting to control their frighteningly unpredictable lives with domination expressed through excessive control and force. Unfortunately, these misguided attempts to establish a sense of safety end up destroying the one and only thing that can ever truly create safety: the intimacy of primary relationships.

For real intimacy to blossom, there needs to be a balance in the containment aspect of our communication style. I've noticed through my work that those of us who grew up in the emotional desert environment are likely to be too contained in our communication style. We don't know how to express; it feels safer to stay within ourselves. We have no idea how to do relationship communication because our parents were just friends cohabiting; we never got to witness any juice.

And those who grew up with the opposite dynamic, those who suffered more of an invasive energy in their childhood, having had their boundaries repeatedly crossed within a loud, abusive, physically confronting environment, usually become *un*contained communicators as adults. They're less adept at holding their emotion—it spills out; it leaks. It's hard for them to witness what they're feeling because they're so *entrenched* in what they're feeling. It may seem that they are more in touch with their authentic cores, but they are not. Unconscious uncontainment is just another clever S.T.U.A.R.T. mechanism for blocking us from our deepest truth.

Often what happens when we enter into a relationship is that those of us who are contained attract those who are uncontained. Subconsciously, we attract a partner who can help us achieve a more healthy balance, though it's obviously challenging to effectively communicate through those different dynamics. The potential exists for us to be of immense service to each other, but we're up against some pretty intensive programming that started very early. In Chapter 9, we'll look at how we can use this concept of containment versus uncontainment to keep our relationships vitally polarized and juicy.

Building Rapport Together

I've talked a lot about the importance of being real, so I want to be sure to balance that with a reminder that kindness is an absolutely essential ingredient in heart-centered communication. When we're intimate, we need to have gentle hearts toward each other always, even when triggered into our own deep pain. If we allow ourselves to become abrasive, we diminish the other's ability to feel us, and we lose the potential for meaningful, intimate, two-way communication.

Successful heart-centered communication depends on building rapport together. One way to build rapport is to be so present to your partner that you do your best to match where they are energetically. If they're in their fire, be present to yours. If they're soft, slow down and share that moment with them, exploring your own capacity to be gentle. You might even notice yourself unconsciously matching your body language to theirs. See if you can deliberately match your partner's tone and energy, but *only do this if it feels authentic.* If it doesn't, and you need to choose between rapport and authenticity, choose authenticity.

You might be thinking that by doing this, it will mean you have to be someone you're not. You might say to yourself, "I'm just not that type of person." However, don't confuse your capacity to access a quality with *being* that quality. To be a great communicator, you must be able to express a wide range of emotion in order to create the intimacy you crave. Thus, if you're not a "soft" person, don't fall into the trap that accessing softness to meet your partner where they're at means that is who you are intrinsically. But then again, what's wrong with being "soft"? If you notice a resistance to accessing any range, it indicates a judgment about what it means to be that, and if you track it, you will uncover a shadow!

You build rapport by earnestly trying to see into your beloved. Stephen Covey advises: "Seek first to understand, and then to be understood." Often we're so desperate to be seen (to be "gotten") that we forget to first attempt to discover what's going on for the other person. Even if you're the one triggered, there are times when the best thing to do is to invite your partner to take space. If you and I are in conflict, and I offer to first give you space so I can hear you out, your sharing might have a dramatic effect on whatever was moving for me in the first place. My sharing might then take a very different form.

Now, if both you and your partner take this advice to heart, it could become cumbersome and even amusing when you get into a stalemate over who will be first to take space. Use your instincts and let the situation dictate who shares first. Take turns going first if it actually becomes an issue for you. That said, an issue I've seen in my clients is the tendency to be so empathic that whenever their partner takes space to share, the anger they might have been feeling evaporates. They feel unjustified to express their true feelings in context to what they have now heard. Their love for their partner creates this interesting balancing act in their psyche. If the good stuff they have said or done outweighs the bad, they feel they have no right to get mad or share their disappointments.

Building rapport means choosing your words with the goal of being understood. Don't use patronizing, superior language to gain a positioning advantage. Communicating with the goal of winning your point is a signal that you are in defense. The goal of communication should always be to understand and be understood. Try to feel the other person, and get a read on their experience of the conversation. See if you can feel into whether or not they're receptive to you so that you can change course if they're not. Make sure you speak from specific parts of you, rather than the all of you. When you share what you track, share with the language: "A part of me feels that . . . "

It helps to be able to understand and discern between knowing something, feeling it, thinking it, or sensing it. A "knowing" is a deep truth about which you are positive. You probably have a knowing that the world is round, even though you've never actually seen it round with your own eyes. A "feeling" is more emotionally based; it's more transient, and may be tied to bodily sensations. A "thought" is also transient, but more related to judgments and ideas that pop up in in your mind. A "sense" is an external read, based on your perception of another, or something going on outside you. You might say to your partner, "I sense you want to say something but you're holding back." It would be more accurate in this example to use the word "sense" than it would be to say, "I *feel* you want to say something . . ." or "I *know* you want to say something . . ." or even, "I *think* you want to say something . . ."

The distinctions may be subtle, but being precise with these terms can eliminate many common triggers and help to keep your communication clear. A common pitfall while tracking is to let your attention slip away from yourself and onto your partner. When you feel into another, it's called a "read," and it's a valuable skill as long as it doesn't take you out of your own experience and ability to give voice to whatever is authentically in play *within you*. Communicating your "read" needs to be done with delicate precision. If you're taking space and you sense anger growing in your partner, the tendency might be to stop and accusingly ask, "Are you angry?"

While it would be an authentic question for you, it could easily put your partner into defense. Your partner might deny it, and that might trigger you into an attitude of superiority. It's better to not even bring your observation up until later, at which point you might gently invite your partner to take space by saying something like, "I sensed some anger in you when I was sharing about XYZ. Would you like to explore that with me?" Or, if your partner's defensiveness makes you realize you're not being received, you may decide it's not worth continuing until you've cleared that energy. You might want to pause and gently ask, "What's going on for you right now?"

If you're the one who is accused of being angry, see if you can avoid going into a defensive reaction right away. Neale Donald Walsch teaches a very valuable rapport-building tool that goes: "Agree with all those who oppose you." It doesn't mean being a doormat and giving up your own opinions; it means being open enough to realize that there are always countless realities available to consider, and your reality may not be a match to another's reality. If your partner senses anger in you, and you don't feel it, it's better to say, "I'm not connecting to that, but you could be right. I'm open to seeing that there may be some anger there, even though I don't recognize any right now."

On the other hand, if you do feel angry, by all means, own it! Don't invalidate your partner's intuition just to make yourself feel right or superior, or to avoid further conflict. Even if you didn't realize you were angry until it was pointed out to you, have the courage to say, "You're damn right. I'm angry."

In most cases, if you are able to clearly and directly communicate what you're tracking, your partner will feel your vulnerability to such an extent that going into defense won't even be an issue. The only time it's likely to happen is when the content of what you're sharing in itself is particularly threatening to the space-holder.

The very best trackers know themselves and also have the ability to tune into others to make sure the person they are tracking with is in rapport with them at all times. When skillful rapport-building is combined with skillful relationship tracking, the result is unbelievably blissful intimate communication. These same skills also form the foundation for becoming a world-class Heart IQ practitioner.

Learn to Speak Each Other's Love Language

In Gary Chapman's popular books on the 5 Love Languages, he describes the top-five ways that people feel loved by one another. Each of us, he explains, will feel most safe, open, and cherished when we are loved in the specific ways we prefer. Once we've determined which of the five "languages" (or which few) we are able to receive most fully, and which languages best resonate with our partner, we can use that information to better love each other. It's about learning to express love in the way our partner is most able to receive it.

The five love languages are:

1. Quality time

2. Words of affirmation (verbally expressing your love and being generous with compliments and words of affection)

3. Physical touch (demonstrating affection physically, not only through sex, but with kisses, cuddles, hand-holding, massages, and all other forms of bonding touch)

4. Gifts (being generous with presents, for special occasions as well as "just because")

5. Acts of service (doing things specifically for your partner, from big things that really show your partner you're there for them, to checking off the "Honey Do" list, putting down the toilet seat, filling the car with gas, cooking, paying bills, opening doors, etc.)

Knowing your top-two love languages, as well as your partner's top-two, is essential! No one can read minds. Take some time to go over this list with your partner so that each of you can feel into it and determine what makes you feel the most loved. Sharing this information with each other will give you so much insight into how to best please each other. Your partner might be thinking they're showering love on you by taking care of household chores, but unless "acts of service" is one of your love languages, you won't be able to feel that love. You might believe you're laying it all on the line by telling your partner how much you love them, but if "words of affirmation" is not their love language, and "physical touch" is, they might be feeling unloved by your lack of physical affection. Knowing each other's top-two love languages clears up so much misunderstanding!

Most of us actually do respond to all five love languages to a certain degree. So the idea is to figure out which ones speak to you the very most. For some, there will be a clear winner. For others, it might be a two-way or even a three-way tie. After you and your partner have determined and shared what resonates with you most, take it a bit further. If it's "words of affirmation" for you, what words specifically turn you on and make you feel the most loved? Share those specific words with your beloved. If it's "quality time" you long for, what does that mean exactly? Does it mean turning phones off and being fully present with each other? Where and how do you like to spend your quality time? If your language is "physical touch," what kind of touch specifically does it for you? You may have a love language that's not on the list. If so, identify that for your partner, with as much detail as possible.

Add depth to this conversation by going over the list and seeing if there's any category where you genuinely feel a lack. If you can do it in the context of appreciation, first noticing and appreciating the areas where your partner truly shines, that appreciation will create the bridge for your partner to better receive your request for more attention in the lacking area. Let your partner know what it would take to totally blow your mind through your preferred love language. Dare to ask for what you really want, and encourage your partner to do the same.

Have these conversations within the framework of relationship tracking, with each of you alternately holding space for the other. In most cases, hearing what you most deeply desire will be juicy and opening for your partner. It should bring joy to both of you to reveal these longings to each other. When you're being open and vulnerable, sharing whatever pops up in the moment, you may find words coming out of your mouth that you hadn't expected! In exploring your love language, you might discover that its opposite has an especially strong effect on you as well. For example, if "words of affirmation" is your primary love language, critical words might have a greater-than-average effect on you, too, causing you to shut down.

While this conversation has lots of potential for juicy enhancement of your relationship, it could unearth some triggers as well. You don't get to control your partner's response to your needs. You might make a request that would be challenging for them, and they might authentically share that with you. While it could hurt to hear it, it's better for them to speak their truth than to appease you with a lie.

For example, your request for more physical touch might trigger uneasiness in your partner. They might authentically share with you that their gut response to that request is that it "sounds like work." Instead of going into defense, you'd want to first appreciate their honesty. That lets your partner know it's safe to be honest with you. Then you can be honest, too. If that response makes you feel hurt, share that. Say, "I'm glad you're being honest, and what's moving in me now is sadness from knowing that."

And here's where you would have an opportunity to really stretch your capacity for heart-centered communication. Can you find compassion for your partner in this situation? Can you set aside your own feelings of rejection long enough to ask yourself, "If compassion had a voice right now, what would it be?" You might suddenly realize how unhealthily contained they must be if they're not capable of enjoying the ecstasy of physical touch with you. What is your partner carrying that is so heavy and restricting and tight that it makes that kind of reaching out burdensome? It's not about denying your own needs, but about looking at the situation in terms of how both of you could stretch and grow and evolve together.

The Healing Power of Acknowledgment and Reassurance

It always takes two to allow disconnection of intimacy. It's important to know this. Even in cases of the deepest betrayals or infidelities—those cases where it's ever so easy to assign a victim and a villain—even in those scenarios, the intimacy has always been lost due to a combination of factors that both partners brought to the table. It's never completely the fault of one person.

I've noticed that one of the primary needs of women in relationships is to have their reality confirmed. Quite often men will listen to a woman's observations about the partnership but will refuse to own or confirm what she's expressed. In many cases, women know the hearts and truth of their men more than the men even do. But it takes a lot of courage for a man to accept uncomfortable feedback and acknowledge where his partner may be right about him. More typically, the man wants to call her crazy for thinking or feeling those things, rather than looking inward to see if there might be any truth to it.

When a woman is continually made wrong in this way, she shuts down. Her intuition is invalidated; her truth is ignored and mocked. After a while, there's no point in her trying to share her reality anymore. Her spark goes out. He remembers that she used to be so bright, full, energetic, and alive. But now she's gone flat, and he doesn't realize it's from all the instances of him defending against her love, not hearing what she had to share.

There is a way back from a scenario such as this, and it is all about each partner taking responsibility for their part in areas of the relationship that aren't presently working and being heard and reassured that their truth is appreciated and that deeper intimacy is the desired end goal.

The art of acknowledgment takes practice. You must build the muscle of stepping to the side of your defensive ego. You want to be strong within yourself when you state your acknowledgment. It's a forthright, "Yes, I do that. You're right. I don't want to cause that kind of pain. Thank you for sharing your truth with me around this." It's not hanging your head in shame and acting like a self-pitying doormat. There's nothing appealing about that for your partner. For it to be healing, acknowledgment needs to be done in your full power, with your full presence. It's naming what you bring that doesn't work, without getting into the drama and the disconnect and the whole pain of it.

The Art of Responsiveness

When I talk about "responsiveness," I'm talking about the way you let your partner know how something has landed for you. Responsiveness is not "your response," so there's no need to "get it right." Responsiveness does not require thought. It's a present-moment, spontaneous reaction that bubbles up from within you without any planning or conscious processing on your part. This kind of natural, organic reaction can only occur when you're able to stay in your heart (and out of your head) in the presence of your partner.

Responsiveness requires a delicate balance of "letting in" and "letting out." If we can't genuinely receive our partner because we're blocked, closed down, or distracted, it won't matter what we say—our response simply won't land. That's because responsiveness is our authentic response to what we feel in *us*, not a reaction to what we *see* in another. We have to let another in, to move us, to touch us, in order to be truly responsive, so it won't work to fake it or train ourselves to say "the right thing."

However, it doesn't end there. If we do let our partner into our hearts but keep our feelings and thoughts to ourselves, staying internal, we are not being responsive either, and our partner will still feel unfelt. I'm sure we can all recognize these two traits: the person who can't let in love, who is distracted and emotionally closed down. They might be charming and charismatic and able to fluently convey their thoughts, but they simply feel *distant*. Then there's the other person who feels everything, yet they are so internal with their thoughts and feelings that they feel *absent*. The first lacks the capacity to receive (which often creates loneliness in their partner), and the other lacks the capacity to express (which creates frustration in their partner). Both qualities are needed for healthy responsiveness.

If you've been deeply wounded in the past, you may have lost the ability to be open with a partner to the extent that is necessary for this kind of responsiveness. In this case, you'd be able to observe your partner shouting, crying, and displaying every extreme of emotion without it ever penetrating your stone-like veneer. You might even be able to say all the right things and go through the "right" steps, but your partner will still feel the lack of authentic emotion stirring within you. In this scenario, you've lost the ability to tune your emotional range to match your partner's. Even if you feel this might apply to you, don't despair. I'm about to offer you some insights that will retrain you and expand your capacity for meaningful responsiveness.

Maybe you feel I've just described your partner. When your partner doesn't seem as responsive as you'd like, it's important not to convey your disappointment as judgment or criticism. The key is to identify the tiny ways your partner *is* being responsive and open-hearted, and to enthusiastically praise those instances while still asking for more. You want to invite more responsiveness, rather than complain about the lack of responsiveness. Your partner may be doing all they are capable of doing given their past experiences and the level of safety they feel with you at the moment. Identifying what they're doing right, and telling them how much you love it and how much it opens you, is the thing that will best inspire them to do more of it.

For many men, responsiveness is the most attractive quality in a woman, especially sexual responsiveness. When a man touches his woman, he wants to feel her let that touch in and for her to express her authentic joy outwardly so he can witness it. It feels less satisfying to touch her only to feel the touch land on a numb, disconnected body, or worse, for there to be an artificial response to it. Likewise, for a man to touch his woman only to have her internalize her joy without letting it show can make the experience of sex less fulfilling. It's clear then with this example, that for a woman to be sexually responsive, she must first let her man into her heart and then be willing to authentically and vulnerably show her joy and open heart outwardly through sound, movement, and breath. Any blockages to this input-output circuit will diminish the polarity and sexual magnetism of the encounter.

Now, although I'm using the example of sexual responsiveness in women, the exact same message applies to men as well. I encourage you both to practice this relationship-changing skill!

RESPONSIVENESS CORE PRACTICE

This exercise allows partners to discover what they like and practice asking for what they want. It lets each partner discover how the other most easily and joyfully receives love. Even though love language preferences will be uncovered, it's important to remember that intimacy grows best when all the love languages are used for giving and receiving love. As a reminder, the five love languages are touch, words, attention, acts of service, and gifts.

You'll want to set aside some special time together for this exercise that focuses on the first three love languages. You'll be offering your partner just one of them at a time so that you can both discover which lands best for your partner. After you've been through them all, you'll switch places so that the giver becomes the receiver.

STEP 1: PHYSICAL TOUCH

Partner A gives physical touch to Partner B, with no words or eye contact.

Note: Partner A's attention should be on their own hands—where they are touching, how they are touching, what it feels like to touch Partner B, being in the enjoyment of their own experience of expressing physical touch to Partner B.

Partner B is receiving and practicing responsiveness with their eyes closed.

Responsiveness can be offered through verbal feedback by stating what would feel better ("I would love it if you'd go a little slower") or through simple words or phrases ("Oh that feels good!"). It's especially important to try to also include *nonverbal* feedback—breath, sound, movement, and facial expressions that correspond to the feeling of being opened, relaxed, and nourished while receiving.

If you're not feeling relaxed and opened from what you are receiving, either give verbal feedback to describe how you'd like to be touched ("Please slow down and use a really light touch.") or move your body into a safer-feeling position to see if it helps your ability to receive. You might try lying down, curling up on your side, assuming a fetal position, or stretching your body out. Experiment to determine what makes you feel safest in your body and most open to receiving.

After each receiving practice, pause for a moment and take notice of:

- Did that feel good to receive?

- On a scale of 1 to 10 (least to most), rate your experience. Note: The number you choose should reflect the degree of ease and relaxation you feel from receiving the touch. It's not about the quality of what you received. This spontaneous evaluation creates a simple anchor. You'll want to remember your answer to the question: How nourished do I feel after being touched?

Partner A communicates how it felt to be in the presence of Partner B's responsiveness or lack of responsiveness. For example: "It was amazing to see how your face lit up when I reassured you!" or "Part of me felt sad when I touched you and you didn't respond, as if you felt nothing."

Note: This practice is about exploring your ranges of responsiveness beyond what currently feels comfortable and safe; therefore, it's important to *amplify* your natural response. If you're not used to making sounds when you feel soothed, use these exercises to practice making an audible sound so your partner can easily hear and recognize that you are enjoying what you are receiving. For example, if you would normally make a small or slight sound, like *hmm*, then make a bigger sound, like *ahhhh!* In the same way, if the touch or attention feels good, let it show by smiling or letting your laughter come through.

The same goes for your movement. Play with stretching your chest forward or curling your spine back as you are being touched. For example, if you knew that it was completely okay to enjoy yourself while receiving your partner's touch (or someone you trust), then what are the sounds, movement, and facial expressions that would feel good to express?

Now try Steps 2 and 3 of this exercise with all this in mind and explore how you can open yourself simply by choosing to amplify your responsiveness when receiving another's words and attention.

STEP 2: WORDS OF AFFIRMATION

Partner A gives compliments and words of reassurance, recognition, and acknowledgment to Partner B, with no touch or eye contact. With this practice, "less is more," so use shorter, bite-sized statements that allow Partner B to take in your words in smaller quantities that don't put a demand on their attention. That means focusing on what you admire in the other and avoiding going into stories about it that would direct the attention on you.

Watch out for the word "because." For example, you want to say, "I'm amazed at how good you are at seeing the best in people." You want to avoid saying, "I'm amazed at how good you are at seeing the best in people *because* I so admire that quality and wish I could be more like that myself, which is so hard for me since no one ever saw the best in me." See the difference? Everything that comes after the "because" may be true, but it's not part of giving your partner the chance to receive the words that declare or confirm your love and appreciation.

Partner B is receiving and practicing responsiveness (still with their eyes closed). Again, this is achieved through both verbal and nonverbal responses. When you give verbal responsiveness, you want to keep it short and present-moment focused. Your verbal response should not include discussion or analysis. Your nonverbal feedback (breath, sound, movement, and facial expressions that correspond to the feeling of being opened, relaxed, and nourished while receiving) is again important to incorporate. Partner B can also practice owning needs, wants, and preferences by offering feedback to Partner A regarding what they would like to hear.

After each receiving practice, pause for a moment and take notice of:

- Did that feel good to receive?

- On a scale of 1 to 10 (least to most), rate your experience. Note: The number you choose should reflect the degree of openness and relaxation you feel from receiving the words of affirmation. It's not about the quality of what you received. This spontaneous evaluation creates a simple anchor. You'll want to remember the answer to the question: How nourished do I feel after receiving those words?

- Notice whether you felt more easily and deeply nourished by words or by touch.

STEP 3: QUALITY TIME/ATTENTION

Partner A stands and initiates slow, gentle body movements while maintaining full eye contact with Partner B, with no words or touch.

Partner B is receiving and practicing responsiveness through movement, giving them a chance to explore what it feels like to receive another's attention and be spontaneously responsive. Partner B may respond by matching Partner A's movement or by following a different desire that arises, such as moving in a contrasting way or not moving at all. The idea is to explore your own authentic expression through responsive movement.

Note: Partner B should only follow Partner A's movement if they feel Partner A being present, *and* if Partner A's attention is feeling good and landing with them. If not, both partners need to communicate what each one needs in order to surrender more to each other's flow.

After each receiving practice, pause for a moment and take notice of:

- Did that feel good to receive?

- On a scale of 1 to 10 (least to most), rate your experience. Note: The number you choose should reflect the degree of openness and relaxation you feel from receiving attention. It's not about the quality of what you received. This spontaneous evaluation creates a simple anchor. You'll want to remember the answer to the question: How nourished do I feel after receiving attention?

- Notice whether or not you felt more easily and deeply nourished by touch, words, or attention.

STEP 4: PHYSICAL TOUCH, WORDS, EYE CONTACT, FOCUSED ATTENTION, AND MOVEMENT

Partner A uses all methods of expression to shower Partner B with loving touch, words, attention, and movement. Partner A will use this exercise to spontaneously follow the urges and desires that arise in the moment.

Partner B practices increasing their responsiveness to receiving the various methods of expression.

Note: Partner A may want to ask Partner B what their preferred method of receiving is and then focus their attention on offering that as the dominant expression during this integration.

STEP 5

Partner A and Partner B switch roles.

THE ACKNOWLEDGMENT PRACTICE

In this powerful intimacy exercise, each partner is invited to take responsibility for whatever they may be bringing to the relationship that is detrimental to the partnership in some way. The beauty of this exercise is that it allows both partners to be seen and validated; it is incredibly heart-opening and powerful. It clears the air of all those unspoken issues that can easily accumulate and fester if we're not mindful of staying open about them. It goes like this:

STEP 1

Partner A says, "One thing that I bring to our relationship that doesn't work is . . ." (Fill in whatever first comes to mind in terms of something that *you* do that harms the relationship, large or small. Follow with genuine words of reassurance to let Partner B know that even though you do this thing that harms the relationship, you are "all in.")

- Share using these words: "What I bring to this relationship that doesn't work is . . ." or "One thing I bring to this relationship that doesn't work is . . ."

- You want to acknowledge first, and add detail later. This means don't go into any stories or explanations while stating your simple, matter-of-fact acknowledgment. For example: You want to say, "One thing I bring to this relationship that doesn't work is that I'm always so stressed." You don't want to add, "and the reason I'm always stressed is because my boss is so demanding and I'll lose my job if I don't get everything done."

- The longer your acknowledgment takes, the more the juice of it will drop, which causes tension and defensiveness to rise.

STEP 2

Partner A acknowledges what they want to bring to the relationship that would work better.

- For example: "One thing I bring to this relationship that doesn't work is that I put myself down a lot and dismiss your compliments and reassurance, and what I really want is to accept the goodness and beauty of me in your presence and to trust you when you tell me that you see me."

STEP 3

Partner A reassures Partner B that they're here and committed to making this area of the relationship better.

- For example: "I'm not offering a guarantee that what I'm acknowledging will change right away, but I want you to know that I'm not going to leave, or avoid, or check out from doing what I can do to make this part of our relationship better."

- Whenever possible, see if you can make the reassurance specific to the thing that's being acknowledged. For example: "What I bring to this relationship that doesn't work is that although I hear your words, I often don't pause to feel you in what you're sharing with me. What I want is to stop more and feel you, and remember how joyful it is to do that! I know it's going to take some practice for me to slow down, but I am committed to being here more often to feel you when you open up to me."

STEP 4

Partner A recognizes what Partner B has had to do, or sacrifice, to cope with the consequences, or fall out, of things not working in your relationship based upon what you've acknowledged that you do.

- For example: "What I bring to this relationship that doesn't work is that I don't speak my truth to you so that you know how I'm really feeling about what's going on between us. Even though I feel afraid to open up, what I want is to take more risks and be more daring in sharing my heart with you. I'm really committed to doing this more often, and I recognize that it doesn't feel good to you to have to hold the tension of what I'm not expressing or saying. You've been holding that for me for so long and I'm really grateful to you for that. I know it's hard for you to risk sharing your truth with me, always having to go first and never knowing if you'll get met and received with appreciation, but I do appreciate you for all the times you've stayed true to yourself and how you've remained hopeful that I would join you some day."

- After sharing your recognition, ask Partner B if they feel recognized and whether you hit the "nail on the head." If not, ask them to clarify what they have had to hold, and then repeat it back to them so they can feel you "getting it."

STEP 5

Partner A recognizes Partner B's willingness to be here in process with you, showing gratitude that you're being met in your desire to make your relationship better right now.

- For example: In addition to the example in Step 4: "And here we are now, and you're still here, and I love you so much for doing your best with what's not been working. I really want to find a way for our connection to feel better more of the time. Right now, just know that I'm so happy we're doing this together."

STEP 6

Partner B acknowledges and reassure Partner A for what's been shared (only if the reassurance is genuine). This is a time to recognize the fundamental truth of your connection and to convey the message, "I'm okay. You're okay. We're okay."

- For example: "Thank you so much for what you've shared. It feels really good to hear you speak to all this. I want you to know that we're okay, and I'm *in* for doing whatever it takes to give our connection what it needs because I know we're worth it."

STEP 7

Partner B acknowledges the part they play in contributing to this ongoing dynamic.

- For example: "I want to acknowledge that I do get impatient with you sometimes when I sense that you have something to share and feel you're holding back. And I can get caught up in wanting to provoke you so you'll get angry and just shout it out. I get so desperate to break the silence. And I can see how that doesn't give you the safety you need to be more daring."

I know this can get tricky, but it's a wonderful way to balance the exchange and make sure both parties are felt. Each partner will state whether they feel complete or incomplete. If there is incompletion, they'll take turns tracking until both feel complete.

Close by each partner stating one thing they are grateful for about the other partner. Then repeat the process with Partners A and B switching places.

This exercise can then be repeated on any other topic or area of the relationship. See if you can come up with at least ten unique sharings.

The Acknowledgment Practice exercise seems straightforward, but in 99.9 percent of cases where I have watched clients do this practice, there is inevitably a blind spot that emerges when Partner B attempts to acknowledge their part in the dynamic presented by Partner A. This is why it's really important and beneficial for a qualified third party, such as a Heart IQ Relationship Coach, to be present. This outside point of view is almost always needed to accurately translate the hidden blind spots each party is bringing to a specific dynamic.

Reassurance is a tremendous factor in the success of this process. If you're the one taking space, you'll want to track and share what's moving for you, but if you're on the receiving end, the last thing you want to do is track your own response. It becomes too cumbersome. It's simply not your turn, in that moment, to track and share your own internal reality. You come straight in with your spontaneous reassurance instead. The goal is to make sure your partner knows that whatever is being shared, you are okay as a couple and all is going to be well. That's what invites further sharing and deepening intimacy.

Again, I want to make sure this lands. Do not track yourself when your partner shares something big with you. First reassure, then, if needed, track what moves in you.

What does reassurance look like? Without using this exact language, you want to constantly be conveying the message: "You're okay; I'm okay; we're okay. I'm in." You do it without a lot of words, primarily with your body language, facial expression, and limited verbal reassurance. If your reassurance is more than five or six words, it's too much.

The only time the focus and actual space shifts to Partner B is when it's time to acknowledge Partner B's contribution to the situation. This is where Partner B shows appreciation for Partner A's vulnerability by giving voice to the portion of the responsibility that is authentically Partner B's.

The Acknowledgment Practice can be quite powerful when both partners understand that the purpose is to repair any issues that are interfering with their ability to feel safe and intimate with each other and commit to that purpose. Therefore, it's important to be aware beforehand of any potential derailments. One such derailment is forgetting to be grateful for whatever Partner A has brought up for sharing and going into judgment or demanding more explanation. Others include waffling around the acknowledgment, not speaking directly to the actual piece that doesn't work, and Partner A's demanding that Partner B own their part in the sharing with expectation and defense.

* * *

When you open to your partner and allow your full range of emotions to come into play and really begin to feel each other and get where the other is coming from, I can guarantee you will have the most flourishing intimacy you've ever dreamed of having. Imagine holding absolutely nothing back—feeling *that* safe in your relationship that you can share your purest, most authentic, and vulnerable self with your partner. If you dare to share, keep reading.

If you would like to see a demo of the Acknowledgment
Practice in action, visit www.HeartIQRelationships.com
using myheartiq as the access code.

CHAPTER 8

Vulnerability in Action: Dare-to-Share Conversations

Intimacy thrives as a direct result of both partners' capacity for raw, tender, honest vulnerability. Vulnerability emerges when the relationship container feels supremely strong and safe, and, therefore, it is something each partner must earn from the other. I've noticed that women in particular often make the mistake of being too vulnerable too soon in a new relationship in the hopes that vulnerability will lead to intimacy and safety. In actuality, it's the other way around. *Only* once safety has been firmly established should vulnerability be offered. It's an honor bestowed upon a partner who has earned it. Through the work and agreements you've made with your partner by engaging in these Heart IQ practices, you have been creating a container of safety. Are you ready to take it to the next level?

Dare to Share All of You

What are you carrying that you believe makes you unlovable? Can you imagine how gloriously liberating it would feel to test that theory and discover that you are indeed lovable after all? Can you imagine how close you would feel to the partner who can love you *right there*—right in the middle of your most deplorable unlovability? Can you imagine how much love and compassion you'd feel for your beloved when they met you in that place of ultimate vulnerability by exposing their most staunchly guarded demons as well?

Maybe the thought of it brings up fear for you. Maybe you're not sure enough about the safety of the container to trust that you would still be cherished and admired if your shadows were exposed. Maybe you're afraid to know what shadows might be locked away in your beloved, and you'd just assume they remain locked away. That's fine. It's a choice. But you're reading this book because you want to deepen your intimacy, your fire, your passion for each other. This is the way to do it. It's also one of the most powerful means of clearing up your shadows and dissolving your core unworthiness.

Daring to share all of you will require some risk-taking. You might even share an attraction you feel for a third party. You might think there's no way that kind of sharing could be beneficial to the relationship, but if it's there and you don't share it, you're holding it, and that can be far more damaging in the long run. This issue came up at one of the Insights to Intimacy LIVE seminars, so I asked the room, "If your partner felt an attraction for someone else, how many of you would *not* want to know?" Not a single person raised a hand. I continued by asking, "If your partner has been withholding something from you regarding your sex life because they didn't want to hurt your feelings, would you want to know that?" Again, everyone said yes. "What about if there's something about your personal hygiene that your partner doesn't like but never brought up?" Again and again I asked the room if there was anything any of them would rather not hear, and again and again the answer was unanimous. We *want* to know these things about our beloved.

The health of your love connection is entirely dependent upon your ability to be real with another. If you're not committed to being as radically authentic as you can possibly be, then there's no point in having a relationship. Even if you feel that you and your partner habitually share what's going on for you, this is an invitation to stretch into something even more profound together. It will skyrocket the safety each of you feels in your container. It will skyrocket your polarity, magnetism, and juice.

When it comes to sharing difficult shadow parts of us, specificity is important. This is not the place for vague confessions like, "I don't always love myself," or "I've never really forgiven my mother." You want your sharing to be directly about the shame you carry, which you would rather your partner did not know about. A combination of excitement and terror usually means you're on the right track.

Before you embark on this dare-to-share conversation, you'll want to make some more agreements. Agree in advance that you're both willing to follow up afterward on any points that would benefit from a good tracking conversation. Agree that whatever is shared will remain confidential and won't be used at a later time as a leverage or evidence. You're doing this as an ultimate expression of your love for each other; it would be an egregious betrayal to use it as a way to gather ammunition. If you have any concern that you or your partner might approach this exchange from that position, do not do it. Sharing at this level is for couples who have built enough safety and trust so that they are genuinely interested in amplifying their love and strengthening their bond with the glue of unconditional acceptance.

Ultimately, this is a test of your relationship container. So, yes, the possibility does exist that you'll discover it's not as strong as you'd hoped. But if that's the case, wouldn't you like to know that now, so that you can work toward repairing any leaks before they get any bigger? Relationship is risky. The only way to take your relationship to new heights is to put it on the line occasionally. However, if you're not ready to go there, you can choose to play it safe and just keep things status quo.

BRINGING IN A WITNESS

Once you have dared to show all of who you are to your beloved because their trust and safety has been rightfully earned, another valuable practice is daring to allow your process with your partner to be witnessed by others you trust—either in a structured setting, such as in my Insights to Intimacy LIVE seminars, or with friends and family who are fans of your love and who want the best for you as a couple. Very often it's most difficult for us to hear uncomfortable truths directly from our partner, but it's easier to understand and digest those truths when we hear them expressed to a third party. Our natural defenses are not as easily triggered in the presence of objective observers, making us more capable of emotional maturity and seeing the big picture. It's human nature, when we're being witnessed, to raise our game. We behave better. We're more likely to bring our best selves to the table.

When Resolution Is Needed

In most cases, sharing at this extremely vulnerable level brings couples to a dramatically healthier, closer, more intimate place. It's an opportunity to do the same kind of shadow work and emotional clearing we accomplish by waiting for triggers to arise naturally in our day-to-day lives, but in a more concentrated, speedy format.

The chance does exist, however, that something shared at this level of honesty will deeply trigger your partner's pain body (or yours). If this happens, your first instinct might be to fear you've gone too far. You might wish you could take it back or start cursing me and this damn book, wondering how you could have been tricked into setting off this landmine. It's an understandable response, but I guarantee you that no matter what has been exposed, it's far healthier for it to be out in the light than stuffed in the shadows.

If you or your partner is in pain over a revelation that's surfaced, don't put it aside for later. Deal with it immediately. Whichever of you is least triggered needs to take control at this point and step into the more masculine role of penetrating the other with love. Do not lose sight of the fact that you both share the intention of deepening your intimacy and connection. The truth will always ultimately do that, but the opportunity immediately before you is to be as accepting of your partner as you can, given what's moving with you. This is a chance for healing, so honor it as such, and be sure to bring all of the skills you've learned thus far into play.

To remind you of those skills, I'm going to take you inside one of my coaching sessions and share with you, partially in dialogue form, some actual conversations that took place when participants were deeply triggered by this kind of vulnerable sharing. My coaching interventions will reinforce the principles we've already learned and give you a better idea how to handle your follow-up conversations when one of you is triggered.

Case Study: Tony and Ellen

Christian: Which of the two of you is least triggered right now, least in their pain body? That's the one who will lead the conversation.

Tony: That would be me. Ellen is triggered because I shared that I'm not always honest about my judgments regarding how she handles her two kids. I know she already has unworthiness issues in this area, so I knew I was taking a risk in sharing it, but the judgments are real for me, and I didn't want to keep them hidden any longer.

Christian: Thank you, Tony. We resolve conflict by having each person honestly track and verbalize what they're feeling. Staying within the framework of tracking, that means not going into blame and judgment. If the urge to blame or judge comes up, as it is likely to, it's okay to share your desire to blame, as a part of tracking your inner reality. Ellen, would you like to start?

Ellen: It hits me immediately, this accusation that I'm not a good mother *(this is her shadow)*. I feel myself wanting to be the best mother I can be, but at the same time, I can also feel exhaustion around it. I can feel a part of me not even wanting to try anymore, just wanting to be free of the heaviness of it. And hearing this judgment from you, Tony, just brings me to the breaking point. When I hear this judgment, what moves in me is almost a feeling of sickness. My body hurts. I feel closed down, like I want to leave, retreat, run away. I feel shame, and I feel helpless to change myself in this situation.

Christian: Ellen, do you believe what Tony has said is true? Is it confirming a fear you have that you are a bad mother?

Ellen: Yes.

Christian: Tony, do you believe she's a bad mother?

Tony: No, of course you're not a bad mother.

Christian: Ellen, Tony has shared a judgment that was not representative of the whole picture, but because it's an area in which you're sensitive, it feels very big to you. It's only affecting you this way because you believe it. Tony, it's your job here to reassure Ellen that you're talking about a part, not the whole. You wanted to be honest about a judgment you have in certain situations, but Ellen has absorbed the message that you think she's a bad mother. You just said that's not the case, so a good way to lead the conversation at this point would be for you to honestly clarify your position. If it's true for you, you could say something like, "There are moments when I don't agree with how you're handling the kids, but overall I think you're an amazing mom." Your job right now is to offer nourishment to feed her since she's triggered and you are not. You're the one who can bring her back.

Ellen and Tony proceeded to do some heartfelt tracking back and forth, and ultimately, Tony did an excellent job of helping Ellen out of her pain body. Their honest dialoging led Ellen to a genuine position of gratitude for Tony's sharing. Once the air was cleared and Ellen knew precisely where Tony stood, he realized that it was far better to have his exact judgments out in the open than it had been beforehand. Ellen described the vague tension and anxiety she had been perpetually experiencing from suspecting Tony was judging her, but never really being clear about when or how.

Ellen felt much lighter knowing that, although Tony had a few opinions about her mothering, these thoughts didn't get in the way of his love for Ellen or his overall admiration of her as a mom. Tony felt much lighter because he had finally been able to say things he'd been holding back that might have festered and led to resentment. He knew now that he could express himself honestly without jeopardizing Ellen's love, and he knew that Ellen was receptive to hearing him out. The heightened connection between them was visible and beautiful.

The biggest thing to watch out for when you're in one of these resolution dialogues is entrainment. Entrainment happens when you're so in sync with your partner that their pain triggers your pain, and you lose your ability to take a loving, clear leadership position. It's like jumping in a hole to save someone who has fallen into that very hole. Now you need a third person to throw down the rope.

It's much better to energetically stay in a place of solid ground. As the un-triggered party, you can't allow yourself to get pulled down by your partner's sad energy. It's easy to get sucked in to meet the person where they are, but it's not the position from which you can be most helpful. I know that sounds like a contradiction to what I shared earlier about "matching" in order to build rapport. However, it's one thing to adjust your emotional thermometer to help another feel felt and understood, and quite another to collapse into sadness because your partner happens to be sad. One is a conscious choice to create a better connection; the other is unconscious entrainment that leaves you both unfelt.

Real, emotionally mature love means loving someone enough to not need them to like you in that moment. You want to be willing to be honest even when it risks upsetting your partner. Real love is not about merging; it's not collapsing into the space of the other, wherever they may be. If that's your tendency, you might have an urge to backtrack once you've said something that triggers your partner. Backtracking is never a good idea. On some level, your partner will never believe that you didn't mean it, and the unresolved tension will interfere with intimacy.

Instead of backtracking, clarify. You need to get clear on the degree to which you meant what you said, understanding that it was received with a far greater impact than you intended. You're clearing up an inaccuracy on your partner's perception of the situation. Don't hold back your reassurance that the big picture is what matters most. For example, Tony's judgment of Ellen's mothering triggered an out-of-proportion response from Ellen, since it was already a sensitive area for her. Ellen didn't hear the information correctly, so Tony needed to clarify with abundant reassurance. As the leader, he needed to activate a little more "masculine" energy to really penetrate Ellen with her love and acceptance.

Being truthful with your beloved is the ultimate expression of love and respect, so you want to stand by your honest sharing, always. When your sharing sends your partner into their pain body, it's simply an indication that this is a hot topic for them, something they feel shame around. That's okay. You've stumbled upon a shadow that's ready to come up for healing.

Now the two of you can work together to release this shadow and heal the long-buried shame that's been causing limitation and restriction of emotional range. Any time an issue feels bigger than it is, you can be sure you've hit upon a shadow and the pain body has been triggered. When you come together, through tracking or quietly holding each other in stillness with the intention to unconditionally love and accept each other, core unworthiness gets digested and healing occurs.

Always make sure that appreciation is given on both sides. The triggered party is due appreciation for being open enough to work through a painful issue. The triggering party is due appreciation for the courage to be so honest.

You may be forming the idea that if your relationship is on rocky ground in any way, it would be best to steer clear of this practice. Not so. Is it likely to stir up uncomfortable issues? Yes, of course it is. And that's exactly what you want. Hiding from what threatens your relationship is the worst thing you can do. It gives those issues power; it gives them room to grow until they become so unwieldy there's no longer any hope of getting them under control. Any couple's counselor will tell you that the biggest predictor of whether or not a troubled couple will stay together is how quickly they begin to honestly, openly address their issues once they come up. Let's go to another coaching session to look closely at what happened when Shelly and Rob dared to share at their most honest level.

Case Study: Rob and Shelly

Rob and Shelly came to an Insight to Intimacy LIVE seminar knowing that there was an intimacy gap in their relationship. They wanted to be together, but they'd been through some troubling issues with leakiness and resentment toward each other. One of the things Shelly dared to share is that she still felt an attraction for a man she'd come to know in recent years. She knew it would be hard for Rob to hear, but she wanted to be truthful.

Rob: I am deeply triggered to know that Shelly still struggles with her feelings for this other man. It's been an issue between us for over a year now. When I track what's moving for me, it's confirmation of something I'd already been sensing, a suspicion that there's still something active there. It's a confirmation of what I don't want to know or feel. I feel very unsafe.

Shelly: I hear you and I feel a longing to resolve this and come together fully with you.

Christian: Shelley, Rob's expressing feeling unsafe because there's a guy you've been having romantic feelings for, and he's wondering if this poses a threat to your relationship. Do you want to be with Rob? Do you love him completely? Is he safe with you? If so, tell him. If not, tell him. You need to take the lead role in this because Rob is triggered and needs to feel your penetrating love if that is true for you.

Shelley: Rob, I can't say you are safe because there's something running in me that I can't control. I don't want to go into a relationship with this other man. I want to be in relationship with you. But I can't honestly guarantee safety.

Christian: Shelley, what I'm hearing is that there are thoughts and feelings that move through you about a third party, that you feel you can't control, and it's interfering. So you can't guarantee the safety of the relationship, yet you want to be in relationship with Rob. So, what is holding the relationship together right now? Is it your commitment, your decision, your promise to him? I don't think any man would want to know you're there just because of some agreement. He wants to know you really want him, that you desire him. If you do, then tell him. Show him.

Shelley: I want a relationship with you because my longing is to be with you. I can't say why.

Christian: Rob, would you like to respond to that?

Rob: I'm noticing that I'm stuck on the fact that you're saying you have uncontrollable feelings for this man. As long as I'm focused on that, the other things you're saying are not really being received. Because my truth is that I just want you to stop with these uncontrollable feelings. I'm fed up with it. I feel angry now. I don't want him in our relationship.

(There is a long silence.)

Christian: Do you receive that, Shelley?

Shelley: Yes.

Christian: Then tell him, "I get it." Even if you don't have a response, you need to acknowledge that the communication was received.

Shelley: I receive that.

Christian: Shelley, do you think these feelings for the other guy need exploration? Do you need to explore them to feel complete, or can you make a clear decision today to just be with Rob? If the energy with this third party is complete, you can control the feelings. But if they're uncontrollable, if they're running you, then you may be incomplete with it, and you'll need to make a decision. Rob is sensing ambiguity in you. You may not be able to decide this firmly until you explore it. I don't know if that's something you want and are denying it, or if it's something you don't want.

Shelley: I don't want to be in relationship with the other guy. But what happens is that with him my heart opens spontaneously. I can't help knowing that, even if I make the choice not to be with him.

Christian: It sounds like perhaps this man is bringing up a longing in you—something that you would like to experience in your relationship with Rob? If so, that's valuable information to share with Rob. You're not attached to this guy, but you've recognized there's some quality about him that you deeply desire to be present in your relationship. It's okay to recognize these needs. Everyone has a right to determine what they want and expect from their primary relationship and to ask their partner for it. If you truly want to create a beautiful, fulfilling partnership with Rob, he needs to hear this important piece of information. But right now, he's in fear, and it's your job to bust that open before you could possibly expect him to receive the information you need to offer him. Can you penetrate Rob with reassurance and love right now? If you can't do that, then that's important for him to know, too.

Shelley: *(after a long silence)* I feel like there's something I would need from him first.

Christian: Okay, so you're inviting him to bring something new into the relationship. It then becomes his choice whether or not to do that. When Partner A wants a certain thing, it doesn't mean that Partner B must bring it. If Partner B decides not to acquiesce, then Partner A gets to decide whether or not the requested item was a deal-breaker. You've yet to express clearly to Rob what it is that you're wanting, but you can still be looking inward to ask yourself,

"Is this something I need in my life?" If so, you base your decision about whether or not to be with him on his decision about whether or not he can meet this need of yours. Can you try to articulate for Rob what it is that this guy brings up for you? If he stirs in you a longing that you want to experience with Rob, tell him. You have to be fierce in letting him know that you're not choosing this guy over him, but that there's something this individual has helped you to recognize that you need, and you want more than anything to help Rob to meet this need.

Shelley: *(to Rob)* I choose you. I'm not in relationship with him. I want to feel opened by you.

Christian: He can't really believe you choose him because you're not really doing that yet. What's true right now is that there's a third-party energy that has come into your lives that has opened you. You say you want to experience that with Rob. You can invite him to meet you there, knowing he may say no. You need to be very clear about this so that Rob can feel your heart and feel that intention.

(Shelley is silent.)

Christian: What's moving with you, Rob?

Rob: I feel triggered in the part of me that's not good enough for who I am. I feel like I need to dance like a monkey to get the banana. Like there's always something else I need to do or be. I feel like you're comparing me to someone else and telling me to be that, do that. But I'm also tracking another part of me that wants to grow and expand. I want to have all these qualities. I want to be able to please you with all these fantastic qualities, and you know that because none of this is new. I feel triggered to an extra degree in my feelings of not being good enough because, on top of my own self-judgments, I hear you judging me as well.

Christian: Rob, it sounds like you're discovering a place within you where you want to say, "Take me as I am or not at all." Is that correct?

Rob: This is who I am today. Shelley knows there are areas where I want to grow and expand. I want to work on being more present, more connected to my fire.

Christian: Shelley, what does this third party open in you?

Shelley: He's got clear direction. He feels defined to me, solid, unwavering.

Christian: Rob, when you hear Shelley list those qualities, does that match the direction you feel you're moving in naturally, anyway, not just for her? Do you even want to be more of those things, or do you feel more like "I am who I am and that's okay"?

Rob: I definitely want to be more of that.

Christian: Rob, I'd like to get a sense of where others feel you are in relationship to those qualities. *(Directing his question to the room.)* Let's get a quick group read: When you hear Shelley listing the qualities she desires in a man, how many of you see those qualities in Rob already? *(Many hands are raised.)* So, Shelley, considering the possibility that Rob does possess some degree of these traits you've identified, what do you think could be blocking you from taking in those qualities from him? Why is it not safe to receive that from him, but it is safe from this third party?

(Shelley remains quiet.)

Rob: I agree with Shelley when it comes to direction. I know that's something I'm missing. I don't think that's the whole issue, but it's part of it.

Christian: When you own that, Rob, it feels very clean. Shelley, when you hear that from Rob, does his honesty relax and soften you? Or does it make you feel like saying, "I know! When are you going to get more direction?"

Shelley: The latter.

Christian: Shelley, if Rob never got more direction, could you love him and be with him? If things never changed at all from the way they are now, even though Rob has expressed a longing to grow in this way, would he be enough for you, right now, as he is?

Shelley: *(after long pause)* Yes.

Rob: That's not the feeling I'm getting. I'm getting the definite impression that I'm not good enough now today.

Christian: It's always dangerous to base a relationship on possibility rather than reality. There's a deep conflict here to be resolved because the surest way for Rob to become that man of clear direction and certainty would be for Shelley to love him completely as he is right here, right now. If the only energy he receives from her is the energy of "I wish you were this and I wish you were that," that's only going to diminish him further and make it harder for him to move forward toward his goals. So a lot of this is up to you, Shelley. You can heal this together if you can give him authentic, plentiful reassurance right here where he is. It's your choice whether or not to do that, and no one can judge you for your decision. It's fine if you don't want to do that, you just need to be clear about it.

Shelley: I'm not sure if Rob really wants to grow. I'm not sure if that's what's in his heart, or if it's just coming from not feeling worthy.

Christian: Shelley, I'm hearing that you're doubting whether he can move beyond his unworthiness to grow into all he can be. What I'm saying is that the difference between him making it or not could be in your hands. Part of a woman's potential in a relationship is to hold her man in the space of having already arrived. If you're constantly holding him in doubt, he's going to see that in your eyes, and be crippled by it.

Shelley: It's just that so often his response to everything is, "I'm not good enough."

Christian: And what do you say in response? Do you let him know you believe in him?

Shelley: Yes, I do that.

Christian: And have you seen any progress in him?

Shelley: Yes.

Christian: So there's been upward movement, then. You see where this is going, right? There's work for both of you to do. Rob needs to continue his own work. But can you see, Shelley, that you being in doubt and habitually voicing that doubt is going to do more harm than good? What's moving for you right now? What is it that you want at this point?

Shelley: I want to be with Rob.

Christian: This may seem a bit harsh, but there's nothing wrong with putting a time boundary around this. For couples who are a bit ambiguous, having doubts, it's often the best thing to bring about clarity. You would need to agree, Shelley, that for a specific amount of time you will put all thoughts of this other man to the side and be fully present, fully open, fully committed to Rob. Because if you let this situation continue this way, it's just going to decay. The reality is you both deserve to be loved exactly how you are. The beauty of relationships is their ability to bring both partners to their fullest potential, but that can't happen until both partners feel fully loved and cherished right at all points along the way.

The hard reality is that sometimes we just outgrow one another or we go in different directions. We don't meet and match anymore. There's no blame in it; it just happens. Rob, you deserve to be with someone who loves you for who you are, not for who you might become. Shelley, you deserve to be with someone who you can open with. You can commit to discovering whether or not you can be that for each other, or you choose to separate so you each can find someone who can. There's so much love here that my suggestion would be to set a time boundary and give it a try. Rob, that means no more dancing monkey, no more banana chasing. Maybe that will begin to provide the kind of certainty Shelley is looking for in her man.

Shelley and Rob ended up committing to a yearlong period of making clear agreements and sticking to them, sealing up the leaks in their relationship, and doing their best to love each other without conditions and unrealistic expectations. Interestingly, Rob first suggested six months, and it was Shelley who insisted she wanted it to be longer, saying, "I really want to be in." To honor Rob's request, they agreed to do a six-month check-in to honestly look at what they'd been able to create by then and to decide at that point whether or not to continue.

Was it a painful exchange for both of them? Of course it was. But if they had not faced into these difficult truths, their relationship would have withered and died. By far the biggest cause of relationship *failure* is relationship *neglect*.

Sharing Disappointments and Unmet Needs

Unmet needs constitute a fragile area that requires delicacy and compassion. When you and your partner are deep in your pain bodies, in defense, it will feel nearly impossible to navigate these spots in a heart-centered way. The only thing that will make it possible is for you to have solid tools in place beforehand, tools so well practiced that they've become second nature to you.

The practice I'm about to suggest is for when you both are in a good enough space to be able to communicate with heart. If you're in an angered, defensive space, don't try this out for the first time. It won't work.

Preparing Yourself for the "Sharing Disappointments/ Unmet Needs Practice"

In just a moment I will be sharing with you the step-by-step guide for the Sharing Disappointments/Unmet Needs Practice, but first I want to give you a little background on this powerful exercise. For this practice, I recommend partners sit back to back, leaning on each other's shoulders so that their heads are side by side. It's so much easier to keep from going into defense this way because there will be no one to face to defend against. When we look at each other, it's easy to project and make the other person the reason for our pain. But when we're back to back, we're energetically more open, which allows us to feel our partner without our emotional closure getting in the way of our communication.

The partner who is taking space first says: "What isn't working in our relationship is . . ." or "A disappointment I'm carrying right now is . . ." or "A need that isn't being met right now is . . ." That partner then shares a truth around a part of the relationship where their needs aren't being fully met, which is a scary thing to do.

These are the kinds of conversations that have the potential to spiral down into defensive pain-body confrontations. Being told you're not meeting your partner's needs can be a powerful trigger for core unworthiness to rear its ugly head. We don't like to feel that shame and guilt, so S.T.U.A.R.T. comes up, and we defend. That is the risk. However, my challenge to you is to do this exercise from such a loving, mutually honoring place that you are both able to set your core unworthiness triggers aside for the good of the partnership.

It's not about blame; it's simply looking inward, then honestly sharing a need that isn't being met. It's a delicate conversation, yes, but if you approach it purely from the position of what you're feeling inside you, as opposed to taking the approach of blame toward your partner, you'll discover that there's a huge difference in those two approaches. One leads to greater intimacy and connection, and the other leads to anger, defense, and disconnect.

You'll want to use your tracking skills before, during, and after you share your unmet needs. Beforehand that could sound like, "My heart is beating so fast. I'm afraid to share this with you because I don't want to hurt you." After you've tracked and expressed your unmet need, the subsequent tracking might sound like: "Let me check to see if it feels like there's anything else."

The partner holding space needs to strive to stay away from defensiveness, instead reaching deep within to find the part that can meet, acknowledge, and confirm the reality of their beloved. Even if they don't agree with what's being said, the primary objective is to make the sharer feel heard and accepted right where they are. As you're listening, give generous spontaneous response. Use all your physiology, all your body, breath, and energy. It makes a huge difference in letting your partner know you're fully present. Once you've given reassurance, it's your turn to track and share. It might sound something like: "There's a part of me that feels hurt, but another part that . . ."

The listener needs to honestly look inward and take responsibility for whatever they've done to contribute to the situation. Without too much shame on one end or defensiveness on the other end; it's a straightforward acknowledgment of their contribution to their partner's disappointment. The key is to meet your partner honestly without being diminished. It's not about apologies or vows to do better. You need to drop into your own energy, your own body, in order for your response to be deeply felt and integrated by your partner. If you're too focused on your partner and too quick to rush in with apologies or remedies, it will feel artificial; it won't land. It's far better to sit and take time to connect inwardly before you offer your sincere response.

I've noticed that often it's difficult for the listener to stay focused because they've gone into fear mode. They're distracted by wondering just how bad it is in terms of where you stand together. There's a really simple step the sharer can take to remove this fear and tension so the listener can focus with better attention. The sharer just needs to communicate in advance, something like: "Even though I need to share this with you, it is *not* a deal-breaker. What I'm about to say is not something that threatens our relationship." Starting with a statement like that allows the listener to more easily stay out of defense and stay open to what's being spoken.

Of course, you only want to offer this reassurance if it's true. Since most couples are highly unskilled at communicating disappointments, issues frequently build up, pressure-cooker style, until they actually *do* become deal-breakers. That's precisely why this exercise is so valuable. When put into regular practice—ideally weekly, and minimally monthly—it becomes a way to stay clear with each other and avoid those pressure-cooker situations. When you have frequent opportunities to deeply hear each other and make any necessary adjustments, this practice won't feel so heavy. It becomes a joyful way to connect and deepen intimacy.

Naturally, reassuring your partner that your issue is "not a deal-breaker" doesn't mean that it won't become one in time. Even seemingly minor unmet needs, if they are continuously expressed and ignored, can eventually become deal-breakers. Reassurance doesn't ever mean reassurance forever, no matter what. It's always in the moment. If there's a need that's not being met, it's important to figure out what's in the way, whether it's a matter of your partner not meeting you, or you not being open enough to receive your partner's efforts. Voicing the unmet need is important, but it doesn't solve the nourishing aspect. We have to figure out why we're not feeling nourished, and we have to do our own individual work to make sure that we are, indeed, available to nourishment from another.

When the individuals in a relationship are in their pain bodies, the way they communicate with each other can amplify their pain responses and bring out more defensiveness than intimacy. Often *what is not being said* is affecting the energy of the interaction more than what's being spoken. This practice is helpful when you and your partner need to communicate your disappointment, undigested pain from the past, or broken trust related to how one or both partners are feeling toward the other. It's particularly helpful when you are dealing with pain from the past that has been triggered in the present through current events.

The Sharing Disappointments/Unmet Needs Practice is a verbal and nonverbal communication practice that:

- Recognizes what the receiver is doing right, along with what's not working.

- Validates your own experience of loss with heart-centered expression.

- Is meant to create an uplifting effect through encouragement, acknowledgment, and reassurance.

- Allows the communicator to find new ways of expressing their needs without using the exaggerations of "always" and "never."

- Helps the communicator to discern, define, and reassure the receiver while sharing their disappointment (For example, "I still love you; this isn't a deal-breaker. I just need to share what I'm feeling.")

SHARING DISAPPOINTMENTS/ UNMET NEEDS PRACTICE

STEP 1

Partner A (the one who is expressing)

- **Reassure your partner that you are still "in":** Reassure your partner with your own words for the message, "This isn't a deal-breaker; I'm still in. We're still okay. But I do need to share this upset that I'm holding toward you." It's important that the partner who's sharing takes responsibility for setting up a safe container to acknowledge and hold the potential unsafety their partner may feel in receiving this upset.

- **Share your disappointment, pain, or mistrust about an area where you feel your needs are unmet or where you currently hold disappointment:** This disappointment, pain or mistrust is usually related to a feeling that your partner has *failed* to meet your needs. It's any place where you feel unmet and disappointed around not receiving what you need. This may be a need that you haven't yet communicated to your partner, or you may have expressed it before, but it's not yet been received. Track your experience as needed, as well as track when you feel complete. Then tell your partner that you feel complete with your sharing so they can be clear when it's time for them to respond.

STEP 2

Partner B (the one who is receiving)

During the sharing:

• **Practice being responsive, engaged, and listening without defense during Partner A's sharing.** Throughout the sharing, hold the question, "What part of me can meet them and agree that this is absolutely the case?" Then share that part of you after Partner A has finished.

• **Listen without defense:** This means to listen without interrupting or interjecting with justifications and excuses and without collapsing into your own pain-body response.

• **Respond, being responsive and engaged:** Respond to your partner fully, using brief verbal confirmation. For example, you might say: "Yes, I get it." You may want to periodically pause and take a breath to let the communication land.

After the sharing:

• **Reassure your partner and confirm their reality:** This is the *reassurance* that you not only see the fact that your partner is in pain but you also see that what you do or don't do is part of why they're in pain. This is the practice of genuinely finding the place in yourself where you can meet your partner in their reality by *agreeing to the truth of what they're saying.* Your partner's perspective or portrayal of the situation may not feel fully true to you. *However,* there is some truth in what your partner is sharing. You must decide that you are committed to finding a piece of truth in your partner's experience and meeting your partner there. For example, you say: "I can really see why you feel so disappointed, and I get why you don't trust me right now."

- **If you truly cannot find any truth in what your partner has shared, then share your truth around that.** Don't go silent and say nothing; don't pretend to agree and offer inauthentic reassurance. For example, you might say: "I see how you would feel disappointed around that, and I don't completely get what I'm doing to have you feel that way. But it's important to me to know that you're in pain, so thank you for telling me, and I'm open to understanding how I'm part of creating this pain."

- **Acknowledge your part in contributing to your partner's pain.** For example, you can say: "I see how you would feel disappointed, and I also get it, because I do that (or have done that) and I see how it creates pain for you. I'm really glad you shared that with me." If you can't acknowledge your part, or your disconnection to seeing your part, or the *possibility* that you even have a part, then your unacknowledged resistance, defensiveness, and denial can be quite damaging to your intimate connection, and potentially to your partner's self-esteem. Whether it's your truth or not, your actions will demonstrate that you think your partner is wrong, stupid, bad, or crazy for feeling something that doesn't exist and for creating so much drama over nothing.

IMPORTANT: If Partner B gets triggered from what Partner A shares, Partner B shares back to Partner A by tracking their experience *only* after they have confirmed Partner A's reality and met them with reassurance. This is not always easy, but it's essential in order to avoid a cascading pain-body trigger that can spiral into a full blowout.

Additional Reassurance Pointers for Partner A:

If you're feeling deeply triggered, but can recognize that you've never told your partner about your need and you can see that your partner deserves to know that you are up against a potential "deal-breaker" point in the relationship, then communicate this awareness along with your disappointment. *Even in your triggered state, you still need to offer that you are "in" in order to create the safety that's necessary for your partner to be present and receive what you're sharing.* After you've shared, pause and tune in to see if you have any more willingness to try again, and if so, reassure your partner again that you're still "in" for now with the understanding of this important boundary.

- For example, you may say to your partner: "I'm at a place where I'm up against my edge. I'm realizing that what I'm feeling is actually a deal-breaker for me, but I also know that I've haven't shared this with you (or shared how important this is to me). So I want to do this now, and I want to start by expressing it with all the frustration and pain I have around it being a deal-breaker. Then, after I've said it, I want to tune back in to see how I'm feeling and let you know what's moving for me in the aftermath of the release. Do you feel like you can listen wholeheartedly for now, knowing that I'm "in" enough to want to share this with you, but I'm also not clear on how much I have left to keep giving to this issue? I really need to take this next step and share my pain with you so that I can feel the truth of where I'm at with us. And I'm here right now, ready to give this my all and let you feel my heart."

If reassurance can't be genuinely offered, it's important to clarify that what you're about to share *is* a deal-breaker for you so that your partner is prepared, as much as possible, to hold your communication with this understanding. In this case, this would be a sharing for the purpose of closing the relationship.

To see the previous practice demonstrated in action,
visit www.HeartIQRelationships.com and put in the access code
myheartiq to unlock your home-study companion course.

The Power of Invitation—Navigating Defensiveness, Shutdown, and Checkout

When we need to communicate an area where we've been disappointed with our partner, it's common for the receiver of such news to become defensive—either outwardly and verbally or by shutting down and emotionally checking out of the conversation. One way to sidestep this defense mechanism is to frame your disappointment as an invitation. Recognize what your partner is doing right, and put the focus on all the times your partner has met this need for you or given you this thing you're wanting more of.

For instance, if you want more of your beloved's time, attention, or physical intimacy, start by giving your heartfelt appreciation for whatever you currently *are* getting in that area. Paint a beautiful picture of how wonderful those moments are for you, so that your request for more of it is coming from a place of how much you cherish these times. That's so much more inviting and likely to make your partner want to step up than if it were presented in a whiny, nagging way.

If it's a situation where you truly haven't gotten any of the thing you want, then give appreciation for the almost-moments, whatever comes closest to what you're wanting. A common example would be the couple that's stopped having sex. You might mention how good it feels to hug your partner and how that makes you long to share more physical intimacy. Remember to steer clear of "always" and "never." The key is to first give love and appreciation for whatever you're getting, then ask for more based on that.

This format works even if your request is more about disengaging than engaging. You can still start with something like, "I really appreciate how understanding you were last weekend when I locked myself in my office to finish up that project. It made me feel you really understand me and support me in my goals. I would love to be able to take more time for myself without worrying about you taking that personally."

It's important to use lots of specific detail when you convey your disappointments and desires. You want to avoid saying things like, "Of course, you already know . . ." It weakens your words. You shouldn't presume your partner knows anything. Just state it truly and definitively, even if you feel you've said it before or they should know it already.

One of the most difficult things to do in relationship is to ask for more love or attention. Sometimes it feels embarrassing or even humiliating. No one likes to be in that position with a primary partner. Because we feel embarrassed for wanting more, there's sometimes an almost subconscious tendency to want to make the other person wrong, to shame them for "making" us feel that way. You need to stay conscious of that tendency because blaming and shaming your partner will do absolutely nothing to move you toward your goal of feeling more love and connection in your relationship. It will have the opposite effect. So instead of saying, "I've noticed you're not doing this," or "I'm not getting enough of that," tell them how important and cherished the "that" is for you, then watch how joyfully your invitation will be received.

＊ ＊ ＊

Do you see now how it is through the witnessing of our pain that healing takes place? When you dare to share your innermost self with your partner, you clear out the emotional debris that has been keeping you stuck in all areas of your life! Remember, most of our pain-body memories were created when we were too young to be able to differentiate ourselves from the emotional climate surrounding us—the doubts, shame, and confusion of others. We took it on as our own, and the burden of it was too great for us to practice, break down, or understand at the time. Our sense of worth became distorted through these stored, undigested experiences.

When these stored pockets of unworthiness are reactivated through our relationship, we revert to the emotional states we embodied at the time of the original wounding, momentarily becoming that disempowered, helpless version of ourselves. Our task is to begin recognizing when we've been triggered, and taking charge of our emotional state by choosing to remain grounded in our curiosity and willingness to explore what's possible in the present moment. Remember, since others were involved in the creation of our pain body, others are required for its healing. And daring to share is the most direct route to that healing!

Of course, there will be times when this practice will stir up anger in your partner, but as you will see in the next chapter, even anger, when it's authentic and channeled through the heart, can be a powerfully beneficial and positive force.

Need help applying this in your relationship?
Visit www.HeartIQRelationships.com for FREE demos
and tutorials using the access code myheartiq.

CHAPTER 9

The Juiciness of Anger and Irrationality

S o far we've talked about communicating our feelings from a place of awareness, consideration, and conscious delivery. But what about the times when you need to express unedited, unfiltered, and uncontained? This is healthy, too! Remember, if you want to increase your joy, you need to be open to feeling more of *everything*. In this chapter, let's explore how you and your partner can find a safe way to share your uncontained anger and irrationality in a way that actually opens both your hearts. However, to do this, you have to better understand your relationship to anger and the other forms of uncontained expression that you've previously made wrong.

Anger Is Vital to Emotional Health

Anger has both healthy and unhealthy expressions. It's one of those words, like love, that can mean vastly different things to different people. It all starts with our earliest associations. It used to be that whenever I heard the word "anger," I'd immediately envision my father's rage and what that meant for me as a child. I've had to learn to uncross those wires and form a new, healthier association to the concept of anger. For someone else, the word might stir up the discomfort of long-stored memories of passive-aggressive behavior—parents smiling sweetly while gritting their teeth and sending daggers with their eyes. To some, anger might mean the complete withdrawal of love and attention from someone of great importance to them.

But anger in its purest sense is a vital emotion to be able to access. In its heart-channeled form, it helps define your clear yes-or-no boundary that honors the essence of who you really are. It could come out fierce. It could be loud. It could even have an aggressive quality to it. But pure, healthy anger is not violent. It is not abusive, victimizing, or martyring—those are dysfunctional qualities of anger. It's also not rage because rage is out of control. Anger, when it comes through the heart, is an expression of your worth and value and the energy itself, although potentially volatile, can be tracked (in other words, you can stay present with it without getting hijacked). If you can't track your anger, you've lost the purity of it. You've become "the Hulk."

The inability to express healthy anger is widespread and debilitating. It often results in depression or frequent bouts of sadness. Sadness is the most common "cover" emotion for anger since it's more comfortable for many people to access. When they feel a boundary being violated, instead of saying no with directness and fierceness, if necessary, they respond with collapse or they look at all the spiritual reasons this person may have crossed the line, and they decide to be compassionate because they think it's better to love than to be angry. Internally, they block the anger from running and probably even feel proud of their self-control and ability to take the "high road."

But martyrdom is extremely unsexy—and unhealthy, too. As soon as someone who is used to playing the martyr feels a flash of natural, fiery anger, it's like the balloon gets popped. All the air rushes out and the anger gets replaced with a sense of diminishment and disappointment. The energy feels like: "Well, I'll just take it on." The unclaimed anger turns into self-justification and even self-righteousness. The inner dialogue goes: "I'll be the bigger one in this couple, I'll do it for you." The expressed emotion is resigned dissatisfaction, but it's just a cover emotion for beautiful, raw anger. I know this dynamic well, and I have to watch for it because I have a martyr-shadow that loves to get self-righteous. Because of what I do for a living, I have a strong fear of ever looking unspiritual or unevolved. I need to practice fiercely sharing my truth without worrying about looking like an asshole—looking like that unspiritual guy who just doesn't get it.

Because here's the problem with unexpressed anger: The anger doesn't stop running; it just runs in the background without your awareness. It eats you up. It decreases your vitality, impacts your physical health, and triggers a whole cascade of nasty side effects. We've been trained to believe that being angry is harmful, when in fact it's the blocking of anger that is harmful. Natural human emotions are only negative when we repress them. Yet, if we're completely uncontained in our anger to the point where we go into projection and "emotional vomit mode," it can be equally toxic. It's the conscious movement of the raw emotion of anger *through your heart* that makes it a healthy expression. It's learning to stay connected to your heart while staying in your full truth and your full power. And then a certain quality emerges. Instead of using anger to blame, it's just used to express what's real for us. There's a very big difference.

We practice this kind of heart-centered anger by using the tools in this book. Anger is part of an emotional range that includes frustration, impatience, creativity, sexuality, passion, and other juicy qualities. If you want to hone your anger skills, set up a regular time to practice uncontainment with your partner. Initially, make it about matters that are unrelated to the relationship—things that you see in the news that enrage you, problems at work, or even old family issues. The more you can practice going uncontained on unrelated matters, the easier healthy anger will come when you need to address something meaningful to your partnership. If you recognize that you both could use help in this area, take turns going back and forth with your uncontainment.

Many of my clients say to me, "I'm just not an angry person. Why does that have to be a problem?" And it's true that some people just naturally have a more calm, nonreactive temperament than others. There's a way to tell the difference between someone who is unhealthily blocking anger and someone whose anger naturally doesn't surface often. The difference is whether or not they *can* go there when needed. If the "non-angry" person can access fierce warrior power in a split second when the situation calls for it, then it's probably someone who's been there to such an extent they've been able to come into peaceful balance with it. They've explored it; they know the darkness intimately, and therefore, are no longer afraid of it. It has simply become a choice for them to not go there very often. The person who is repressing anger would be unable to *step into anger* with that kind of ease, fluidity, and, most important, joy.

Celebrate the Juiciness of Irrationality

Sometimes we're triggered by things that we know in our rational minds should not warrant our anger. If we feel that flash of anger anyway, we often make ourselves wrong about it and usually don't want to admit it. But when you and your partner have set up a practice of exploring the depths of your healthy anger together, you can make wonderful healing use of these moments. You tell your partner, "I know that my anger over this is unreasonable so I truly am not blaming you, but I do feel anger running nonetheless. I would like permission to get irrationally upset about it, with you holding me in my uncontained expression." Then express what you're holding while being thankful for the opportunity to do some emotional clearing!

When handled like this, your anger doesn't need to be justified in any way. It doesn't have to make sense. You and your partner can agree in advance that there are times when you need permission to see the unreasonableness of your trigger and just get full-on furious even when it doesn't "make sense." The more you can allow anger to run in such a way that it has permission to not make sense, the more you'll be able to come into balance with it.

We all have some things inside us we've never given voice to. Take advantage of this chance to give a richer voice to anything you've habitually contained—anything you've never dared be fully unfiltered and free with. It works best when you sandwich your uncontainment with tracking. So you track first, then go wild, then track what you're feeling in the aftermath of your expression.

You might set it up with your partner like this: "I've got so much moving right now; I need to give it voice. Would you hold space for me while I say what I need to, unfiltered, so I can let this energy out? I may project onto you unfairly, and I don't want you to take it personally. I have no idea how it's going to come out, but I want to be able to give full voice to what's there, and I apologize in advance if it lands really heavy because that's not my intention. Is that okay?"

You track that there's something moving for you, you ask for permission to express it, and your partner gets to choose whether to say yes or no. If it's a no, then you don't do it. But if your partner is willing to support you, you go for it. There's no tracking during the uncontained portion—just the purity of whatever wants to come out. You can blame, victimize, and/or project. Nothing is held back. There's no trying to sound right or be spiritual. It's just full explosion of your realness and truth. After you've done it, you're likely to feel lighter and infinitely better, then you give thanks to your partner for holding that container, and you track and share whatever's moving now in the emptiness of what you released.

As the receiving partner, you get to step into the task of loving the energy of your partner's expression rather than the content of what is being shared. You may hear a bunch of blame and "wrong-making" that you could take personally, but instead, you choose to appreciate the fire in your partner. This is critical, insightful, and life changing, offering you an opportunity to uncross important neurological wiring here. Love the passion and how your partner comes alive! Love the full-throttle expression of your partner's truth! It's so beautiful to see this fuller emotional range given voice!

Once you've offered that appreciation and acknowledgment, you can track your experience to go back and address the actual words. You might have heard some inaccuracies you're dying to clear up. You might be feeling battered by something your partner shared. This is the time to remember that you *invited* this kind of unfettered releasing. It's important to acknowledge prior to sharing that the content will likely be exaggerated and over the top, so you can stay present to receive the inner workings of your partner's stored energy, which is ultimately healing and intimacy-building for you both. You want your partner to know that you *can* hold this and that you're solidly here.

I've noticed a lot of women don't want to open fully because they don't know if their man can hold them. They're afraid to test the container. But once they do, and they see that they can be held there, it takes the relationship to a whole new level. So don't try to read your partner to see if you think they can hold it all. Just go for it and give them the chance to step up.

If you're the one holding space and you've been hurt by what was expressed, you can share that. Offer your reassurance first, and then say something like, "I want you to know that I'm holding some anger or hurt from what you've shared." Check in with yourself to be sure you're not running any kind of revenge energy ("You've hurt me so now it's my turn to hurt you.") If you're sure that's not the case, you can then ask for your partner to hold you while you now go uncontained! As long as it's invited by both of you in this way, the potential for deep, unresolvable triggering is minimal.

"Holding" means staying present and embodied when the energetic emotional fierceness is coming toward you from your partner. It's being big enough to stay out of defense for the moment. It's engaged eye contact. You're not trying to fix, hug, or touch the other. You're enjoying the practice to the best of your ability. You're not numb, shut down, or checked out. You may find that it's so intense, you feel yourself wanting to check out, but you just pull yourself back to the moment to the best of your ability. If you truly don't feel like you can hold the space, you'll want to honestly share that without shutting your partner down.

Try to always hold in your awareness that whatever is being expressed likely has very little to do with you. When emotions run this high, the cathartic, emotional release that takes place is usually more about clearing resentments from the past—from parents and prior relationships. Our triggers are so often based on projections from our childhoods and are primarily energies that were never cleared about our moms and dads. This practice clears away those old energies and allows us to enjoy cleaner, more unencumbered, and projection-free partnerships!

When you both fully understand the miraculous value of this practice, you can even get playful with it. Your invitation might start to sound more like this: "I feel ashamed that I'm judging you, but this is what I'm holding right now. I'd like to share my inner dialogue around it so you know what goes on inside me, given that I'm acknowledging I can see that this judgment isn't fair to put on you. I'd really love to move the energy of my judgments so I can see the pain-body trigger that's running them. So, can I show you the judgmental 'crazy bitch' that I hold inside me sometimes?"

As the one being asked to hold space, you accept that invitation because you know that this uncontained projection is really not meant for you! You're just there to fill the role. That's why you don't take anything personally as the receiver. You may hear it as personal; they may even make it personal to what you've been doing recently. However, the original wound and trauma really has nothing to do with you. If you start to confuse who you are with the projections your partner holds around one of their parents, it can be a dangerous undertaking. But if you can separate their wounding from who you are, you're going to be in a much healthier place in your relationship.

Another option to consider for your uncontainment practice is to try it nonverbally. Sometimes when we're deeply triggered we can't think of how to articulate the words, or we notice that trying to put words to our feelings is taking us too much into our head and away from our emotions. If you sense that happening, try going uncontained simply with sound. Take all of that churning, anxiety, fear, or whatever is unexpressed in you, and just scream it out, with your partner holding space. It might come up as a "Noooooo!" or maybe just as a howl of some sort. This can be exceptionally cathartic! Hold nothing back. It can involve some physicalized expression if that feels right in the moment. For example, try standing up and moving your body freely to complement your sounds and your voice. Just don't let the physical movement be a replacement for the sound; the sound is necessary to move the energies up and out. Be sure that your nonverbal expressions are directed toward your partner so that you can experience yourself being witnessed and received in the expression of your truth.

If you're the one holding space for your partner's uncontained sharing, be very generous with your supportive spontaneous response and reassurance. This is vulnerable stuff, so really be clear in sending the message: "I love when you're on fire like this, sharing your raw truth. More of this, please!" Going to these tender places together is what allows your relationship to maintain delicious, juicy magnetism and polarity.

EXPANDING YOUR EMOTIONAL RANGE WHILE BEING WITNESSED

For your intimacy to deepen without barriers or limitation, the boundaries of safety within your intimate relationship container must be tested. One of the best ways to do this is to work with a certified Heart IQ Relationship Coach to practice stretching the range of what can be held within your connection. Working with a relationship coach is not just about resolving problems; it's also about exposing your inner battles by expressing your pain-body triggers while being witnessed. A coach can guide you to learn new ways of feeling and processing undigested pain, and if needed, teach you how to fight together in a healthy way.

Preparing for the "Sharing Uncontained Truth Practice"

Another way to stretch the boundaries of safety within the container of your relationship is to try the following practice for sharing your uncontained truth. It provides an excellent opportunity to practice giving an authentic voice to the emotional energy that's being held by each of you *and* a chance to practice holding the upset and hurt with reassuring presence.

It's important to note that pain-body triggers are likely to occur during this practice. There is the risk that the interaction may ignite familiar battles. However, doing this practice together is also a chance to go through the practice of healing the pain-body response by learning how to hold, track, acknowledge, and reassure.

This practice need not be reserved exclusively for your primary couple relationship. It can be used for sharing about any relationship either of you is in. For example, you may find it therapeutic to share your truth about a relationship in which you've been hurt by a friend, sibling, parent, or past partner, so you can be witnessed in the expression of your full truth with compassion and acceptance.

This practice can include anything you've been holding on to in relationship to the other for fear of hurting your partner or being rejected. It can even work when you're afraid that what you've shared might be too much for the relationship to recover from and might potentially bring about its end.

Here are the things you'll need to understand before you start:

For Partner A

Partner A will dare to share what they want to express to their partner *without* having to filter or package it, take full responsibility for it, deliver it heart-intelligently, or monitor how it lands. The point of this practice is to give you permission to vent, blame, judge, yell, scream, and cry. You can be bitchy, judgmental, irrational, and inconsiderate of the other's feeling because your partner has agreed to hold you in whatever kind of expression emerges.

This expression can be done sitting or standing, using gestures, and moving the body in whatever way is needed to embody the truth of your experience with words, sounds, and movement.

Movement can be used to complement the words and sounds being expressed, but does not replace the words and sounds. You don't want to remain silent while using movement to express your truth. The practice of uncontainment requires sound.

Partner A is practicing how to express the *full range* of their truth, whether this means anger, sadness, grief, hostility, blame, victimization, hopelessness, doubt, etc. It's only in the vulnerability of your full range that your partner can experience a larger part of themselves being called upon to show up for you.

For Partner B

Partner B is practicing how to "hold" and does not need to fix or change what's being shared. What does it mean to hold? First of all, it *doesn't* mean to check out or go numb, although that is often a natural tendency. If it does happen, track yourself to the best of your ability, pause the practice once you notice you are checked out, and tune in to what you need in order to come back to being present. "Holding" is the quality of staying present and embodied when the emotional-energetic fierceness of your partner's expression is coming to you, and *to the best of your ability*, not taking it personally.

"Not taking it personally" means not becoming defensive or tracking the part that gets triggered, but staying present and embodied while noticing the defensive part of you. "Staying present and embodied" means showing engagement through your eye contact, not trying to sooth your partner through touching or hugging, being in a neutral and relaxed body posture, enjoying the energy of your partner's sharing, and being tuned in to yourself and your partner.

Partner B will never know how good they are at holding unless Partner A takes the risk to open. Partner A has to test the intimacy container of the relationship by opening so that Partner B can discover their holding capacity and practice strengthening this muscle as part of a present-moment meeting of needs. Certainty is called forth when uncertainty is revealed, so Partner A needs to give it their all as they express their truth in order to create the vacuum that calls forth Partner B's capacity to hold what needs to be held. Holding can be learned and honed with practice; however, the full range of emotional energy needs to be encountered to improve this skill.

SHARING YOUR UNCONTAINED TRUTH PRACTICE

STEP 1

Partner A tracks what's moving about their need to share.

- For example: "I've got so much moving right now, I don't know how to share it with you in a way that's all nice and neat without losing my authenticity. I really want you to hear my heart's truth about what's moving in me, so I don't want to manage how it comes out. I can definitely track that I have some blame running and some judgments that I need to share with you. I know they're mine, but they're wrapped up in a projection about you, so I'd like your permission to just say it how it is for now, knowing that if this part of my experience can be met with acceptance, by me and by you, then it will likely move in some way that won't be so sticky between us. Do you feel like you can listen and hold while I just let it all come out, and then we can deal with any part of it that may land heavy for you afterward?"

Partner A prepares Partner B for what's coming: For this to have a chance at being a successful exchange, you must not railroad your partner and offer your uncontained truth without warning or agreement. If permission is asked, but there's no agreement, then you do not share at that time. You practice your own holding ability to contain or manage your expression until a time where there's more safety and receptivity, whether it's with your partner or with someone you and your partner trust.

- For example: "If you're unwilling to hear me now, can we make time for me to share this sometime soon?" Or, "If you're unwilling to receive me, I'd like to share what I'm feeling with [third party] so that I can move my energy and see what opens up in me once I'm not needing to hold this anymore."

Partner A asks if Partner B is willing to hold while they share. If the answer is yes, continue to Step 2.

IMPORTANT: Often, Partner B won't know if they can actually hold their partner because they don't yet know what's coming, or they may know, but they're holding a memory of an unsafe version of the uncontained expression from Partner A.

When facing the uncertainty of not knowing if you really will be able to hold for your partner, it's important to say yes to the practice of holding, but with an honest disclaimer. You will only know if you can hold, and get better at your holding capacity, by practicing.

- For example: Partner A asks, "Do you feel like you can hold while I just let it all come out?" Partner B might respond, "I honestly don't know if I can hold you. I know I feel scared about what may be coming at me, and I can track that I'm afraid to let you down, but I also feel how much I want to try. I'm never going to learn how to hold you if I don't just jump in and practice. So can you be okay to know that I'm practicing, and I'll be doing my best to hold you, even if I lose track of myself from time to time?"

STEP 2

Partner A shares their truth, with no story, justification, or tracking.

- Just communicate the plain and simple expression of your emotional truth, with as much authentic emotion as it warrants. There is no need to say, "I feel this way *because* . . ." Just express yourself fully without trying to justify your reasons.

Partner B holds the space.

- While Partner A is sharing, you have the opportunity to practice loving their energy rather than focusing on your partner's words. Too often, we let the words that get said or don't get said be what we focus on and how this can match a past memory of feeling unrecognized, misunderstood, or wrongly accused. In this exercise, Partner A is *daring* to share their truth, which requires immense courage, strength, determination, passion, and fierce love and dedication in listening to and following the integrity of one's own heart. It is this fierce love that needs celebrating. With practice in both expressing and holding this energy, the effect will shift from draining to enlivening, and become a source that can inject new aliveness into the intimate connection.

- As you practice holding, hold your attention on the energy of the sharing. Even though you may hear blame and projection, do you enjoy feeling your partner come alive and daringly reveal their authentic heart's truth?

STEP 3

Partner A tracks where they are *after* sharing their truth, which includes *acknowledging* and *appreciating* Partner B for holding them.

- For example: "Wow, it feels really good to let that go! I had no idea how much energy I was using to hold that in. Thank you so much for listening to me and feeling me in my upset. Even though I could tell that some of that was hard to receive, I could feel you staying with me. I really needed to feel that, so thank you."

Partner B offers reassurance. Meet your partner here first, before you begin to track yourself and speak to anything that was shared with you.

- For example: "I hear you loud and clear! That felt really good to feel you so alive and passionate and focused! I did feel challenged by some of the things you shared, but I really want you to know that I want to hear your raw truth more often. Your fire lights me up and helps me to understand you, and I want our space to be cleared out like this more often so stuff doesn't come between us."

STEP 4

Partner B tracks their response if hurt arises in response to Partner A's sharing. This part can be tracked as a disappointment or need, or can be shared as Partner B's uncontained truth in response. In this case, Partner B takes on the role of Partner A, and the steps are again followed.

Need help applying this in your relationship?
Visit www.HeartIQRelationships.com for FREE demos
and tutorials using the access code myheartiq.

CHAPTER 10

Putting It All Together with a Daily Practice

The first nine chapters of this book have likely been a lot for you to digest. If you've been trying these practices with your partner and have been checking out some of the videos on www .HeartIQRelationships.com to see these processes in action, you've undoubtedly gained some key insights into how to deepen the intimacy of your relationship and begin to heal some of your past wounding with your partner's support. In this chapter, I'll offer further insight to incorporate Heart IQ into your relationship.

The 3 Stages of Intimate Relationship Connection

You may find that some of the processes you've learned are more appropriate at different stages of your connection with your partner. Although you'll want to feel into which process is best for you at each juncture and trust your instincts on that, I'll briefly describe some stages I often encounter with my clients. You can see if you spot any similarities in your own relationship or its progression.

Stage 1: Recover

Stage 1 is the recovery stage. At this stage, you both need to regain the connection you've lost with yourselves and your own stability. It feels like, "Once I'm stable in my ability to feel me again, and you're stable in your ability to feel you again, then we can begin to recover our connection with each other." The key distortion that needs to be cleared at this stage is the idea that you are causing each other's pain. The truth is that you are necessary to each other's healing; you are each there to reactivate the other's pain so that this pain can be seen, heard, felt, witnessed, and digested *in relationship with each other*. Given that this pain was originally activated in an unsafe relationship with another in the past, it must be *reactivated* in a safe relationship with another in the present. The energy of this pain must be active for it to reengage its mission of delivering the insights and wisdom it was always meant to bring.

Stage 1 is about having the resolve to stay "in" so that you can remain present to your pain without running away or trying to hide, fix, rescue, or blame. The first step to "staying in" is regaining stability in your individual self-connection. Without this stability being intact, your efforts to focus attention on your relationship will always run the risk of retriggering the pain-body response that's trying to heal in the potential safety of your connection. The safety of your connection is fed from the stable intimacy of your self-connection, so this is where you must begin. Otherwise, your connection will be at risk for becoming a drain to you both.

Stage 2: Reconnect

The second stage is needed when you're ready to repair your intimate connection after having lost touch with the joy of your own awareness. The connection may have been rerouted through your pain temporarily or for a lengthy period. It's important to discern if the length of your disconnection from yourselves, and therefore with each other, has been acute or chronic. Your job is to begin to feel each other again. This stage is about reestablishing a heart connection and gentleness with your renewed intimacy until a tangible, embodied sense of safety and trust is reestablished. The core value to embody in this stage is reassurance.

The key distortion that needs to be cleared in this stage is the idea that your connection requires hard work. In this stage, it's likely that a pain-body trigger has occurred in the relationship's history, but it was never resolved and yet you've found a way to move around the uncertainty and normalize your drop in polarity and impassioned engagement with each other.

You may have channeled your unacknowledged heat into either a more overt expression of constant arguing, bickering, and blaming or a more passive expression of taking shots at each other, which may present as playful but are delivered with an undercurrent of anger and dismissal. Even though your pain-body response is not presently active, your connection has suffered and has likely gone flat as a result. You may be getting by as a couple, but only with a lot of hard work. It's even possible that you can maintain the goodness of your connection for periods of time, but then repeatedly move back into pain (stage 1), even though years may go by between "episodes."

Stage 2 is about building your skills at reassurance. Your connection is trapped in a power struggle because neither of you feels felt by the other. Uncertainty has taken over and muted your intimacy. *Expressing vulnerability* and *receiving compassion* is the healing combination that's needed in this stage in order for reconnection to feel safe. It's a medicinal blend that has the power to regenerate your depleted connection. When vulnerability is expressed, compassion is called forth, and when compassion is present to hold what's shared, vulnerability is easier to access. When the unacknowledged uncertainty is met with a genuine, heartfelt expression of reassurance, the breakdown of intimacy can repair, and it becomes safe again for your hearts to reconnect.

Some particularly effective practices at this stage are the Acknowledgment Practice and Sharing Your Disappointments Practice.

Stage 3: Rediscover

Stage 3 is all about reigniting passion through responsiveness. It's when you're ready to expand the potential of your intimate connection and your expression of joy by using your relationship intimacy as fuel to explore the expanse of *divine intimate union,* where deep and sustainable joy becomes activated and accessible through the

intimate relationship. This stage is about helping you to rediscover the unlimited potential of your intimacy by reorganizing your
vision of what's possible and reigniting your passion for realizing
this vision together. The key to this stage is responsiveness.

The distortion that needs to be cleared in this stage is the idea
that there's a limit to the joy and goodness you deserve. This is
the stage when core unworthiness can be healed because there's
finally enough safety, compassion, tenderness, genuine dedication,
and fierce love present to hold this deeper pain with certainty of
its core goodness. In this stage, all levels of your connection—
including your disconnection—can be used to accelerate healing, expand spiritually, awaken sexually, transmute trauma, and
embody boundless joy.

Stage 3 is about increasing responsiveness skills. The quality
of your intimate connection in this stage is held back only by
degrees of embodiment. As your degree of embodiment increases,
so does your intimacy, and that's accomplished through amplifying
your responsiveness. There are an unlimited number of emotional-
energetic ranges that each partner can physically embody as a
means to awaken new ranges of shared intimacy. And the potential
doesn't stop there! As you dare to become more vulnerable *and*
fierce in your expression of love, your intimate connection will
create a bridge for the expression of Divine Embodiment. This is
the process of integrating your highest spiritual essence with your
humanity. In this way, your intimate relationship connection acts
as a constant source of nourishment that gives each of you exactly
what you need to live out your deepest truth in a grounded, practical, measurable way that ignites transformation in all those who
are ready to receive it. This is the kind of relationship modeling
that can change the legacy of a generation.

Creating a Relationship "Check-Up" Routine

The exercises in this book are meant to break down the complexity
of intimate communication. They are designed to make it easy to

learn the skills to speak from the heart. However, the practices I've shared with you do not have a specific "order" and it will not work to be militant about the rules of what comes first and how you use them. An organic, natural approach to integrating this heart-centered approach into your life is best. That said, in order to have the freedom to flow, we need a container to safely explore these practices. Therefore, the first step is to make agreements with your partner as outlined in Chapter 5.

Next, I recommend you set a "check-up" routine that includes a daily practice, a weekly check-in, a monthly clearing, and a yearly detox. Each component of this routine is critical for relationship health. We seem to think that relationships should just "work" and continue to work without care and attention, but that is wishful thinking. Relationships require presence, awareness, attention, and consistent effort. If we neglect them, we will need to spend more energy repairing the damage than it takes to maintain it. So the choice is yours. Commit to a regular practice of connection and clearing, or risk waiting for something to break, perhaps irreparably.

Each practice session, check in, or clearing requires you to create a safe container. Your agreements lay the groundwork for this, but each time you spend conscious time together, you need to "open" the space and "close" it. A wonderful method for doing this was introduced to me by one of my mentors, Tej Steiner, the author of *Heart Circles, How Sitting in Circle Can Transform Your World.* I'll share it with you now:

It begins with a tune in. Take your partner's hands while you both close your eyes and just drop into yourself and see how you feel. Take notice of your breathing and feel yourself inhaling and exhaling. If it's hard to notice your breathing, let your face relax by dropping your jaw a bit so it's easier to exhale from your mouth.

Continue breathing in through your nose and out through your mouth. Notice how the air feels moving into your body and then flowing out. Notice where your physical body is in space—feel your feet on the ground, your bottom or back touching the chair or wall, and your head sitting on top of your shoulders. Notice the space you occupy, as if you have a bubble of space around you. See if your body wants to stretch or adjust its position so you can keep settling and relaxing into your bubble. Continue breathing into the space inside your body and the space inside your bubble, and let yourself be in your own space for a few moments of silence and stillness.

Whichever partner is ready to open their eyes first squeezes the other partner's hand. It can be as short as 30 seconds or so or longer if you'd like. When your eyes are open, notice what feels different in this moment of now.

Next, you'll share with your partner by briefly stating what's moving with you in the present moment. This is like a mini version of the relationship tracking exercise. This short status update is like a thermometer, a temperature read, to let your partner know where you stand. It could be as simple as, "I feel energetic. I'm well rested. I'm eager to tackle the day. I'm in." Or it could be, "I just want to let you know I feel very tender today. I didn't sleep well and I have a lot of emotion stirring in me right now, so it feels like just about anything could make me cry. And with that, I'm in." It's not about going into the reasons for feeling tender or any kind of long explanations or assumptions about why you feel the way you do. It's just a quick reporting of your status. Notice the way you end your sharing by saying the words "I'm in." This allows your partner to know when it's time to say thank you and begin with their own brief update.

When you hear your partner's sharing, it's not your job to investigate it or try to fix it. You simply say, "Thank you," and then share your own experience of your present state. It's a matter-of-fact exchange. No rambling or digging around in it. That's it! That's how you open the space.

Once complete with your practice, check in, or clearing, you need to close. You do that by simply holding hands again and saying whether you feel complete or incomplete with what has happened and one thing you are grateful for. This is not a statement of whether you feel complete or incomplete with your life, your relationship, or even your process. It's whether you feel connected and open in spite of everything that might have moved.

If you do feel present and connected, just say so by saying, "I feel complete, and I'm grateful for XYZ, and with that I'm out." Notice the words "I'm out" to let your partner know that they can now start their own completion. If, however, you feel *incomplete*, it will simply sound like this, "I feel incomplete, and what I'm grateful for is XYZ, and with that I'm out." Notice that you don't give a reason for your incompleteness, nor does your partner try to figure out why you feel that way. Just by naming your incompleteness it will complete you.

Now that you've taken the time to make your sacred agreements and you know how to open and close a time of conscious sharing, let's go deeper into the routine of your daily, weekly, and monthly practice.

Your Daily Practice

Most couples do not have the same schedules. You might get up and go to bed at different times. If possible, find a time when you can both be available. I recommend the evening, before you both retire to sleep. Here's a great example of a daily practice that takes 10–15 minutes:

1. Open the space by tuning in and sharing what's moving for you both (2–3 minutes max).

2. Share something you are holding on to (a resentment or a "withhold") and then switch. This does not need to be connected to your relationship (although it definitely could be). For example, "I'm holding resentment toward my boss because he promoted Frank, when I thought it should have been me." An example of a withhold could be, "Although I've been acting as if everything is okay with your family coming to stay, I'm actually holding a judgment about them and I've been secretly dreading it. I've realized that I have withheld how I truly feel about it because I didn't want to hurt your feelings."

3. Share an acknowledgment of your partner, then switch. An acknowledgment of your partner may sound like, "I acknowledge that you've been stressed and working really hard recently and that it's been difficult to juggle everything in our crazy life. I acknowledge your capacity to hold it all together while remaining so loving."

4. Share an acknowledgment of yourself, then switch. An acknowledgment of yourself may sound like, "I want to acknowledge that in spite of having a cold, I produced some great content today for my blog."

5. Close the space by having you and your partner share whether you feel complete or incomplete and one thing you feel grateful for (in relationship to each other or the life you share).

By taking these 5 simple steps each day, you will be building a strong container for you to express your love and truth with each other. Sometimes it's easier to see this in action rather than reading about it. I've included a video demo and tutorial on www .HeartIQRelationships.com if you want to learn more. Remember, simply put in myheartiq as your access code for the home-study companion course to this book.

Your Weekly Check-In

In addition to your daily practice, each week, set up a time for 30–60 minutes to check in with each other. I recommend the weekends during a time when both of you are free from distractions. Also, make sure you don't do your weekly check-in under the influence of alcohol or drugs. The weekly check-in includes four components: 1) Tune in, 2) Check-in, 3) Relationship Tracking/ Dare to Share/Responsiveness Practice, and 4) Closure.

First, open the space by tuning in and sharing what's moving for you both. Second, take turns checking in. This is a powerful time for expressing and receiving what you need—asking for attention from your partner, receiving it, letting it in, and then expressing your truth while being witnessed and received by your beloved. You may discover that you open when receiving the focused, loving attention of your partner, even at times when you first feel closed. You also might discover that you feel like closing at times when resistance and judgments come to the surface. No matter what comes up, it's a chance to practice using the muscles that connect you with each other. Just like our physical muscles need to be worked out to become strong and flexible, we have to flex our emotional-energetic muscles of receiving and expressing ourselves authentically to keep fit. It's part of developing and maintaining our overall health and wellness.

Checking in is a tracking practice in which you express aloud what's real for you in the present moment in relationship to where you are and what you want. Often, you'll find that your judgments, resistance, and closure will lessen just by giving voice to these parts of your experience. It's so important to feel the reminder of how these seemingly dense and unchangeable states can shift just by acknowledging them—that we can return to being in the flow of life by having others witness us in these states while recognizing them in ourselves. This is so contrary to what most of us have learned, and it's hugely relieving and relaxing to experience the opposite being true!

With that in mind, here are some new rules to live by:

➤ When you're real with what's moving for you, you give yourself choice around how you want to be in relationship to your experience.

➤ When you communicate what's true for you to another, you're practicing opening and sharing your heart.

➤ Taking in another's loving attention and receiving their spontaneous response to what you share allows you to feel seen, heard, and felt, which brings about relaxation on every level— emotional, energetic, mental, and physical.

➤ Being seen, heard, and felt is essential for your healing and growth as a human being.

Checking in with your partner is one of the simplest ways to increase intimacy and connection. Here are the steps:

1. State what you want and ask for the attention. "I would like to check in. May I have your attention, please?"

2. Take in your partner's attention without rushing. Do this silently. See if you can relax into the moment without bubble bursting or defending with your S.T.U.A.R.T. strategies.

3. Share what you're feeling and what you want or need right now to be more present (more "in").

4. Finish with "With that, I'm in," or "Thank you, I feel 'in' now."

5. The other partner, the receiver, shares their spontaneous response to what's been shared.

6. The second partner now begins with Step 1 and checks in.

As you take these steps, notice how it feels to connect to your partner in this way. When we give each other our focused attention, it creates a natural amplification for us to tune in to what's moving in real time. The practice of tracking in an amplified field gives us a chance to feel what it's like to have the volume turned up on our senses so that we can see, hear, feel, and notice things moving in us that might be too hard to recognize in daily life. Then we get the chance to express what's happening within us live in the moment to another and feel them receiving us as we are—we don't have to perform and be a specific way to be received. Checking in is an invitation to "come as you are" and dare to have your goodness seen, heard, and felt by others—so you can know what it's like to be authentically received!

After you have both checked in (10 minutes max), it's time to practice sharing yourself with your partner and vice versa. You do this by simply doing the relationship tracking practice described in Chapter 6 while combining it with the Dare to Share Practice in Chapter 8. You can also add the Responsiveness Practice here as well, which can be a great way to end your sharing. Combining these three core practices forms the bulk of your time together, and if you are doing it correctly, it will feel extremely joyful, nourishing, and connecting!

When you both feel "full," simply close using the closing instructions shared earlier.

Monthly Clearing

Monthly clearing is an essential part of your relationship routine. Plan ahead and put time in the calendar each month to sit and have a clearing. A clearing is an opportunity to reset your intimacy, clear out any disappointments, and share any unmet needs. The longer we sit on resentments, the bigger they become and the harder they are to clear in the future. If you keep on top of your miscommunications and stay present to communicating your "stuff" early on, you'll avoid 99 percent of all intimacy issues and will prevent relationship breakdown. I know that pain sells better than prevention, which is why so many of us don't take action on a preventative strategy until we're hurting. Please, do what it takes to keep things good between you before your intimacy decays to a point where emergency intervention is required.

Your monthly clearing session should be scheduled open-ended. That is, don't do it just before bed or just before an important meeting or appointment where you'll need to pause or cut off your conversation prematurely. Leave approximately one to two hours for this time, but be aware that it can also be longer or shorter. The clearing practice is built on a similar structure to the other practices. You'll first tune in, then check in and share, wrapping up with closure.

During the main sharing part of the clearing practice, you'll warm up with the Acknowledgment Practice, followed with the Sharing Disappointments/Unmet Needs, and Sharing Your Uncontained Truth Practices. I recommend you begin with the Acknowledgment Practice on page 154; its easy-to-follow structure will open your hearts to each other, creating a safe space for deeper conversation to follow. If you choose to start with this practice, it's really important to follow the steps in this process without derailing. If we don't make sure to diligently follow the structure of this process, we can easily veer off and trigger our pain bodies. The steps outlined for this practice will keep you in the energetic space of acknowledgment.

To make your acknowledgment statements land better, you'll want to be sure to keep them brief, yet specific. When you state what you want to bring instead, make sure it's connected to the acknowledgment you shared. And always be reassuring about your commitment to the relationship. If something lands well for you, be sure to thank your partner for sharing it. It feels wonderful to the sharing partner to be met in this way, and it helps them to go further. You'll know the acknowledgment practice is working when you both feel lighter and better from this experience.

Once you have both gone through two or three rounds of the Acknowledgment Practice, begin sharing whatever disappointments and unmet needs you're running, using the steps outlined on page 180. We all have needs that we'd like met by our partners, but for most of us, those needs can be categorized as primary or secondary needs. Naturally, having our primary needs go unmet will affect our relationship more profoundly than having our secondary needs unmet. When a primary need (like the need for touch) isn't being met, it can make you feel unloved and undesirable. You start to feel bugged by little things like the way your partner leaves the toothpaste tube or neglects household chores. Attention to these little things is often heralded as a miraculous relationship-saver, but I don't subscribe to that theory.

It's my position that you would never be bothered by such trivial things if not for the fact that one (or more) of your primary needs is not being met. You need to ask yourself, "What's actually not happening here, at a deep, deep level?" Most people argue about the trivial nonsense because it's safer and easier to spot than the actual core issue. If you were able to discern and actually communicate the core issue, your partner would most likely say "thank you," and look for a way to meet it. When you don't share your core disappointments, year after year, they can become a heavy weight of locked tension in your body.

Combining the processes of Sharing Disappointments and Uncontained Truth can often help you get to the underlying issues in such cases. You want to be as straightforward as possible. It might sound like this: "I want to express to you a disappointment I'm having in our relationship. I really need to be touched and physically nourished, and I've realized it's a core need for me that hasn't been met in our partnership. It's been going on for so many years now, and I take responsibility for leaving it unspoken. I haven't shared it clearly with you so I don't intend to blame you here or make you wrong. I just really feel this huge well of tension, energy, and anger around this issue right now, and I don't want it to get projected onto you in passive-aggressive, resentful ways. So I want to give voice to it now, and it might actually come out as though I'm blaming you and making you wrong, but I want you to understand that's not my intention. I just need to move this energy. Can you hold me in that without taking it personally?"

Once you've gotten the buy-in, you thank your partner, and then you go uncontained. You use words, sound, energy, and/or breath—whatever it takes to let it all out—and then you sigh and say, "Thank you. That feels so much lighter." Your partner reassures you that it was all okay and even welcomes the information.

If you're the receiving partner, you let the uncontained partner know that you appreciate them giving voice to that. And then if there's pain running in you, you get to track that and share that back. That's how the Sharing Disappointments process can blend beautifully with the Uncontained Truth process. Nearly all disappointments need an uncontained truth component when shared authentically. But pain needs direction, even when it's uncontained. Don't fall victim to the tendency to go within yourself and bypass the opportunity to direct your pain onto your partner. When you're uncontained you want to use the word "you." It's not the time to say, "I'm feeling anger moving in me right now."

It's also important to remember that we have different parts. Sometimes we go the heady route of saying, "I don't want to put this on my partner because I know I played my part, too, and I know he was just doing the best he could do, coming from his own experiences," etc. Certainly there is a place in your relationship for that kind of compassion, but if another part of you has been holding a lot of anger over a wound that your partner has been inflicting, it's okay to recognize and give that part of you a voice by asking your partner to hold you in an uncontained expression of that part, directed *specifically* at them (even if a part of you knows you are projecting from the past). As long as you both recognize that both of those parts exist within you, it won't be too threatening for your partner to hold and receive you in that.

It might sound like this: "I'm tracking a part of me that's feeling so much guilt over expressing this to you because I know I play a big part in this disappointment. Yet the part that's holding all this tension and pain is still here, and I want to be able to bring it to the front and give it full authority to take over, so that I can discharge this tension. I want you to know it's not all of me—just a part. Are you willing to receive this part?"

Now a very different experience can be had. People can hold anything if they're very clear about what they're holding. It's the surprise ambush that causes deterioration of the relationship, not the well-tracked exchanges of genuine emotion. This is an example of tracking the relationship to the content. The content is a "part," and your awareness of how it could be received is the secondary component.

Remember, you'll need all the skills developed from practicing your relationship tracking to be successful. Track your judgments about what you're sharing, as you're sharing it. Even if you feel tension or discomfort, or the words aren't coming out the way you want them to, share that as you track it. It speaks to the unspoken and helps to relieve the tension that the unspoken creates in the space. It's okay to say things like: "I feel like I'm blocked, I feel like I can't do this, and I'm afraid you're going to judge me for that and think I don't want to be close to you, but that's not true." Tracking these feelings out loud will often turn any frustration your partner was feeling into compassion for you instead.

Responsiveness should always be a part of this process as well. Be generous with your brief verbal and nonverbal encouragements, love, and compliments. When you are ready to close, look into each other's eyes and simply state, "I feel complete," or "I feel incomplete." Then each of you will share one thing that you are grateful for, and the session is closed.

Yearly Maintenance

To make sure your relationship gets the attention and care it needs, I highly recommend attending at least one Insights to Intimacy LIVE seminar per year as a couple. As valuable as the practices in this book are, there is no way to describe how much more you and your partner can accomplish in the energy of a safe amplified field. It's one thing to read about these practices and another to actually get trained in doing them well, under the expert guidance of someone who knows all the ways the process can derail.

Need help applying this in your relationship?
Visit www.HeartIQRelationships.com for FREE demos
and tutorials using the access code myheartiq.

When It's Time to
Say Goodbye

Are you staying too long or leaving too quickly? As a general rule, men tend to leave too soon and women tend to leave too late. That's not always the case, of course, but it's definitely a pattern I've observed. When we stay too long, it's usually the fearful part of us that's blocking us from the clarity that the relationship is no longer serving us and needs to be closed. Making that decision can trigger our deepest, most painfully held traumas.

When you fall in love with someone, it's like all these spaghetti strands connect your two hearts, and there are plenty of them. The strands represent every aspect of your love and desire to be together and to fight for the relationship. But they're fragile. Every single barbed comment from your partner that doesn't land with you, every insult, every dismissive tone, action, or facial expression cuts one of the spaghetti strands. At first, it's okay because there are so many of them. We feel like we can spare a few and still carry on. We might even be able to build some back with goodwill gestures that balance out those jars to our emotional well-being. But if the jars continue in excess, or over a long enough period of time, the day will come when there is just one strand left. Once that final strand is cut, there is no going back.

When the couple remains together after this point, it's only out of guilt, desperation, or fear of being alone. The heart-centered connection is gone.

Closing a Relationship Using Heart IQ

Before closure is even possible, you have to confront the fear of leaving. This is critical. There is often confusion over whether or not to stick with it because we can never know for certain what the future will bring, no matter which path we choose. Our fear around making that choice keeps our commitment to the relationship in an ambiguous state. Our ambiguity keeps us in the procrastination cycle. It can even start to feel comfortable there.

You need to acknowledge and confront the fear of leaving by having an honest dialogue with your partner. It might sound like this: "This isn't working. Here is what would need to change in order for it to start working for me. This is what I would need to happen differently. I want to commit fully to making it work with you. I'm willing to commit for this period of time, and then if it is not working when that time is up, I will leave."

Don't make the mistake of waiting for the moment when you're both in agreement that it's time to separate. It's a common pitfall, and it gives far too much power to the other partner. If you are the one who has recognized that your needs are not being met, then you need to be the one to clearly say, "Change, or I am leaving." It's a very powerful statement, and many people avoid saying it because they believe it's wrong to give an ultimatum. I believe it's wrong to stay in a relationship that no longer serves you once you've tried everything to make it better. This requires honesty around both what isn't working and what is required to make it work. It's about honoring the relationship enough to give it a fair chance to turn around.

You'll have to decide how long to give it, and you may not easily come to a consensus on that. If one of you suggests a month and the other would like to give it six months, you might feel like you need to split the difference and agree to a three-month period. But it really comes down to the honest desire of the partner who is suggesting the shorter time frame. It only works if both of you are completely dedicated to giving it your best for this amount of time, so guilting your partner into extending the time frame won't ultimately serve either of you. That said, if you are the partner who wants longer, fight for it. Make your partner feel how important it is to you, and you may very well inspire the other to authentically share your vision.

However long you decide to stay "all in," this is your chance to find out once and for all if the partnership is salvageable. During this period, you're committed to riding the waves of the ups and downs without weighing things on a daily basis to see where they stand. You've declared that you're all in, so let that be your dominant intention. But keep in mind that it's more about *you* than it is about your partner. All that's expected is that you be full of presence or love. Ironically, you'll want to maintain a healthy detachment from needing anything from the other. You want to be focused solely on what *you* bring, what *you* can give, without placing any demands on your partner. Imagine how effective it is when both partners do this!

If you try to persuade, impress, or manipulate in any way, you've lost. The journey is not really about the other; it's about you coming into your joy, your self-love, your self-confidence. It's about you shining for your beloved. It's not about trying to get the relationship to work; it's not about fixing the problems. It's just about being the most amazing human being you can be in the presence of the other. It's you dropping into you, if you dare. It's not about your heart reaching out; it's about your heart reaching back *in*—knowing that you're enough, that giving all of you to the other is always enough. That's what your partner longs for: for you to be happy and full of presence and full of you doing what you want to do with your life with all your joy and all your fullness. Remind your partner of this if you feel it's become too much about salvaging the relationship.

In Search of Conscious Uncoupling

After the declared period of time, if the partnership is still causing you more pain than joy, you'll know you need to move on. Please stay clear about the fact that it's you making this choice. Often our guilt leads us to take the approach of pretending we're doing our partner a favor. It can sound like: "I really think it would be best for you if I leave," or "You deserve someone who can love you better than me." Don't do it. It's a cop-out. It's not honest. If you are the one ending the relationship, you do need to be kind, but also straightforward. You need to do it from a soft place, but still from a place of power, not in a place of collapse.

It might sound like: "Even if I love you, this isn't working. We've done our best to make it work, but I'm still not in a place where my needs are being met and I've come to clarity that this relationship isn't serving me and I need it to end in its current form. There may be a possibility that a friendship can be born out of this, but not immediately." Do not promise your partner that the two of you will be friends. It doesn't serve either of you. I've successfully befriended most of my exes but only after having a clean break where we both had the space we needed to heal and grow. It doesn't work to go directly from romantic relationship to friendship. One of you may be fine with it, but the other one will likely stay stuck, unable to go on with their life. Before you can consider friendship with an ex, you need a clear break with no phone calls, texting, or emails—no communication of any kind.

In terms of the actual act of closure, it's important to first consider that status of each partner concerning the relationship's demise. If it's you who wants to end things, your partner is either in agreement with you or is upset with your decision. Assuming you would like to close consciously, in either scenario, it's your partner who will have to make the choice between joining you in creating a conscious closure or simply disconnecting. A conscious uncoupling tends to be more painful at the start, but far more healing and comforting in the long term. Unconsciously disconnecting saves a bit of pain up front, but it is much harder and more painful in the long run. Even worse, it causes you to have to reignite patterns and themes in your next relationship that could have been avoided if you'd taken the time and care to consciously close the present one.

You can't force your partner to meet you in heart-centered closure. Ultimately, you don't want to delay your own heart-centered closure just because they're not ready to meet you there. You don't need to be met when you're breaking up. It's probably why you're breaking up—because you're not being met! And there is, of course, the possibility that even though you've agreed to a certain number of months, you come to crystal clarity before that time that you no longer want to be in the relationship. Whenever one person is very clear that it's over, it's time to close.

When kids are involved, it's even more critical to bring a heart-intelligent methodology to your closure. Often children provide a new level of excuse not to close a relationship, but this is erroneous thinking. People who say, "I won't leave because of the kids," are assuming it's emotionally healthier for their children for them to stay in an unhappy marriage than it would be for them to go through their parents' divorce. The absolute opposite is true. Children are energetic beings and they don't have to see their parents fighting to sense the energy of the household. A safe, loving environment is what they need to thrive, but a home with two parents in a loveless, disconnected relationship is far less likely to provide that kind of safety than a situation in which each parent is happy and fulfilled on their own. Even though trauma will likely be caused by the divorce initially, the long-term benefit of having two happy role models outweighs that short-term trauma, especially when the parents take care to close the marriage consciously.

Attaining Heart-Centered Closure

Good closure hinges on authentic gratitude for each other and for the relationship, and sometimes steps are required to get to that place. As a partnership comes to a close, each party often has resentments or disappointments that have been stored up for some time, so there will likely need to be some exchanging of uncontained truth to clear out of the way. It's important to share whatever may be holding either of you back from feeling gratitude.

A lot of people won't let go until they hear from their partner that they're sorry. And it's not just the words, "I'm sorry," that do the job. It has to come with remorse and a sincere message of "I get how I've hurt you." Remorse heals. It's the secret sauce to heart-centered closure. It requires deep introspection from both partners and a willingness to own how they have hurt the other. It's not about regret, shaming, blaming, or wrong-making. It's about what you've learned. It might sound like: "In spite of doing the best I could do, I see that I've hurt you. I'm so sorry for that. I love you and I never wanted to hurt you. But I get that you hurt, and you've been hurting. Thank you for this lesson. I'm going to be more conscious of this dynamic in my next relationship."

A conscious closure requires a declaration, done either alone or in the presence of others. Some couples I've known have even made a ritual or ceremony out of their closure. One way to do this is to sit with a bowl of water and use it as a cleansing symbol as you declare your gratitude and closing intentions to each other. The words should be your own, but they might include language like this: "I am consciously and gratefully closing our romantic connection and I cease and de-role from any projections or roles I have played for you. I claim back my sovereign self and I take back any parts you've been holding for me in our sacred container. I reclaim them now."

It's important to renounce the roles you've played for each other and the projections you've carried for each other. If you don't take this energetic step, you could continue to carry pieces of your ex-partner(s) for decades! Some energy workers maintain that any time you have sex with anyone, you carry that person's energy in your system for several years. Whether that's true or not, whatever you don't close will remain open in your next relationship, so to ensure a clean clear and fresh start, do everything you can to close your past.

Another critical ingredient to a good closure is the takeaway. What medicine has this relationship brought you? What were the lessons? What were the healings? Every relationship heals, and you need to recognize and honor the healing for it to stick. You want to authentically communicate to your partner, "I could never be the person I am today had we not taken this journey together."

This paves the way to eventually having an enduring friendship if that's what you desire with this person. But you have to first be willing to go into the black hole of separation and loneliness before you can know if you can be friends. You need to cut those cords fully and feel the vacuum of this person no longer being in your life. Only then can you fill the vacuum back up with yourself and only then are you able to create a healthy new relationship or establish a clean friendship with your ex.

I once dated a woman who had a feeling of unsafety around her father because he was ambiguous, absent, and distant. She was unable to drop into her heart because of this enormous anger toward her dad for not feeling felt and seen as special. As I've described, in relationships, we tend to project our parental incompletions onto our partners, so I started to receive some of this uncontained anger. As perfect matching would have it, I also had a father who was unsafe, but in a different way. He would lash out and become angry without warning, which would put my nervous system into paralysis and shock.

Then, as an adult, whenever I received my partner's anger, I'd go into this little-boy collapse. She'd get upset about that and tell me to "Be like a man! Show up! Don't collapse into my power; step into your greatness!" Her words would only serve to trigger me deeper into feelings of "I'm not enough; I'm not acceptable." This is an example of a pain-body cycle of triggers. I could have said, "I've had enough of this! Your anger is not okay, and you're horrible and I dump you!" But if I had ejected from the relationship abruptly while making her responsible for my pain, I would not have dealt with my inability to hold anger, with my diminishment into a little boy, or with my inability to deal with that dynamic.

I likely would have gone on to find someone excessively sweet, gentle, and calm. But I'd only be in bliss with that partner for a short time before I'd start to feel bored, lifeless, and unable to access the juice and spark of this new relationship. When we run away from one energy to try to find the opposite, we rob ourselves of the opportunity for growth that the more difficult energy was providing. We end up avoiding something critical in ourselves; some piece in us that is in need of healing. And yet that is what happens when we don't take the time and care to close our relationships properly. Either we run away and create a relationship that's the total opposite of what we had (but doesn't satisfy us) or we find ourselves in the exact same position of the prior relationship.

Life will continue to bring you a lesson until you learn it. If you close your relationship with a genuine attempt to own, feel, take responsibility for your part, see patterns, and digest the medicine that's been offered, you will be free to create a healthier next experience. Then, when you attract somebody new, it will be with the benefit of having integrated that medicine. That's how the Laws of Emotional-Energetic Couple Dynamics works. We're always given what we're ready for and what we need. If there's a lesson we've failed to learn, we'll get another opportunity to learn that lesson—and another, and another, until we recognize the medicine. The only way to escape it is to deliberately run to the opposite extreme, creating a flat, passionless union where we cease to grow and evolve.

Taking Your Medicine

To close this topic on closure, let me repeat a final word of warning. After your relationship has ended, you must stay completely separate from your partner, as well as steer clear of developing a new relationship, for at least the first few months. Make it part of the agreement. Don't keep connected and hooked into each other, no matter how much easier you believe it might make the transition. Nor should you have someone "in waiting" to transition to immediately after you close because you think you've found an "upgrade." You must completely let your partner go, even if you fear it might mean you'll never see them again. When there's an unwillingness to fully let go, you block the ownership you need to have around what parts you need to start filling for yourself. You have to take the medicine.

I have been through several heart-intelligent closures; I know this art. If there's anything I've mastered, it's how to close a relationship well, while ultimately keeping people in my life and sharing profound friendships and deep love with them. It *is* possible, but whenever I've tried to stay in contact during those first few months it's been painful, crushing, and counterproductive in the long run. Push through the discomfort of that threshold because the freedom and beauty waiting on the other side of it is incredible.

Need help applying this in your relationship?
Visit www.HeartIQRelationships.com for FREE demos
and tutorials using the access code myheartiq.

How to Become Sexually Magnetic

CHAPTER 12

The Secrets of Sacred Sexuality & Magnetism

If you've ever doubted there would be significant perks to practicing the steps and gaining the insights I've outlined for you throughout this book, let me put those doubts to rest for you. Not only will you have mastered the most direct means of healing old wounds and coming into ever greater serenity and joy, and mastered the secrets to sublime emotional intimacy with your partner, but you'll also be poised for the most mind-blowing sexual connections you've ever imagined. You may have heard about sacred sexuality, but you may not have known that this extremely rare and special brand of sexual experience can only be enjoyed once all of the preceding practices have been incorporated into your relationship. Without that foundation, sex is nothing more than a release of tension and, in some cases, even a way to *avoid* intimacy.

The Juicy Dance of Sexual Magnetism

"Polarity" is a term commonly used to define the juice that keeps your relationship alive, vital, and sexually charged. In order for you to feel an ongoing electromagnetic, chemical charge of sexual polarity between you and your partner, you need to be in full mastery of your own internal emotional expanded range. Any time we make any natural part of us wrong, suppressing it, we end up suppressing the whole emotional spectrum available to us. We can't access our fire anymore, and we become denser, heavier-feeling, and numb. Our internal furnace flickers out and our engine slows down. It's so common for a once-sizzling partnership to dissolve into two individuals who don't connect in a magnetic, sexually polarized way.

Does it surprise you to learn that most people are tapping only a fraction of the sexual potential available in their relationships? Would you like to hold the key for unlocking the rest?

Throughout this book I've talked about the need for expanding our access to the emotional-energetic range that each of us embodies so that we can be present to all of what's moving in us. As I've explained, any energies we're holding that are hidden by shame, guilt, or judgment are shadows, and whenever we're able to expand our capacity for acknowledging and owning that energy—whenever we're able to heal by releasing the shame and judgment around it—we call that shadow work. Shadow work is the secret to maintaining juicy, luscious polarity between you and your beloved.

Each one of us, no matter our gender or sexual orientation, has the full range of masculine and feminine energies within us. Somewhere on the spectrum, however, we each have a place we call "home." Home is an optimum place of relaxation and resourcefulness. It's where we get to be our best, easiest, most natural selves. It's rare to find one's "home" dead center in the middle between masculine and feminine, neutral to either energy, but likewise, neither is anyone 100 percent masculine or feminine. With every bit of yin exists some degree of yang, and vice versa.

Polarity Is an Inside Job

Before we go further, I need to bust one last myth. If you are under the impression that relationship polarity depends upon men cultivating their masculine energy and women cultivating their feminine energy, you've missed the point. While it's easy to find misinformation that fosters that inaccurate notion, the truth is that long-term, meaningful, enduring relationship polarity can only exist when both partners are committed to increasing the polarity *within themselves*. It's all about the relationship *you* have to both the masculine and feminine within *you*.

Before we proceed, read the following list of common traits that are associated with "masculine" and "feminine." This isn't *my* list, based on my personal idea of what it means to be masculine or feminine. Instead, it was generated from multiple polls from hundreds of men and women who have attended my Insights to Intimacy LIVE seminars.

Feminine traits are: responsive, opening, yielding, mystery, birth, vastness, expressive, fullness, movement, flexible, emotional, sensitive, surrender, flow, radiance, creative, receptive, beauty, uncontained, mother, darkness, nurturing, communication, relational, vulnerability, connection, sensitivity, inclusion, compassion, life force, nature, and chaos. Femininity is the energy of the ocean— deep, dark, mysterious, and unknown.

Masculine traits are: presence, light, detachment, competition, assertiveness, control, penetration, force, stillness, containment, vertical, focus, structure, specificity, action, clarity, freedom, power, confidence, delivering, conscious witness, analytical, logical, sharp, angular, breakthrough, assertive, persistent, laser beam, death, predator, nothingness, father, and leader. Masculinity is the energy of the land that holds the ocean's depths and the shore that receives the ocean's changing tides.

As you read the lists of masculine and feminine qualities above, were you men thinking, *I should have these masculine qualities,* and were you women thinking, *I should have these feminine qualities?* If you noticed that you possessed traits that were on the opposite gender's list, did it strike terror in your heart? Relax. We all have every bit of it within us, and the more we can become comfortable with owning the entire spectrum, the more we'll increase our *internal polarity*. When we disown a trait that naturally exists within us, we collapse the polarity potential for connecting to another.

It's purely a myth that women should try to connect more to the feminine side, and men should try to connect more with the masculine side, and I don't just mean in terms of alternative sexual preference situations. Every one of us—male, female, heterosexual, homosexual, bisexual, and so on—needs to have an integrated alliance, an expanded connection to both energies. Before you can have juicy, real polarity with anyone outside yourself, you must first learn to have polarity within yourself. When you connect to and expand this range within your own experience, it creates an incredible amount of juice and energy.

Internal polarity is what makes certain people so charismatic and alluring. Every one of us has the capacity to connect to our fire, this burning, bright light that allows us to be inspiring, naturally charming, and magnetic to joy and adventure. Those with internal polarity are the ones who light up a room just by walking into it, the ones with the crowds around them at every social gathering, the ones who make authentic connection with fellow humans look so effortless and enjoyable.

Increasing Polarity

To generate this charismatic potential in your life, you need healthy access and ownership of the broad spectrum of light and deep energies within you, as well as the masculine and feminine. But often large segments of our life energy are bound and unavailable to us. As we've discussed, past trauma can cause us to wall off these energies with our S.T.U.A.R.T. strategies. We carry powerful (and often subconscious) underlying beliefs that certain parts of the spectrum are wrong for us to feel, or we've learned from experience that it's unsafe to allow ourselves to go there.

Let's say for example that you've read that one aspect of the feminine is to be able to fully express emotion, including being fully in your anger or other uncontained emotion. But let's say you've had childhood experiences that taught you that showing anger or sadness is wrong or unsafe. Instead of expressing yourself fully, you know you only go about 50 percent in your expression of these energies. You might have a desire to express more, but you simply don't have access to that fuel; it's locked away, stored, bound in your body as repressed memory and trauma. Maybe you can even feel the stored tension—as a lump in your throat, a pit in your stomach, an ache in your heart—but you don't know how to begin to release it more completely.

When you do your work to release these energies, they get to flow freely. The greater you're able to expand your emotional-energetic range, the more space you create for movement. It's the amount of contrast between the highs and lows, the light and dark, the positive and the negative that provides that space. Picture a waterfall about ten feet high. As the water rolls over the edge of the waterfall, it gains momentum. The force with which it hits the ground is dependent upon the distance it's covered, right? So a higher dropping point will result in more force and greater energy. Similarly, increasing our internal polarity is a function of doing the inner work that will lead us to feel more of our true selves and expand our emotional-energetic range. Again, we need to claim *all* of it, not just our masculine if we're men, and not just our feminine if we're women. We have to get out of this idea that if you're a woman you should have feminine energy and if you're a man you need to show up and be more masculine. It's harming our relationships, and we're judging each other when we don't show up that way.

Your relationships become magnetic when you generate the internal polarity to expansively own and express both your feminine and masculine essences. This wakes up the people around you; they begin experiencing you differently. You have an edge. You're tapped in, turned on. You're dynamic and clear. You're not stuck in an ultra-masculine frequency, too hard around the edges, inflexible, boorish. And neither are you stuck in ultra-feminine energies, too wispy, soft, and willowy to exude any sense of power or purpose. You're balanced, effective, and at peace.

I want to be clear though, that just because we all have the full spectrum of masculine and feminine energies within us, it doesn't mean our home base needs to be right at neutral, or we need to have precisely balanced access to both ends of the spectrum. We all have a different comfortable range of masculine and feminine that's unique to us. You might be comfortable with 80 percent feminine energy and 20 percent masculine, or vice versa. You just need to be able to incrementally push the boundaries of your comfort level in both directions to expand your internal polarity, which is just another way of saying, "expand your emotional-energetic range."

First you'll want to determine where you feel most at home. Imagine a line with the word "feminine" at one end and the word "masculine" at the other. Somewhere in between those two extremes is a point where you feel most relaxed, a place where you can comfortably rest, most easily receive from others, and simply feel good. Give yourself a moment right now to consider the lists of feminine and masculine qualities shared earlier. Which ones pull you in the most? What feels most like home? If the majority of the words associated with feminine energy are speaking to you, and you have very limited affinity with the words on the masculine list, you're "at home," on the extreme feminine end of the spectrum. If the reverse is true, then your home base lies at the extreme masculine end. If the words that call to you most are evenly distributed between the two lists, you are likely somewhere in the more central, neutral range on the spectrum.

Once you determine your home base, I want you to notice how your day-to-day activities often take you away from this comfortable place. Perhaps your home base is on the feminine end of the spectrum, but your job requires you to embody many more masculine traits. It's great to be able to move around on the spectrum to best suit the various requirements of your life, but it's equally valuable to know where your home base is so that you can invite yourself there as much of the time as possible. It's an aspect of your self-love, your self-care, of acknowledging and accepting yourself precisely as you are.

When you're with your partner, there may be moments when you recognize that your partner is more in their masculine or more in their feminine, and you can make a conscious choice to meet your beloved in a contrasting energy. If your partner goes all "he-man," you may playfully decide to go to the most extreme feminine point you're comfortable with. This will create instant polarity in the moment and could just as easily happen in reverse. When your range is limited—when there are many aspects you cannot access and express—it limits your opportunities to be able to meet another in intimate connection.

CLAIMING YOUR PARTNER

For safety to prevail within the container of our relationships, we have to know that our partner is committed to us. There is something so nourishing about feeling fully claimed by your beloved—being able to relax into the certainty that you, above all others in the universe, are valued, cherished, and honored by someone you have chosen to value, cherish, and honor as well. This concept of claiming is a two-way street. While the role of claiming is presumed to be the man's role, for it to work, the woman must be claimable. Men and women are both susceptible to some very common forms of trauma that make the ability to claim, and to be claimed, challenging. Claiming happens naturally when two open hearts come together, but cannot happen when either heart is partially closed due to prior damage. When trust has been repeatedly broken, we need to work harder to create the right emotional climate for claiming and being claimed.

For men, the key is containment. Men who are guarding their hearts will find it difficult to be fully committed to one partner in a way that creates a safe container. Their energy may leak toward other women in their lives, not necessarily as direct, open romantic attention, but just as small flirtations, ogling, or exchanges of subtle sexual energy. This kind of activity, while often assumed to be harmless, will be felt by the woman as a lack of safety. The container of the relationship will feel weak and vulnerable as a result. For women, the key to being claimable is having an open heart. No matter how safe a man makes the container, and no matter how much love and attention he lavishes on his woman, if her heart is not open, she won't be claimable. If she's been badly hurt before, she may have a closed heart that has nothing to do with her current partner and everything to do with her past history. She's programmed herself not to trust, and S.T.U.A.R.T. fiercely guards her heart's threshold.

What often happens is that a man with poor containment capacity attracts a woman with this kind of unopenable heart. Always, we attract partners with energy that matches our own, so this is a very common scenario that plays out as a difficult relationship fraught with power struggles. She's thinking, *If he would only stop being so leaky and claim me, my heart would open to him.* He's thinking, *If she would only open her heart to me, I would be more contained with my energy.* This is the exact impasse I witness frequently at my Insights to Intimacy LIVE seminars. When the whole dynamic is brought to light, both partners can come to a new level of compassion and understanding with each other, and from there, they can choose to shift into a new capacity for claiming and being claimed.

The biggest challenge with claiming, for both men and women, is the level of vulnerability it requires. The irony is that nothing creates safety like an ironclad relationship container, and yet to create one, a certain level of personal safety must already be in place for each partner. If you're still very much entrenched in your prior wounding and core unworthiness, you won't be able to access the emotional courage to claim and be claimed. If the woman does not love herself or the man does not respect himself, true claiming will be more difficult to achieve.

A Ball Does Not Roll Uphill—Relighting the Spark

If you don't work on your polarity, your relationship will go flat. All energies in life seek the lowest level. A ball doesn't roll uphill on its own. The unpopular truth about polarity is that any relationship will naturally move toward greater and greater dissipation of polarity until it comes into neutrality. That's just the nature of things. It requires energy to maintain the polarity that keeps the spark alive. It requires deliberate attention. It's work, but very joyful work.

My colleague David Deida explains that we all have shells that we build up around our natural home-base essence. In Deida's work, he explains that our essence is the home base we've been talking about. It's our true nature; it's where we fall on the spectrum between masculine and feminine extremes. This essence is not developed through conditioning; it's already defined at birth. As a result of our childhood experiences, we develop shells around our true essence as a means of protection from the trauma of disappointing others or incurring their harsh judgment.

For example, there are some cultures wherein society demands women demonstrate very feminine characteristics, and men demonstrate very masculine ones. If you were born in such a culture, and your true sexual essence happened to fall on the side of the spectrum that didn't match your biological gender, you'd likely build an artificial shell around your true essence, and that shell would be what you'd show the world. Or it could be less about your culture, and more about your parents' expectations.

Consider this example: There's a family with two daughters. One is naturally quite beautiful, and the other is quite intelligent but lacking in the physical assets displayed by her sister. Imagine that both of these girls were born with deep feminine essences. The parents treat them differently, however. They buy the beautiful one sparkly, lovely clothes, and the more intellectual one an encyclopedia set. The second daughter starts to feel that her feminine essence is somehow wrong for her. She begins to disown and crush her feminine core. She starts building this shell around her core so that she can project a more masculine energy, even though it's not her true essence. This masculine shell serves her for a while, but then she reaches high school and realizes that the shell she's been projecting doesn't attract boys. She wants to become more feminine, but because her feminine core has been crushed, she develops a fake shell around her masculine shell so that she can project an artificial feminine energy.

Unfortunately, this is a very common dynamic, and the same happens with boys who are born at the very masculine end of the spectrum. They might be punished harshly for their physicality or not being able to sit politely in the classroom. They might internalize the message that their masculine longings for action and movement and exploration make them "bad boys," and so they adopt a shell of feminine attributes in order to better fit into the circumstances of their lives. Then, later, for fear of appearing too soft, they create a macho false shell so that they can project artificial masculinity.

Since attraction is based upon energy, what happens next is that the falsely macho male attracts the falsely feminine "bimbo." You will always attract your reciprocal. These two false shells will have a relationship with each other, and it might even be a steamy and passionate one since they're representing opposite ends of the emotional-energetic range. But the relationship won't have staying power or depth or bliss because it's not made of two real people, but two false shells. For the real people beneath the shells to come together in blissful union, they'll have to do the work to heal and dissolve the false masks until nothing is left but their core essences. Since this kind of work is still relatively unknown, couplings formed from this all-too-common dynamic usually fail once the thin veneer of chemical attraction wears off.

Most people are actually born with a true essence rather close to the masculine and feminine extremes, but our culture has made unrestrained masculinity and femininity unpopular, causing us to develop shells that neutralize our more masculine and feminine essences for the sake of political correctness. It's not uncommon for us to go through many shells before we learn to discard them all and relax into our true essence. Becoming conscious of how it works is the first step toward a far more satisfying relationship. Luckily, just *being* in relationship with your partner will bring up your shells for healing. If you stay conscious to the practice, you'll have plenty of opportunities to heal and work through the shells.

Watch Out for Polarity Killers

Maintaining a juicy, magnetized state of polarity with your partner requires conscious effort and deliberate management of your energies and actions. There are myriad polarity-killers that can pop up in your daily life to pull the plug out of your connection, even when you've been feeling alive, turned on, and hot for each other. A few of the top polarity-killers identified at my seminars are: nonresponsiveness, partner's leakiness, children, codependency, micromanagement, being drunk or numbed by addiction, being too heady, being overworked and exhausted, and using coded communication in our initiation attempts and expecting our partner to be a mind reader.

Pornography is a common polarity-killer. Once you start to objectify sexuality and divert your attention there, it's a leaky distraction. Same with high-frequency masturbation; it can satiate your sex drive, which will make you less inclined to have polarity with your partner. Just stopping masturbation for two weeks will dramatically increase polarity with another. Remember that there's a vast difference between having heart-centered sexual interaction and having sex that's disconnected from your heart. Even having too many conventional tension-release orgasms with your partner (but without heart connection) will decrease polarity over time.

Spending too much time with your partner can also kill polarity. We need time apart to solidify ourselves as independent beings. Merging is one of the sneakiest contributors to happy couples losing polarity with each other. A magnetic attraction requires two separate poles. When you've merged completely with your partner, there is no room for electric spark or magnetic pull. A good way to safeguard your relationship from this pitfall is to be sure that when you do your check-ins with each other, you each make a point to share what is authentic and moving for you in your own life, separate from your life together. While it's naturally valuable to do tracking and check-ins that focus on the two of you as a couple, you need to be equally interested in what is happening for each of you as individuals. That's what keeps the spark alive.

In the physical realm, other polarity-killers include lapses in personal hygiene like failing to consistently bathe or brush your teeth. Sexually, they include lack of foreplay, as well as too much speed, disconnection, or self-centeredness during the sex act. Emotionally, a big polarity-killer is not feeling desired enough by the other, or feeling that sex is a favor, a service performed for the exclusive benefit of one partner, or as a reward for good behavior.

How you connect sexually is truly one of the most critical parts of relationship success and a barometer for the totality of the partnership. When you have a heart-connected orgasm, your whole body feels lit up energetically. If you aren't feeling that, you need to look at how you can open more of your inner emotions through your own personal work. You might need to work on owning your shame. Your shadows (particularly the shameful ones) are the biggest polarity-killers in the world. Shame is all about not being able to feel your goodness in all that you are. If you carry shame, you automatically are shielding your heart, and that means sexual energy can't move through it. The more you practice sharing your shame—having it witnessed so that it can be digested, the closer you'll get to being able to experience heart-centered lovemaking. It happens automatically when you practice Heart IQ, but it doesn't happen overnight. You must commit to the practice.

Spiritual Expansion Through Your Sexual Connection

Mastering polarity is the secret to enjoying sacred sexuality. It's not just about the physical act of sex, or even the act of making passionate, present love to each other. It's realizing that your entire body becomes a doorway to the divine when you actually allow yourself to flow with all that is available inside you.

Practicing sacred sexuality is all about recognizing the tension and blockages that show up in our system through good tracking, and opening those blocked areas so that we can come into whole-body bliss. It's not just about intercourse, but an exquisite experience that starts as soon as you wake up and look your partner in the eyes. From there, the whole day is about making love; your life together is a sensual dance that doesn't end.

On some level, we all recognize that sex can be a stress reliever;

we just haven't learned how to make the most of this amazing tool. What normally takes place as we go through our day, week, life, is that we encounter situations that overtax our nervous system's capacity for handling them directly and immediately, so these tensions become stored in our bodies. Bits of this stored-up tension get discharged every time we have sex, and that's why we have the term "tension-release orgasm." When we're sexually aroused, tension builds up until the eventual release takes place, carrying a bit of our stored tension along with it. The release feels good, so we're content for the moment. But we haven't created intimacy. The release might feel momentarily pleasurable, but it's superficial. It doesn't meet our longing to go deep into blissful connection with another. That's accomplished only when we learn to clear these two channels so that our sexual energy can powerfully open us to divine bliss.

Sexual energy, when it's *not* connected to the heart, can be as addictive as heroine or cocaine. Research carried out by Marnia Robinson, author of *Cupid's Poisoned Arrow,* has found that the chemicals released in the body from a conventional tension-release orgasm stimulate the same parts of the brain that are stimulated when you inject heroine. It triggers the same addictive response. It also creates a cascade of chemical reactions that flood the body with dopamine. Dopamine is a mood enhancer, but it can create serious problems for you when it's out of balance.

When sex is just sex (when there's no real love involved) the moment you have an orgasm, dopamine spikes. Since it's a pleasure chemical, this surge of dopamine makes you feel really, really good. But here's the problem: After the initial spike, the dopamine level doesn't just return to its status-quo elevation; it caves far below normal. You feel the imbalance as an agitation, a hunger. Sometimes that hunger is expressed as a need for more sexual interaction, but unfortunately, it's not a heart-centered need. It's more of a primal, "give me my fix" kind of hunger. When you're in this state and you touch your lover, the touch is not the nurturing kind of touch, but a hungry, self-serving kind of touch.

Sometimes the dopamine dive that follows a tension-release orgasm is expressed through other kinds of frustrated hunger as well. It could trigger a need to eat sweets or create a sense of loneliness, helplessness, and depletion. It's often the cause of depression. According to Robinson, a single non-heartfelt orgasm can destabilize your dopamine balance for up to two weeks.

Perhaps the most insidious aspect of this chemical reaction is that dopamine imbalance affects men and women differently. Typically, it makes men feel like they want to disconnect and get space from their sexual partner. For women, on the other hand, it triggers their insecurity, their core unworthiness, which makes them overly clingy, needy, and demanding. It leaves women with an empty feeling they don't know how to fill. That is the effect of disconnected, non-heart-centered sexual interaction. It's what happens when sexuality is not channeled through your heart. Earlier we discussed how anger that isn't channeled through your heart can turn into unhealthy, unnatural rage that's toxic to your energetic system. It's the same with sexual energy.

Making Love Through Your Heart Channel

The most remarkable finding from research done on brain chemistry during orgasm is this: When you make love through your heart channel, an entirely different chemical is released—oxytocin. Oxytocin stabilizes us, nourishes us, uplifts us, and creates incredible connection and intimacy. It promotes well-being in all of our body's systems. It doesn't spike and then crash, bringing us to emotionally unhealthy states the way dopamine does. Our bodies are miraculously designed for healthy, heart-centered lovemaking. Any other kind of sexual act actually creates unwellness in our systems.

I do not want to make wrong the red-hot, fierce passionate experience of making love with great power and enthusiasm. It's not like I'm suggesting the only right way to make love is to be calm and passive and gentle. I'm talking about learning to be able to tell in your body whether or not you are fully in your heart when you make love. For a man, if you are inside your woman and you're only feeling the stimulation genitally, that is your clue that you are not in your heart. If you find yourself in that position, I suggest you stop what you're doing and find a way to connect with her so that you can become engaged energetically and make love to her from your whole being.

For a woman, it's the same. But also if you are offering your sexuality in any way as a favor, through service, or as a reward for good behavior, stop. You need to be present and aware enough to stop *any* time you don't really want to be sexually engaged, even those times you feel you "should" have sex for some reason. If you're not feeling a genuine longing to be sexually intimate with your man in that moment, simply don't do it. All of the above scenarios will result in an unhealthy dopamine release, as opposed to the nourishing oxytocin release you'd get from a heart-centered sexual experience.

When you realize the longing isn't there, however, avoid making false excuses or simply saying, "I'm not in the mood." Use the situation as an opportunity to invite intimacy! Use it as the valuable warning flag that it is. You now have a full arsenal of guaranteed connection practices to choose from! Choose to make your time together about meaningful connection instead of about a sexual experience that will leave you both chemically unbalanced. Be open to what might genuinely feel wonderful to you from there.

Always let yourself lean into sexual activity only to the extent that it feels good and authentic and right for you. But do try to stay open to the possibility of that at all times. There's often this idea that any sexual behavior that gets started must eventually culminate in orgasm. I'd like to dispel that notion. Often, for women in particular, this underlying assumption makes them unwilling to start anything because they don't feel like finishing it. It's important to understand what a delicate situation this can become. Failed initiation attempts and feelings of rejection associated with sex are tremendous hot buttons for emotional wounding and spirals down into our core unworthiness.

I've seen many men and women who were once confident and clear in their relationships, but who, after consistent sexual rejection, became shut down, afraid to dare ask again, afraid to be open about their desires. My recommendation is to find times within your relationship when you can plan to just connect without agenda—not with a plan to have sex, but with an agreement to stay open to that possibility if it feels right. Don't say no before you've even had a chance to be opened by your beloved. You want to be *open to being opened* at any moment and not predict anything in advance.

What often happens when there has been sexual pressure in a relationship is that before they even get into the bedroom, one partner will say, "I just want to let you know I'm not in the mood tonight." It's meant to spare the other partner the embarrassment of being rejected, but it can do more harm than good. Making that kind of prediction cuts off the potential for any intimacy that might have spontaneously arisen between you. There might have been the opportunity for an absolutely incredible experience that didn't even have to end with sex, but it's thwarted before it's even had the chance to develop.

Sex as a Tool for Conflict Resolution

Once you have become very practiced at heart-centered relationship skills, you can actually use sex as a means for resolving conflict. It's tricky and requires excellent ability to read into your partner, but when it works, it works beautifully. I'm not talking about make-up sex or even angry sex. Make-up sex is when you feel better after arguing, so you have sex to make up. Many people think sexual intimacy should be the result of feeling connected, loved, and open, as if sex were the reward for being in an open, loving space. But what if sexual intimacy could also be used as a way to dissolve your pain body to get *back* to a place of intimacy when intimacy has been lost?

It's been my experience that sex *can* be a practice of nonverbal dissolution of the pain body. It requires a huge leap of faith because, often when we're triggered by our partner, having sex is the last thing we want to do. There has to be a willingness to explore whatever arises. It could turn into angry sex or passionate, soft tender loving sex. It can be enormously liberating to express ourselves in this way through our lovemaking.

You want to ask yourself, "So if all this pain I'm feeling had an expression through my physicality, my sound, my voice, my sexuality, what would it be?" Maybe you both get naked and you feel you want to push at each other or roll around on the floor together, expressing your defiance physically. All the power dynamics of wanting to be right can be expressed through sexual play, even if actual sex is not the end result. Maybe you recognize wanting to be on top, and you roll your partner into a more submissive position. Then maybe your partner rolls you around to the bottom. In this way, you can choose to enjoyably play out your battle rather than staying in hostility.

It would seem obvious that such a scenario would require a full buy-in from both partners. But there are actually situations where partners know each other so well that one may decide to override the other's stated wishes. There may be moments when your partner knows your deepest heart's longings even better than you know them yourself. An example would be when a woman is so triggered by an argument that she tells her partner, "Leave me alone!" and storms off into another room. Despite her declaration, she may be desperately longing for closeness with her man and just be too triggered to ask for it. But perhaps he can feel underneath her defense. Perhaps his intuitive read would be to disregard her words, charge after her, and pull her into an intimate embrace. He would need to be completely clear that he was not operating from his own agenda, desires, or needs. It would have to be about the partner, or it would be a violation of the relationship.

Some advanced couples do make these kinds of prior agreements with each other. If you recognize that you frequently close down and you're able to track yourself in your closure, and you know that what you really want is to not be closed, but to be opened by your partner, then you might feel safe enough to invite your partner to penetrate your closure when it surfaces. You create a new level of openness and intimacy when you reach the point where you're able to see that your partner can feel your heart better than you can. You trust their read of your heart better than your own read of your heart, and you invite them to lead you to openness.

Sexual Magnetism Requires Surrender

The concept of surrender can elicit a mixed bag of emotions, particularly for women. It can stir up feelings of powerlessness, weakness, losing control, or being defeated, submissive, and frighteningly vulnerable. But, at the same time, the idea of surrender can possibly have the positive connotations of letting go, trusting, relaxing, being taken care of, being able to receive and freely exploring, or being taken to bliss by a partner.

Surrender is ultimately a sacred experience with the divine. Do you trust and allow your partner to open you into the deep places where you cannot go on your own? Do you want that? It's interesting that the answer is not always an instant "yes, please." For some, the initial reaction is more of a hesitant "I'm not sure. Where would I be taken?" But if you knew, then it wouldn't be surrender, would it?

I'd like to give a bit of shape and form to this concept of surrender. Through my extensive background as a martial arts instructor I came across a concept I called "Dynamic Tension." This concept has given me a whole new perspective on how to relax into total surrender. This concept involves yielding, the act of consciously choosing to be guided and led. Imagine someone pushing you and you resisting them with all your force. In this scenario, it's a battle of strength. The stronger party "wins." The one that can push you over will feel dominant, and the one being pushed around feels weak and submissive. This is how many view surrender. However, a force can only exist when you resist. If you choose to move with the force that is directed at you, the fight becomes flow and the struggle becomes a dance. You are not collapsing when the force comes, but consciously yielding because it feels joyful to do so. When you understand this concept, your relationships and sex life become utterly transformed and magnetized.

When you're totally tense, you can't really feel another. And when you're fully collapsed, you can't feel them either. But in a state of dynamic tension, you're perfectly poised to experience your interaction with your partner. You can take turns consciously leading each other and enjoying the full sensation of being led. This kind of surrender, this conscious yielding, is extremely healthy and enjoyable. For exercises on how to access more surrender and polarity with your partner, please visit www.heartIQRelationships .com and enter the access code myheartiq.

SUCCESS STORY FROM PRIYA & AKASH

Priya and Akash attended the Insights to Intimacy LIVE seminar in 2014. Priya says, "Heart IQ has given us the tools to work with our own stuff, rather than throwing it at each other because we don't know what to do with what we're feeling when it comes up."

Akash says, "The tool of tracking has expanded my ability to go deeper and be more honest. Before, when my partner would tell me what was going on with her, I would get defensive because I felt like I had done something wrong. Now I'm able to hold her without getting triggered, and it feels great to be able to be there for her."

Priya says, "From this work, my partner is more embodied and confident in his masculinity, and this allows me to feel more safe in our connection. Plus, as I've been continuing to practice surrendering, trusting, and letting go, he has become more expansive and still, and even more present to me. That's made all the difference. I've never felt so safe as I do in this relationship. I am so grateful to this work, from the bottom of my heart!"

Need help applying this in your relationship?
Visit www.HeartIQRelationships.com for FREE demos
and tutorials using the access code myheartiq.

So What Do I Do Now?

So what now? What do you do? Where do you start?

I've said it before, and I'll say it again: You can't read yourself to an experience. I hope you enjoyed reading this book, but more important, I hope you use the practices to dramatically enhance your life and relationship. In my experience, however, reading alone will not make the difference you are looking for. Reading is a start, but if you want to actually make a shift in your current or future relationship, it's going to be your actions that count.

Remember, Heart IQ communication is a practice. For change to occur and for it to stick, it needs to be automatic and unconscious, where the change has occurred on a cellular level. Make sure you set time aside to actually apply this stuff! However, be smart about it. If you're in a relationship, commit to the schedule provided in Chapter 10 for four weeks. That's just one month of your life . . . and the rewards from doing this will provide years, perhaps *decades,* of enjoyment and relationship bliss. Of course, if you get benefit, don't stop! Keep going!

However, before you start putting all these wonderful tools and practices to work, make sure you both sit down and make your sacred agreements together. This must be your first step. I know it's not a sexy conversation, but it will save you plenty of heartache. This way, you're starting with a clear intention and a strong container, one that will create a huge amount of safety for you both over time as you drop deeper into your vulnerability.

So let's recap what we've covered. In Part One of this book,

I introduced the concept that we are intrinsically good, and that over time, we disconnect from this goodness. We mistakenly buy in to the idea that we're unworthy after years of neglect or in some cases abuse, whether consciously remembered or not. As a means to protect us from feeling bad all the time, we developed some sophisticated strategies for disconnecting from our disconnection. I call these strategies S.T.U.A.R.T. Some of these strategies include addiction, codependency, and being too independent. These defensive behaviors sabotage our intimacy, keeping us from the love we crave. To lower this resistance, we need to embrace and love what is, accepting who we are, as we are, without making ourselves wrong. When we do this, we automatically are able to love our partner in the same way. The idea is not to focus our attention on our issues or our stuff, but to open our hearts to feeling more joy. When we do this, however, it activates our core unworthiness, which offers an opportunity for healing. Core unworthiness is not something to fix or be removed, however, as its presence becomes our depth when we learn to integrate it.

If you only apply the previous paragraph to your life, you will already notice a huge shift in the quality of your relationship with yourself and others.

In Part Two, we rolled up our sleeves and got to work with some powerful communication practices. All Heart IQ practices are built on your capacity to effectively track—that is, watch with joy and presence your internal reality, judgments, feelings, and intuitive "pop-ups." Through great tracking, you get to identify clearly what's yours and what's someone else's stuff. You begin to notice your S.T.U.A.R.T. strategies and shadows, and because you now see them, you can navigate around them, choosing to open, when before you would automatically close. We then explored the art of relationship tracking, which offered you an opportunity to build intimacy with your partner by sharing your tracked reality aloud, so that you could be witnessed and received in your truth, which, as you discovered, is a critical ingredient to healing your core unworthiness and feeling your own goodness again.

From a solid foundation of relationship tracking, you discovered ways to increase your responsiveness, as well how to reassure your partner so they can feel felt. We then explored the Acknowledgment Practice as a way to take responsibly and unmerge from your partner through sharing all the parts you bring to the relationship that don't work. Finally, we went on a journey to better understand how to share difficult truths, disappointments, and unmet needs, including how and when to become uncontained in your expression. This was all wrapped up with an easy-to-follow schedule, which offers daily, weekly, and monthly opportunities to put all of this into action. In this part, you also learned how to consciously close a relationship that is no longer working for you or your partner.

Wow, that's a huge amount we covered, just in the second part of the book. But we're not done yet! In the final part, we looked at how to build a healthy sexual connection by becoming aware of the fact that there are two types of lovemaking: connected and disconnected. When we make love from a place of heart connection, energy flows and we feel close to our partner. Making love opens us to more joy and releases plenty of nourishing oxytocin into our systems. When we make love from a disconnected place, energy will accumulate around our genitals and sex becomes more of a tension-release mechanism than a joyful celebration of our divine essence merging. Instead of the feel-good wholesome quality of oxytocin being released, a big dump of dopamine floods our system, creating an unstable emotional wave that can last up to two weeks. During this time, we are susceptible to addictive behavior and compulsive urges that are sponsored by an empty hunger that's hard to fill. We also looked at how sexual magnetism is created by first expanding our own range of masculine and feminine qualities within *ourselves*. This is key because a big myth to having more polarity is for men to be more "masculine" and women to be more "feminine." Finally, we can just be ourselves and build our magnetism from an authentic, deeper place.

This book is a lot to digest in one go. To get maximum benefit, it's so important to take the time to reread it and actually *study* this material. In fact, I recommend you reread this book every month for the next year. Why? Because repetition is the mother of all learning and Heart IQ can't be absorbed at speed. It needs time, stillness, patience, and pacing for it to fully land.

If you know in your heart that you're not going to reread the book every month for the next year, then register yourself and your partner for the next Insights to Intimacy LIVE seminar, and use the rich Heart IQ amplified field to shortcut your learning.

You can struggle on your own, trying to find your way, wasting months, even years to apply Heart IQ effectively. Or you can schedule five days out of your busy lives to accelerate your awakening and connect with other like-minded people while learning one of the most important life skills you can ever develop. Couples who come to this experience fall in love all over again. In fact, we've had a surprisingly high number of proposals and reconfirmation of vows take place, right there during the event! This is the healthiest environment for couples to be in to open their hearts, heal their past, and take the next step of their journey together. If you can't attend in person, we offer a fabulous livestream option so you can practice in the comfort of your own home!

Finally, let me remind you that I've filmed free demonstration video tutorials on the core practices covered in this book. There are so many nuances to witnessing this work in a live setting, such us timing, pause, tonality, and energy, that it can be easily missed when simply reading about it. All these tutorials can be found at www.HeartIQRelationships.com using the access code myheartiq.

Well, that's it for now. Thank you for spending your precious time reading this book. I wish you tremendous success and true happiness, and I look forward to meeting you in person soon.

Be gentle with yourself,
Christian Pankhurst

Share This Wisdom with Others

This book teaches you how to master relationships. That's no small thing. We know that our relationships with others can only be as good as our relationship with ourselves. But at some point, after we've taken in what we need to learn just for us, we must turn to face the world and ask what, if anything, we can do for others who are struggling with the same issues.

In essence, transformation only begins with you, but ultimately, it is not about you at all. It's about the entire world and the direction humanity is heading. Just like you are me cleverly disguised as you . . . so is everything and everyone on this planet.

All of life is a mirror to our own inner reality. Our world is nothing more than a reflection of all the people who make it up. As each individual raises their consciousness, the world raises its consciousness—moving from fear to courage, from hatred to love, and from scarcity to prosperity for all.

It is therefore up to each of us to enlighten ourselves so that we may add more light to the world. If you want the world to be a certain way, then start with you being that way. If you want the world to be a better place, start with you *being* better.

I therefore ask you to share this message of love, healing, and empowerment with others. Get the message of this book out to as many people as possible. Commit to telling at least ten of your

253

friends, family, or associates about it or consider getting it for them as a life-changing gift. Not only will they be introduced to powerful intimacy-building concepts, they will learn to track how their hearts have closed and how to open once again. With each open heart, we add a little more love to the world. It would also be incredible for them to join you at the Insights to Intimacy LIVE seminar. It is truly a blessing to have your friends and family share this extraordinary experience with you. I know that with your help, we can spread Heart IQ far and wide and that we *can* change the world. . . . I ask for your support in making this dream a reality. Thank you.

Heart IQ Events & Courses

Visit **www.HeartIQ.com** for more information and pricing about upcoming courses, events, and programs.

Insights to Intimacy
LIVE Seminar Testimonials

"As guys, we don't know how to access our emotions, but the work of Heart IQ has made it safe for me to go there."

—*Marc*

"This work has been paramount in helping me to find this amazing relationship. It feels like the work I've done in circle has helped my nervous system to recognize my partner when he showed up in my life. In doing Heart IQ retreats, I got the chance to experience different qualities in men that I wanted in my next relationship. Then I met Marc, and I'd never felt so met and matched in my yearnings. Something in me finally relaxed and said, 'At last!' I couldn't put into words exactly what I was looking for, but my experience in circle helped me to know him when I met him and felt him. I've loved learning to work with the masculine and feminine dynamic, and understanding how polarity is created and diminished in a relationship. This has been transformative."

—*Natasha*

"I feel so deeply connected to myself and my beloved. I'm taking away the realization that sometimes it's best to say less. I realize that I've used words as a mask, and sometimes, it's better to just move together in our bodies without words. This is a real way that we can understand each other. I think that's what all women long for—to be felt so deeply and held in a loving and safe way that allows them let go and surrender. If all women got to experience even a little bit of what I'm experiencing, of being loved in relationship, the world would be different."

—Priya

"I had become blocked in my feelings for my wife and children. With Heart IQ, I started having more space inside me to feel how much love I have for all of them. I've learned that I have to keep my inner space clear so that I can feel what's important to me. It's the space inside me that allows me to let them in more deeply."

—Simon M.

"I can now feel what I want and then ask for what I want. This has made a huge difference for me to feel safe and secure in my relationship."

—Sue

"I can't really remember feeling so joyful before; I'm wide open! I feel like I've been present to a coming together in such a beautiful way through this work."

—Simon G.

"These days, I have shared things with my husband that I haven't shared in seventeen years, and it feels so great and relieving—and he is still here! To have all these tools and to experience that people can go through things and feel more joy, all this is encouraging me to know that I can do this more in my life."

—Andrea

"I'm taking away an acceptance that it's okay and safe to embrace all of me. In fact, I relish it now because that's when my heart smiles!"

—Eugene

"Through this work, I know that it's safe to speak my truth in the moment and that I can rely on my own safety within."

—*Satya*

"I feel joyful, light, still, and allowed to drop deep in my feminine power and vulnerability. I thank you for having such a clear program, and in such a short time, getting to the core."

—*Atar*

"Sometimes, I end up getting stuck on what I want, and I can't see the whole picture. Through this work, I've realized I have such a great relationship with my partner. We have a wonderful life together!"

—*Josefina*

"There have been so many 'Oh My God!' life-changing moments; it's fantastic!"

—*Christina*

"This is one of the best personal development experiences I've had in my eighteen years of working on myself. You incorporate the whole experience—body, mind, and spirit. It was so rich!"

—*Mathias*

"The most important thing I take away is to be able to track my own thoughts and feelings and not to immediately judge them or diagnose myself after ten seconds. I don't have to follow old patterns, and it feels really good! It's been a confirmation that all the things we've done to this point have brought us here, and I know I'm on the way now."

—*Olle*

"I realize that it can be joyful to work on my shit!"

—*Karen*

"I'm taking away a clear and constant heart. I'm taking away tools that can make my really good relationship great!"

—Dan

"I feel really open—I feel like I have love for the whole world. I never thought it would be possible in such a short time to get insights that I've been trying to find for so long. I've been trying to let go of an old relationship that was so painful for me, and I could finally release it through this work."

—Anne

Acknowledgments

Thank you to:

Sumir Brown, for your unwavering love, dedication, and support.

Jerry Post, for showing me what Heart Intelligence looks like in the world.

Tej Steiner, for showing me the beauty of circle work.

Stephanie Fabela, for your wisdom, depth, and support in creating the content for this book.

Lisa McCourt, for your gifted writing skills.

Carol & Gary Rosenberg, for helping out with the editing, formatting, and cover.

All my past romantic partners, for helping me become the man I am today.

To the Heart IQ Community, for your loving support and passion for wanting to see this work grow and expand.

About the Author

Christian Pankhurst is a world-leading authority on heart-centered communication and heart-intelligent relationships. He is the creator of the Heart IQ™ Method, a coaching framework that specializes in group dynamics and intimacy development. This methodology utilizes "circle work" to create incredible results by leveraging the Heart IQ™ Amplified Field to accelerate awareness and inspired action.

In 2009, he was awarded the title of "Britain's Next Top Coach" after winning a national coaching competition with a majority of votes from ninety-two countries and landing a £100,000 media-production package. Following this success, Christian opened the Heart IQ™ Academy in 2011, creating a professional training organization that has certified over 300 personal and small group coaches as well as large event facilitators in over twenty-five countries around the world. The Heart IQ™ Academy offers a one-of-a-kind education by combining professional coach training in both online and live event formats along with embodied application of these training principles through Christian's unique circle work method for personal and group awakening.

Graduating as a chiropractor in 2002, Christian has worked closely with many world-leading experts in the field of personal transformation. In 2006, after extensive study with mentors from multiple disciplines, he began developing a new approach to coaching individuals and couples that integrates practices from natural healing philosophies, various spiritual teachings, therapeutic psychology, dance and movement modalities, martial arts, embodiment practices, nonviolent communication, circling, and numerous healing arts disciplines. This grand synthesis provides students with a deep understanding of the human condition and gives them the essential tools they need to help individuals and couples both heal and awaken.

Christian lives in the Netherlands with his partner, Sumir, at the Heart IQ™ Headquarters—a stunning four-hectare retreat and community center near Groningen, Netherlands. Together, they lead the dedicated Heart IQ™ Network team to spread the work of Heart IQ™ around the world.